A New Century of Social Housing

A NEW CENTURY OF SOCIAL HOUSING

Edited by
Stuart Lowe and David Hughes

Leicester University Press
Leicester, London & New York

First published in Great Britain in 1991 by Leicester University Press
(a division of Pinter Publishers Ltd)

Editorial offices
Fielding Johnson Building, University of Leicester,
University Road, Leicester, LE1 7RH

Trade and other enquiries
25 Floral Street, London, WC2E 9DS

British Library Cataloguing in Publication Data
A CIP cataloguing record for this book is available
from the British Library
ISBN 0 7185 1353 3

For enquiries in North America please contact PO Box 197,
Irvington, NY 10533

Library of Congress Cataloging-in-Publication Data
A New century of social housing / edited by Stuart Lowe and David
　Hughes.
　　　p.　　cm.
　　Includes bibliographical references and index.
　　ISBN 0-7185-1353-3
　　1. Public housing—Great Britain—History.　　2. Working class-
　Housing—Great Britain—History.　　I. Lowe, Stuart, 1950–
　II. Hughes, David, 1945–
　HD7288.78.G7N49　　1991
　363.5'85'0941—dc20   90–23112
                                                                CIP

Typeset by Florencetype Limited, Kewstoke, Avon
Printed and bound in Great Britain by Billing and Sons, Worcester

Contents

List of figures

List of contributors

Richard Best, is Director of the Joseph Rowntree Foundation at York

Trevor Buck, is Lecturer in Law, Department of Law, University of Leicester

Jane Darke, is Senior Lecturer in Housing, Department of Urban and Regional Studies, Sheffield City Polytechnic

David Hughes, is Senior Lecturer in Law, Department of Law, University of Leicester

Peter Kemp, is the Joseph Rowntree Professor of Housing Policy and Director of the Centre for Housing Policy, University of York

Stuart Lowe, is Lecturer in Social Policy, Department of Social Policy and Social Work, University of York

Peter Malpass, is Senior Lecturer in Social Policy, Department of Surveying, Bristol Polytechnic

Jane Morton, is an Associate Consultant, Centre for Housing Research, University of Glasgow

Patrick Nuttgens, is an Honorary Professor at the University of York, and was formerly Director of Leeds Polytechnic

The late Roger Smith, was Professor in the Department of Surveying, Nottingham Polytechnic

Paul Whysall, is Senior Lecturer in the Department of Business and Management Studies, Nottingham Polytechnic

Peter Williams, is Professor of Housing Management, Department of City and Regional Planning, University of Wales, Cardiff

Acknowledgements

The photographs of Quarry Hill, Leeds, in the body of the text and on the dust cover are reproduced by kind permission of the Local History Library, Leeds City Council.

The photographs of New Earswick, York, are reproduced by kind permission of the Joseph Rowntree Foundation.

The photographs of early LCC properties are reproduced by kind permission of the Greater London Record Office.

The photographs and illustrations of Liverpool Corporation housing are reproduced by kind permission of the Local History Collection, Liverpool City Library.

The photographs and illustrations of Glasgow housing are reproduced by kind permission of Strathclyde Regional Archive.

1 Introduction: one hundred years of social housing

Stuart Lowe

The realisation that the Victorian market economy offered no solution to the housing needs of millions of working-class households was painfully slow to develop. The appallingly high mortality and morbidity rates in towns justified an initial intervention into market processes on public health grounds, but it was not until the 1890 Housing of the Working Classes Act that a distinctively 'housing' focus was given to the alleviation of urban squalor. The 1890 Act was not itself a seminal statute but was consolidating legislation, typical of much housing policy that was to follow, and is primarily significant for bringing together a range of existing powers whose combined provisions created the framework in which public authorities could intervene positively. As Gauldie points out it was the social and political climate in which the legislation was enacted that is crucial to its interpretation and its impact (Gauldie, 1974). It roused a storm of protest from free-marketeers, and it is certain that with very few exceptions the local authorities did not want to be involved, not least because the powers to build were not supported by a realistic financial subsidy from central government. At the same time it was far from clear who the developers of the new 'social' housing would be. The model housing trusts and the voluntary and philanthropic movement pioneered the first experiments in social housing provision and were widely regarded as the appropriate agencies for this task.

In 1990 there is more than an echo from the past in the tone of the debate on social housing, and the policies adopted. After one hundred years of social housing it is still argued that state provision is inefficient and causes dependency. The market and the expansion of the property-owning democracy is the solution to housing need. Housing associations (the successors of the nineteenth-century voluntary housing bodies, and in some cases the same organisations) have been given the leading role in social housing provision, while the local authorities after decades as major developers, are now regarded as 'enablers' and managers of the remaining council housing stock.

As the wheel of history comes full circle, there is an urgent need to learn from the lessons of the past, and this can only be done by scholarship which is sensitive to the sources and development of social housing provision. Despite the five million dwellings that have been built by 'social landlords' since 1890 the sober story to be told is often one of lost opportunities, wrong turnings, and above all of a continuous battle to establish the legitimacy of social renting as part of the solution to the nation's housing needs. The development of home ownership as the twentieth-century substitute for nineteenth-century private landlordism is probably irreversible but the general, long-term outlook for the housing market is uncertain. Viewed from the early 1990s, the attempts to establish social renting as a second stream of housing provision, with an equally desirable appeal to most consumers, appears to be a story of qualified successes mixed with outright disasters. This is not to disparage, as is currently fashionable, the achievements of council housing and the smaller contribution of the housing association movement in providing good-quality housing for some people (see, for example, Saunders 1990). Compared to the poor conditions that many people came from, the new council housing was a very distinct improvement and in domestic life provided a haven for thousands of households. The grandiose visions of some architects incurred, however, great costs in social and community life. To view social housing from the point of view of the consumer provides a very different perspective on its attributes and disadvantages compared to the blanket conclusions of sociologists and architects who rarely, if ever, lived in council housing. An appreciation of these sorts of issue should not be read as an uncritical defence of social housing but rather as an attempt to take seriously the gains that have been made, the better informed to seek explanations of the wrong turnings and faltering progress.

This is a work of evaluation, not celebration. In a small way it is hoped that the text may help to clarify and contribute to the assessment of what has been achieved, what has been lost and what the future might hold for social housing. The chapters do indeed suggest an agenda for the future, based on more market-sensitive, consumer-orientated, smaller-scale forms of provision. There will always be a significant minority of our citizens who do not seek to meet their housing needs through owner occupation and those who cannot afford it. The chapters in this book demonstrate that there is a future for social housing, if only because millions of people will continue to be tenants of the public authorities. More than this, all the evidence suggests that the need for it is increasing.

The rest of this chapter provides a brief commentary on the progress of social housing provision over the century since 1890 in order to put the more specialised focus of the essays in context.

The 1890 Housing of the Working Classes Act

Two important elements of the 1890 Act were the collections of quasi-housing legislation known as the 'Torrens' and the 'Cross' Acts, after their parliamentary sponsors. The Torrens Acts (Artisan and Labourers' Dwellings Act of 1868, amended in 1879 and 1882) provided for the demolition and closure of dwellings unfit for habitation. This legislation applied only to individual houses, being in essence a 'public health' rather than a 'housing' measure. The powers were difficult to enforce because no provision was made for rehousing the occupiers of the unfit dwellings, but the Acts were incorporated into Part II of the 1890 Housing of the Working Classes Act. Of greater significance than the Torrens legislation were the series of amended Acts collectively known as the Cross Acts (Artisans and Labourers' Dwellings Improvement Acts of 1875, 1879 and 1882) which provided for the demolition of whole areas of insanitary housing. Cross was Home Secretary in the Disraeli Government and his seniority was an important factor in challenging the accusations of 'socialist' interference in the rights of freeholders. It is particularly important to note the rebuilding powers which were contained in this legislation. Local authorities were empowered to buy sites and rebuild, but there was a clear preference for the redevelopment work to be undertaken by charitable trusts and 'model housing companies'. The Cross Acts were consolidated into Part I of the 1890 Act.

Together the Torrens and the Cross legislation form a major part of the more comprehensive view of housing policy which gives the 1890 Housing of the Working Classes Act its main historical significance. The approach was typically incremental and in this regard was a precursor of much of the housing legislation that was to follow. The Act consolidated all the existing dwelling improvement legislation and the slum clearance powers. Thus Parts I and II of the Act were no different from legislation that had existed for several decades. Part III referred to so called 'Working Class Lodging Houses' which local authorities were empowered to build, and also to renovate and improve. Lodging houses were very broadly defined and included separate houses and cottages. As Gauldie suggests, it was clear that after 1890, 'it was legally possible for an enlightened local authority to pursue an enlightened housing policy' (Gauldie, 1974, p.294).

Given that many of these powers were not new, the key point about the 1890 Act was the new political and administrative context in which the legislation was enacted. Politically, there was a much wider franchise in local government after 1884, and the emergent Labour Movement ensured that housing was kept on the political agenda. Administratively the Local Government Act of 1888 created the framework in which the *ad hoc* provisions of urban services of the previous fifty years were gradually incorporated into a system of local administration, based on counties and county boroughs, which survived until the next major reform of local government in 1974. A further important reform was the powers to make by-laws granted to local authorities by the Local Government Board in 1877. Although by-laws were not mandatory, their gradual adoption, particularly with regard to certain aspects of building design and internal layout, was a significant base for improving standards. The public health inspectorate had a new role in the interpretation of standards in local by-laws, which gave new prestige and authority to the profession, although it had the effect of increasing building costs (Holmans, 1986, p.28).

At the outset most local authorities neither sought powers nor actively used them on any scale. Jane Morton suggests in her chapter that only 25,000 houses were built by local authorities in England and Wales (a further 3,000 in Scotland) before the outbreak of the First World War, using the powers under the 1890 Act. The new London County Council was easily the most innovative authority. The outer London boroughs were also able to take advantage of the Act to plan for a longer-term building programme under terms which allowed London authorities to buy land for improvement schemes without the necessity for all houses in the area to be declared unfit (a provision later extended to other authorities in an amendment to the Act). During the quarter of a century between 1890 and 1914, the orthodox political reflex was to look to voluntary and philanthropic effort rather than the local authorities for new building. Furthermore, it is not difficult to imagine that clearance of slums was much more easily fulfilled than rebuilding; so that the 1890 Act almost certainly led to a net reduction in the nation's housing stock, particularly housing that was accessible to the poorest families. When replacement dwellings were built, they were often unavailable to those in greatest need because the development costs—even including a cheap land subsidy and inexpensive development loans—and management charges put rents above the reach of low-income households.

Thus the progressive intentions of the 1890 Act were severely hampered by its financial instruments, which still carried the assumption that housing investment should be self-financing. Local authority housing budgets were, to use the current idiom, 'ring-fenced' (i.e. meant to be internally self-financing with no support from ratepayers) and it was assumed that 'balances of profits' would be used to support other spending programmes. It was also assumed that housing built by local authorities would be sold into the private sector as quickly as possible, and certainly within ten years of construction. Thus the 1890 legislation is curiously contradictory in its intentions, reflecting the unresolved and highly equivocal attitude of the day towards state intervention. This ambivalence, in both the policy and practice of social housing provision, finds more than an echo in the 1990s.

Richard Best's chapter on the development of housing associations, and Peter Kemp's chapter on the rise of the local authorities, both discuss the rise of local councils as the primary suppliers of public rental housing. But it is important to establish at the outset that, in the decades before and after the turn of the century, the model housing trusts and some local authorities were both actively engaged in the provision of low-rent housing. Neither at this time had become a dominant force, and each enjoyed some elements of subsidy. Indeed, the charitable trusts were clearly favoured as providers, and had for many years benefited from being able to buy slum clearance land and other sites cheaply. They were also given favourable borrowing facilities under the terms of the Labouring Classes Dwellings Act of 1866. A few local authorities, notably the London County Council, took their chances to build, but most authorities felt themselves already overburdened with expensive duties, such as the provision of elementary education, and did not willingly seek an expansion of functions into the field of rental housing. At the same time it is transparently clear, despite the laudable efforts of the Quaker industrialists, Peabody Buildings and others, that the efforts of the model dwelling companies and the housing trusts were hopelessly inadequate to address the national task of supplying low-rent accommodation.

By 1914 housing had emerged as a major political issue, one which was particularly high on the agenda of the emergent Labour movement; but it was from the trauma of the First World War that local councils emerged as the main providers of social rented accommodation, initially to build 'homes fit for heroes'.

The inter-war period

By 1917 only about 28,000 houses had been built by local authorities and 50,000 by the model dwelling companies and charitable trusts. Almost certainly far more dwellings had been demolished than built, although how many were cleared is not known. While the threat to public health had been reduced, it was rare for the displaced and low-income households in general to find refuge in the new 'social' housing. These were houses for 'the better class of poor' (cited in the Royal Commission on the Housing of the Working Classes, 1884). This theme, of the use of state intervention to support the 'deserving poor' is continued in various guises throughout the inter-war decades.

The war itself created a completely new social and political climate. It is clear that the rapid increase in housing production by local authorities and rent control in the private sector were as much a consequence of the threat of civil unrest and the spectre of continental socialism as any positive will by the state authorities to become more involved. As Swenarton points out, money spent on housing was as much 'an insurance against Bolshevism and Revolution' as it was to provide 'homes fit for heroes' (Swenarton, 1981, p.71). Thus it was impossible after the Armistice, at least initially, to revert to full-level market rents (which had been controlled in 1915 following the famous rent strikes in Glasgow); but it was precisely this problem—of how to regenerate the market for private renting and stimulate building for rent—that accounts for the uneven response and equivocal attitude to provision in the public sector. Daunton argues that the surge in the supply of council housing following the 1919 Addison Act was widely understood to be a temporary measure designed to sustain the rental market until 'normal' conditions returned (Daunton, 1983, p.298). It is clear, however, that real rent levels had fallen even in relation to their 1914 levels and that the underlying logic of private landlordism was in abeyance. Even so about 900,000 new dwellings were constructed by private landlords between the wars, not far short of the number built by the local authorities themselves. This temporary return of private landlords to building for rent was mainly a phenomenon of the period between 1932 and 1939 and was due to the very low level of building costs at the time and the decline in house prices during the 1920s and 1930s. The proportion of houses built for private renting as opposed to sale to individual buyers grew from 11 per cent to 30 per cent in that period (Merrett, 1982, p.13). Against this, however, well over one million private rental properties were sold by landlords to sitting tenants or on vacant possession. When this figure is added to the 1.8 million houses built for owner occupation, mainly by 'spec' builders in the 1930s, then it is clear that the dominant force that had emerged in British housing between the wars was not council housing but owner occupation.

The orthodox interpretations of the part played by council housing in this period point to the emphasis on 'general needs' provision under the 1919

Addison Act and the Chamberlain and Wheatley legislation in the 1920s. The 1930s is characterised as a period of reversion to a more residual role through the emphasis on slum clearance. Merrett, however, shows that the council house building programme fluctuated very considerably due to cuts in subsidies, particularly in the late 1920s (Merrett, 1979, p.48–50) and various strategies were adopted to cut costs, notably by reducing building standards and using unconventional designs. There was no sustained support for council housing. The Chamberlain Act in 1923, for example, provided building subsidies to private developers as well as local authorities. The latter were only allowed to expand their programme if private sector activity was not meeting local demand. Only 75,000 council houses were built under the Chamberlain legislation compared to over 360,000 in the private sector. Furthermore, as Marion Bowley shows, there was a very vigorous programme of rehabilitation and reconditioning of properties in the privately rented sector, which was regarded as an alternative to new building in the public sector. Bowley estimates that in every year between 1919 and 1930 some 300,000 houses were made fit for habitation—by statutory orders against landlords (Bowley, 1945). Moore argues that this massive programme of renewal was seen at the time as an alternative to slum clearance and council house building. (Moore, 1980). Thus the switch of policy to subsidies supporting only slum clearance in the Greenwood Act of 1930 was a logical progression of the generally prevailing attitude to council building and not a major break. For local authorities, powers to build were no more than residual.

Two further points need to be made about the inter-war period. First, council housing was not, and was not intended, to meet the housing needs of the poorest social strata (at least until well into the 1930s). As Bowley shows, throughout the 1920s and up to 1932 council house rents were set at a level which precluded most unskilled manual worker households from access. The market for council housing was, in the main, 'the better-off families, the small clerks, the artisans, the better-off semi-skilled workers with small families and in fairly safe jobs' (Bowley, 1945, p. 129). It was only with the introduction of the Greenwood slum clearance programme that poorer families began to benefit from council housing. But even here it has to be noted that despite the achievement of building over 250,000 council dwellings under this legislation between 1932 and 1939, this total was reached at the expense of reduced standards of materials and space, a very utilitarian approach to design and the appearance of large-scale peripheral estates. Rents were, as a result, more affordable for the slum-cleared families but as Malpass and Murie observe, one of the factors underlying the reduction of standards, 'was probably to make council housing less attractive to people who could afford to secure private accommodation' (1987, p. 48). Indeed, the private sector was building houses for sale at this time at breakneck speed (nearly a million houses in four years, between 1932 and 1936), at a time of low building costs, but at prices above the affordability threshold for most manual workers (certainly unskilled workers) even with more abundant building society credit. The massive scale of private sector building during the 1930s (without subsidies) is also an important measure by which to evaluate the council house building programme. The quarter of a million 'Greenwood' houses are only a small fraction of the massive output of the private developers; if the Wheatley subsidies had continued, the scale and the quality of the public sector contribution would have been significantly greater.

A second point to note is that of all the inter-war housing legislation the only unequivocal support for general needs public sector housing for rent was provided during the minority Labour government in the 1924 Housing Act, and this was largely the product of the political vision of one man, John Wheatley, the Minister of Health. Wheatley was a Glaswegian Catholic socialist who had been hardened by years of political campaigning without power (Keenan, 1990). His ideal was to use the municipal construction and ownership of 'council' housing to replace the privately rented sector. He was also a pragmatist and knew that he had to proceed by small steps and without cutting himself off from political and economic reality. It was largely his contact with and lobbying of the building industry that allowed over 500,000 council houses to be built under his improved subsidies.

The Wheatley Act gave the local authorities a much higher level of subsidy from the centre, and also allowed them to subsidise the building programme from the local rates fund. Many of the best inter-war dwellings in either the public or the private sector were built under this legislation, although rent levels still exceeded the affordability threshold for many low-income households.

After the Second World War

The Labour Party won the post-war election on a tide of popular belief that the sacrifices of the war years should lead to a new beginning in Britain's social and economic life. The housing crisis caused by war damage, the cessation of building during the war, and rapid household formation at the close of hostilities was a key issue in domestic politics. Aneurin Bevan, as Minister of Health, shared with his predecessor from the 1930s, John Wheatley, the belief that municipal housing should provide for general needs, be built to a good standard, and at rents affordable to working-class households. In the six years after 1945 local authorities built over 800,000 dwellings compared to only 180,000 in the private sector. Private sector construction was limited by a system of licensing. However, a very high proportion of the new council housing was constructed by private construction companies. After the disruption and dislocation of the war years the reorganised and more corporate private building industry emerged as a formidable force in the subsequent history of council housing. 'Bevan' houses were popular and were built to standards in excess of the Dudley Committee recommendations. On average, Bevan houses had nearly 40 per cent more floor space than the pre-war 'Greenwood' dwellings. Yet, in terms of quality, but not quantity, the return of the Conservatives to power in 1951 marks a major shift of policy and fortunes for council housing. Housing was a high-profile issue in the election, which had been fought on a 'numbers game', with the prospective Housing Minister, Harold Macmillan, claiming a target of 300,000 new dwellings a year by a mixture of private and public provision. This was a period in which quantity of production was the main theme in housing policy. In essence local authority housing was allocated a makeweight role with priority given to the private sector as the 'normal' supplier. In accordance with this residual function building and space standards in the public sector were drastically curtailed. Building licences were abolished in 1954, leading to a gradual acceleration in private sector building, from 90,000 in 1954 to over 200,000 in 1964. Large numbers of council houses were also built, more, indeed, on an annual rate than under the Labour Administration. Up to 1964 council house completions never fell below 100,000 a year. This expansion in the public and the owner-occupied sectors was at the expense of private renting, which declined rapidly following the reintroduction of the slum clearance programme in 1955. Moreover, the 'revival of private landlordism' through the new Rent Acts, principally the 1957 Act, failed due to the persistently uneconomic returns and the threat that a new Labour government would reintroduce rent controls. The Rent Acts failed to stem the gathering tide of sales by landlords as house prices began to accelerate; indeed the easing of tenants' rights encouraged an increase in the pace of sales on vacant possession. Even in the 1990s, the spectre of Rachmanism still haunts what remains of this sector of the housing market.

In short it is clear that, despite the numerical scale of building, the role given to council housing at this time was essentially residual. Local authorities had the function of making up the numbers and of providing replacement houses for demolished slums. They had no other function, and certainly no general needs function. Macmillan's view was that, 'Local authorities and local authorities alone can clear and rehouse the slums, while the general housing need can be met, as it was to a great extent before the war, by private enterprise' (quoted in Samuel et al., 1962). No doubt most of this new council housing provided a better quality of housing than the worst of the slums, but the evaluation of this achievement is tarnished by the lower standards of building, the wrenching up of settled working-class communities, and the switch at an early stage to the widespread use of mass housing solutions to the building programme.

The change to prefabricated technology, combined with the corporate interests of a relatively few very large construction companies, led to the increasing use of high-rise and slab buildings. Local authorities were encouraged at this time to chase this option through changes in the subsidy system in the Housing Subsidies Act 1956. Le Corbusier's idea of building 'machines for living in' suddenly developed strong support, although it was a tradition of building which was very much opposed to British vernacular architecture. The result was a disaster for the already fragile legitimacy of public housing. This housing was on a scale completely out of keeping with the urban built environment, and was out of touch with the shape and pattern of the local communities it replaced. At its peak in 1966, blocks of flats over five storeys high accounted for over a quarter of local authority building approvals, but the proportion declined rapidly in the wake of the Ronan Point disaster in 1967. Prefabricated flats of less than five storeys and maisonettes also formed an important part of the programme and after 1967 took an increasing share of new council housing, up to nearly 40 per cent of approvals in 1970. Dunleavy

(1981) points out that a high proportion of this mass housing was built by only half a dozen large-scale construction companies. Financial packages were offered which tied local authorities into massive debt repayment costs. This was one of the reasons for the change of policy in the early 1970s to an emphasis on renewal and renovation, as well as increasing the pressure for a rent regime which incorporated a bigger proportion of these costs.

Mass housing options were continued and supported under the Labour Government of 1964–70, which maintained the concept of the residual role of the public sector. Better building standards and dwelling sizes were encouraged as the result of the adoption of standards laid down in the Parker-Morris report, dating from 1961 (MHLG, 1961). However, the gathering financial crisis and the escalating costs of high-rise building (which was never cheap) meant that there was no return to the ideals and standards of Wheatley and Bevan. On the contrary, the Labour Party was consciously trying to shift its identification as the 'party of council housing'. Richard Crossman, Housing Minister in 1964, wrote in his diary that, 'we only build council houses where it is clear they are needed' (cited in Boddy, 1980, p. 19). Crossman went on to say that he considered the main aim of Labour's housing policy was to encourage owner occupation. Indeed during the course of this government home owners were exempted from paying capital gains tax on house sales, tax relief was retained for home improvements, mortgage interest tax relief was retained when general reliefs were abolished, and the option mortgage scheme aimed to make owner occupation more accessible to low-income households.

A consensus also existed through most of the post-war period that the voluntary housing movement should have a small and subsidiary role in housing supply. While the local authorities were the major suppliers of general needs and slum clearance housing, housing associations had a particular role in renovation and the provision of special needs housing, principally for the elderly and disabled. An important development for the voluntary sector was the establishment of the Housing Corporation in 1964 to register and fund co-ownership and cost rent housing schemes. Two-thirds of the mortgage costs still had to be funded from the building societies. A major step was taken in the 1972 Housing Finance Act when housing associations were included in the 'fair rent' system and the Housing Corporation was given powers to lend to housing associations. Although somewhat overshadowed by the political turmoil caused for local authorities by this legislation (see p. 79), the 1972 Act in effect set up a 'third arm' of housing provision, with substantial subsidies paid to associations. Local authorities were no longer the only subsidised providers of social housing, and after the 1974 Housing Act the associations enjoyed an almost complete write-off of their development costs (apart from that which could be sponsored by the collection of fair rents). The financial regime for housing associations was completely different from the historic costs approach to financing council housing and is indicative of the willingness of governments of all political complexions to support a form of subsidised provision not controlled by the local authorities, though on a relatively small scale.

The period from the mid-1960s up to the end of the 1970s is thus marked by a considerable degree of consensus by the main political parties on the position of council housing as a necessary but subsidiary source of housing supply. Housing associations were a small but expanding new arm of provision that central government could more easily control, with the primary role remaining with the private market. The national economic crisis also imposed a major shift in policy away from new building and towards renovation of the existing stock, principally, though not exclusively, through the voluntary take-up of improvement grants. Resistance had built up to the worst excesses of the mass slum clearance 'rolling programmes', now threatening areas which by no stretch of the imagination could be considered slums. In most of the large cities residents' associations and community action groups sprang up to resist the onslaught of the bulldozer (Lowe, 1977). A significant difference between the political parties still existed, however, and this was most visible in their attitudes to rent policy. When the Heath Government was elected in 1970 it moved quickly to bring council rents into line with the 'fair rent' system which had existed for private tenants since 1965. In essence this was a step towards 'the market' and was combined with the revival of an earlier policy of allowing council house sales. Low-income households were protected from more market-oriented rents by the reintroduction of means-tested rent rebates. The reversion to means testing was fiercely resisted up and down the country in a vociferous campaign of mass action (Lowe, 1986, Ch. 5). But the commonly adopted tactic of rent strikes was difficult to enforce and it is clear that the campaign against the move towards market rents and rebates for low-income families was not a success. On the contrary, the reduction in the building programme, the move towards market levels of rent, and the policy of sale of council houses are indicative of the new phase in the fortunes of council housing; though large quantities of public rental housing had been constructed, its detachment from the logic and method of market ideology was to be limited, and where possible its complete incorporation into the market encouraged.

Social housing in the 1980s

In this context, the aggressive policy of the marketisation of council house rents and council house sales which followed the election of the first Thatcher government was not an innovation but an intensification of an existing attitude towards public housing. The former has in effect been achieved in the 1989 Local Government and Housing Act, and the latter principally through the terms of the 1980 Housing Act. Nearly 1.5 million council houses have been sold into owner occupation, involving massive expenditure on discounted prices and the sale of public assets worth in excess of £7 billion, making it by far and away the biggest privatisation programme of the Thatcher era. At the same time, subsidies to local authorities have been reduced to a small fraction of previous levels of expenditure, and until the recent 'ring-fencing' of local authority housing revenue accounts, three-quarters of local authorities in England and Wales received no central funding but were reliant on the receipts from the sale of their housing stock.

Council housing now accounts for less than 25 per cent of the nation's housing stock, and is declining relative to home ownership (which in large swathes of the South of England accounts for 80–90 per cent of households). A large part of the best suburban council housing stock has been sold, leaving local authorities with a high proportion of flats in high-rise blocks and houses on the most run down of the 'traditional' estates. Because of the pressure on the quantity and the quality of the stock many authorities, especially in the South of England, are able to make very few re-lets to households from the general waiting list and often are unable to meet their statutory obligations to house homeless families. At the same time the sales policy has mainly shaken out relatively affluent skilled manual worker households, leaving council housing with a much more socially homogeneous profile (and making owner occupation more socially heterogeneous). Council housing no longer provides accommodation, in Bowley's words, for 'artisans and better off families'. The pace of the residualisation of this sector of the nation's housing stock has intensified in the 1980s in a quite dramatic fashion, but it should not be thought that what happened was new or based on some innovatory 'Thatcherite' ideals.

The innovation of the Thatcher years was to inject an aggressive programme of sales and a rent regime designed to capture as much of this housing for the private sector as possible. The four million council houses that remain have taken on the role of the former privately rented sector as the housing of the nation's poor and most socially deprived people. Ring-fencing the housing revenue accounts makes council housing a more or less isolated and self-financing system, including housing benefit. Targeted housing benefits, originally funded as a means-tested income maintenance benefit, have thus become absorbed into mainstream housing finance, to be paid for largely by better-off tenants. There are virtually no 'bricks and mortar' subsidies for new building and councils have ceased to be the major developers of social housing that they had been since 1919. Housing associations have taken over as the main providers, no longer the small third arm but the primary suppliers of the much reduced social housing programme. The new grant system is, however, based on a fixed proportion of subsidy (currently 75 per cent), with development costs topped up by private finance. In this system the flexible element in the financial equation is not the subsidy but the rents, and the question for the housing association movement is whether the small traditional associations can continue to exist, let alone supply affordable low-rent housing in a climate dominated by large-scale commercial interests. The 1990s may well see housing associations emerging as a new form of large-scale private landlord, providing market lettings with little public capital subsidy, while by a curious turn of history the local authorities will take responsibility for providing accommodation for those in the most severe housing need.

In some parts of the country the ghettoisation of a high proportion of low-income and socially deprived households into council housing has already led to the merging of housing and social services departments. This might be considered a logical outcome of the role of housing departments with no development function and as managers of difficult-to-let estates and an under-resourced, and increasingly pauperised tenant population.

This, of course, is not the end of the story. Housing needs in the 1980s have increased. Waiting lists are growing and homelessness is increasing. Social housing is still in demand. What has happened to the provision and management of social housing, and what might happen in the future, will be discussed at the end of the book. For now, the scene is set for the following chapters to provide a greater depth of insight into the first hundred years of social housing.

References

Boddy, M (1980) *The Building Societies* London, Macmillan.

Bowley, M (1945) *Housing and the State: 1919–1944* London, Allen and Unwin.

Daunton, M (1983) *House and Home in the Victorian City* London, Edward Arnold.

Dunleavy, P (1981) *The Politics of Mass Housing in Britain 1945–75* Oxford, Clarendon Press.

Gauldie, E (1974) *Cruel Habitations* London, Allen and Unwin.

Holmans, A (1986) *Housing Policy in Britain* London, Croom Helm.

Keenan, P (1990) '*We trust that you will see no obstacle put in our way': Wheatley and the 1924 Housing Act* University of York.

Lowe, S (1977) 'Local politics and community groups' in R Darke and R Walker (eds) *Local Government and the Public* London, Leonard Hill.

Lowe, S (1986) *Urban Social Movements : The City After Castells* London, Macmillan.

Malpass, A and Murie, A (1987) *Housing Policy and Practice* 2nd edn, London, Macmillan. [A 3rd edition of this work was published in 1990.]

Merrett, S (1979) *State Housing in Britain* London, Routledge and Kegan Paul.

Merrett, S (1982) *Owner Occupation in Britain* London, Routledge and Kegan Paul.

MHLG [Ministry of Housing and Local Government] (1961) 'The Parker-Morris Report' in *Homes for Today and Tomorrow* London, HMSO.

Moore, R (1980) *Reconditioning the Slums: the Development and Role of Housing Rehabilitation* Polytechnic of Central London.

Samuel, R, Kincaid, J and Slater, E (1962) 'But nothing happens', *New Left Review*, **14**, footnote 42 on p. 55.

Saunders, P (1990) *A Nation of Home Owners* London, Unwin Hyman.

Swenarton, M (1981) *Homes Fit for Heroes* London, Heinemann.

2 The 1890 Act and its aftermath — the era of the 'model dwellings'

Jane Morton

In August 1890, under Part III of a new Housing of the Working Classes Act, the Salisbury Administration issued an invitation to the local authorities of the country. They possessed a power, the Act reminded them, to 'erect buildings suitable for lodging houses for the working classes'. The expression was to be clearly understood to include 'separate houses and cottages'.[1]

Part III is one of the milestones in the history of social housing. It marks the origin of the local authority housing sector. More important for the longer term, it marks acceptance of the case, tentatively advanced by the Royal Commission on the Housing of the Working Classes six years earlier, that there might need to be a positive intervention in tight housing markets when they failed to clear at a pace or in a way that could be regarded as acceptable.

The nature of the invitation should not be misunderstood. There is no question yet of operating on other than restrained commercial terms, even of sustained building programmes. 'Model schemes', to give the builders a lead, were thought likely by most who argued for the power before the Commission to be enough.[2]

And yet the Act is a breakthrough. What authorities are being offered is an opportunity to participate on equal terms with the philanthropic bodies to whom governments had looked until then for this role. Lord Salisbury had set the brief himself at the time of the Commission. What was required, and he believed it to be possible, was 'to provide healthy and decent dwellings, without loss, at a rate cheaper than the average which obtains under the Peabody Trust'.[3]

Whether this was possible and what contribution such dwellings stood to make were to be questions of mounting importance over the next twenty-five years. The conclusions reached, by 1917, would shape the forward development of social housing policy.

Within the period, however, a key question is also the relative performance of authorities. How they responded to this invitation stood to determine who would ultimately emerge as principal agents of a later, more proactive administration.

The Royal Commission of 1884–5

Two separate shifts in perception, gathering strength throughout the 1880s, can be seen to have prepared the ground. The Royal Commission on the Housing of the Working Classes plays a critical role here, by tracing deteriorating conditions in the inner areas of London and other towns to an acute and particular shortage of affordable housing. By 1890 it was appreciated that this had to be addressed, if authorities were to be expected to apply their powers to clear and close the homes of the poor, consolidated and sharpened up in Parts I and II of the Act. The second shift takes place in the image of the local authority, following the reform of county and London government in 1888.

Salisbury, then in Opposition, had asked for such a Commission, alarmed by levels of overcrowding in some inner London neighbourhoods, which Lord Shaftesbury confirmed to be worse than he had ever known in sixty years of work among the London poor. Households of five and more were to be found living in single rooms in former family houses equipped to house no more, now occupied by up to twenty families. The risk to health was apparent.

The Commission was a remarkably heavyweight body, chaired by Sir Charles Dilke, Gladstone's President of the Local Government Board, with Salisbury and the Prince of Wales among its members. All leading housing reformers, from Shaftesbury to Octavia Hill, came forward to give evidence.

Most remarkable, in restrospect, was how far it penetrated in its analysis of what was taking place. The year of its hearings was truly a learning experience for the nation. In its report, the symptoms of the situation were relatively rapidly disposed of, mainly prompting a conclusion which undoubtedly some Victorians required to hear: that it was 'the stye that made the pig' and not the reverse.[4]

There was close attention to rent and income levels in affected neighbourhoods. In inner London, average income here was found to be 18s., well below Booth's 'poverty line' of 21s. for a moderate-sized family.[5] Dockers in the East End took home 8s.–9s. when there was work, costermongers 10s.–12s. At a time when the middle class expected to pay 12 per cent of income in rent, 88 per cent of these people were paying over 20 per cent , 46 per cent over 25 per cent.[6]

The explanation offered was particularly perceptive. Essentially, the Commission concluded, there was here a major if probably temporary mismatch between housing demand and supply. The inner urban poor were being driven outwards by a conversion of city centres to public and commercial uses but were being halted in their tracks by lack of access to newer, cheaper housing further out, of the kind which had eased similar congestion and high charges in the middle years of the century.

The Commission, equipped with information only from the early 1880s, was unaware of the full extent of the access problem it had identified. Its report lays undue stress on 'pull' factors as a consequence, such as the difficulty a docker or costermonger would face in moving any distance from his work. In fact, movement outwards was generally becoming more difficult.

The house-building boom of the 1870s, which had opened up so many new working-class suburbs to those who were able to move, ended abruptly in the early 1880s, in part as a response to stricter building regulations following the Public Health Act, 1875. It would not be followed by another boom (facilitated by a transport revolution which opened up further cheaper areas) until the middle 1890s.[7]

There was no doubt in the Commission's mind that the market would adjust, as it had done before. Its report urged the railways to put on more workmen's trains. Even so, it considered that the state had a duty to take action to improve the supply of housing in the interim when shortage resulted in such conditions. At the very least, there had to be 'restitution' when homes were lost, as Salisbury put it, 'for purposes of public ornament or utility'. Additional provision was to be encouraged where conditions were worst.[8]

The new local authorities

This raised the question of suitable undertakers. In London, local government emerged as a large part of the problem. At this time, enforcement of sanitary legislation in the metropolis lay with a network of vestries and district boards. Even when not actually corrupt, like the Clerkenwell vestry found to be run by the very 'housefarmers' exploiting the poor, they were patently not up to a larger role.

Major clearances were a responsibility of the Metropolitan Board of Works (MBW), created over thirty years before to rebuild London's sewers. The Board relied principally on the Peabody Donation Trust for any rehousing deemed necessary. Peabody was found to have obtained eight sites cleared at a public cost of £1.25 million from the Board for some £350,000. The average income of those it housed was found to be over 23s. a week. Only the East End Dwellings Company, among the philanthropic organisations, sought at this time to house any poorer group. The railway companies, despite undertakings given, were providing virtually no replacement housing at all.[9]

The provincial cities outside London were a striking contrast. Equipped with unitary corporations since the 1840s, increasingly responsive to their communities since the franchise reforms of 1867 and 1884, they had tackled the whole problem of urban change more constructively and responsibly. Liverpool and Glasgow as early as the 1860s and Birmingham in the 1870s had secured their own private Acts of Parliament which gave extensive discretionary power to clear, improve and, if need be, rehouse those displaced as part of the process of modernising their city cores. National legislation had for years been modelled on their innovations.

The Commission was to recommend that London, also, be equipped with a strong elected central authority. It questioned representatives from the cities closely as to how they had coped with rehousing problems. Birmingham and Glasgow felt good management had thus far averted crisis. In Glasgow no more than 500 homes were demolished at any time to avoid putting too much strain on the market. Birmingham had at one point, however, held a site in readiness in case a rebuilding scheme were required.

Alderman Arthur Forwood from Liverpool, where conditions in the dockside areas were close to those in London, aroused interest by disclosing that this city was planning to build. Liverpool had built an experimental block of flats once before in the 1860s. Like the Peabody Trust, they had found themselves housing artisans. They now knew, said Forwood, that one had to build down closer to the rent those displaced could afford in order to help them. They hoped to be able to offer homes at 2s. per room.[10]

In the course of its enquiries the Commission discovered that Shaftesbury had succeeded in getting a statute through in 1851, which would have permitted any authority to do likewise. He ascended to his peerage in that year and had steered it single-handed through both Houses. The Labouring Classes Lodging Houses Act had been invoked once only, in 1853, for the provision of hostel-type accommodation, probably out of confusion with his better known Common Lodging Houses Act, also passed in 1851.

By the time of the Commission, Shaftesbury did not believe 'that there was any man living, except myself, who knew that such an Act existed'. But he thought that it might now answer the problem, if the government of London were first dealt with. The Commission, cautiously, recommended that it be given a 'trial'.[11]

The 1890 Act

Despite his concern, Salisbury was uneasy about the suggestion. He came to power briefly in the summer of 1885, following the Commission's final report, and steered through an amending Housing Act which picked up a number of the Commission's recommendations. The 1851 power was redefined to apply to the MBW, thereby bringing it generally to attention again.

But it was a messy piece of legislation. 'Unintelligible to the ordinary lay mind', said one Peer. The Commission had asked that housing law be consolidated and updated in a single measure which would give authorities clear guidance as to what they should be doing. It had discovered that they were not applying a number of the powers they had because they were buried in such an accretion of statutes.

Salisbury returned to power more securely late in 1886, to remain for the next six years. He made his first priority the reform of local government. The London County Council and the administrative counties were created in 1888.

Salisbury had expressed his reservations in a Memorandum appended to the Commission's report. He thought authorities might well crack the problem of building 'cheaper . . . than Peabody'. He thought they should have the chance. But he did not wish to see them move on from there to 'general provision of cottages'. That, he thought, could be justified only where 'some exceptional obstacle has arrested the action of private enterprise'.

He was uneasy also that they might be tempted to use the power to provide 'cottages at rents which did not represent the real cost of their erection'. If that were to happen, he predicted that it would have the effect of 'driving everyone else out of . . . [the] field'. Parliament had echoed both arguments in 1885 and had cut back the Commission's proposals. The Metropolitan Board of Works was not to be allowed to get redundant prison sites, for example, at less than 'a fair market price'.[12]

The event which seems to have precipitated a decision occurred as late as February 1890. The London Liberal group of MPs tabled a Bill on behalf of the new London County Council (LCC). It proposed wide-ranging development powers, including a power to build outside the metropolitan boundary, using compulsory land acquisition powers where it saw a need.

There was to be no obligation to obtain the customary 'best return'. When setting rents, LCC was rather to 'take into consideration the character and condition of the district' and, in so far as it could, was to 'provide for the poorer classes of the population the best available accommodation at the lowest rent'.[13]

This Bill's chances were not strong. The LCC 'Progressives' were a fairly distinct political group. The Liberals generally at this point were warier of tampering with property rights than the Conservatives, who had thus far led on housing reform. But it signalled a certain impatience. Salisbury must by now himself have been aware of how supply was tightening. Both Glasgow and Birmingham had recently taken a decision to build, following Liverpool's example.

He is also likely to have learned about the original and economical design work of the LCC architects, as they prepared to build on the former MBW's unsold clearance sites. He took a close interest in such matters. The plans for the authority's own first clearance scheme at Boundary Street in Bethnal Green, approved in November 1890, were even then under discussion.

The Queen's Speech for the 1890 session which coincided with the tabling of this Bill, included a promise to consolidate. The Government's own proposals were tabled in May. The version that finally won approval in July 1890 spelled out a much more positive role.

The doubts remain in Part I of the Act, which deals with clearance arrangements. Here, finally, there is provision that an authority may redevelop a site directly if no other undertaker shows interest and, also, that another 'equally convenient' site may be substituted. But authorities are expected to 'sell and dispose of all such dwellings within ten years', unless relieved of the obligation. On rents, they are now free to make 'such reasonable charges as they think fit'. In 1885 they were expected to seek the 'best reasonable' return. But written in is a requirement that any tenant who falls on poor relief must leave his accommodation.

Under the Act, towns and cities are the providing agencies, as before. In rural areas, authorities must seek the consent of the new county councils. In London, the authorised agent is LCC. Outside London, consent for building schemes has to be obtained from the Local Government Board. Up to 1905, LCC has to obtain the consent of the Home Secretary.[14]

The financial challenge

The Commission had appreciated that cost of site would influence rents. Hence the provision that another cheaper site might be substituted in central area clearance schemes. For the longer term, however, the cost of borrowing was recognised to be the key. Though opposed to anything that might have the effect of being 'a rate in aid of wages', it considered that the state had an obligation to make funding available 'at the lowest rate without loss'.

Authorities and others seeking to provide for low-income groups were therefore permitted under the Act to borrow from the Public Works Loans Board at cost for approved schemes. In 1890 this was to mean a rate of about 3.125 per cent, over forty years in London, thirty years outside London. Those who could obtain better terms were of course free to do so. Birmingham had been able to raise a loan privately in 1886 at 3 per cent.[15]

In addition there was some scope for relieving the cost within the context of a large area improvement scheme, cross-subsidising from land sales. This was open to Glasgow and Birmingham. Beyond this, as Salisbury had been aware, lay the rate fund, to which at the very least operating losses could be charged.

Authorities were in fact very wary of annoying their ratepayers in 1890. The Glasgow provost who steered through the city's central area improvement scheme had lost his seat. Rates were paid, moreover, by the poorest house-holders, with no provision for relief. They accepted completely at the outset that schemes should be self-financing. In both Glasgow and Manchester, officers were even required to indicate what return was to be expected when a project came up for approval. A return of less than 4 per cent was liable to be queried. Any implications this might have for rent levels and hence the class to be housed were also largely accepted. LCC had pledged itself to a return of no more than 3 per cent, based, moreover, on a marked-down site cost, reflecting its value as an area of working-class housing. The calculations still indicated rents above those previously obtaining, if anything of quality was to be built. Using the pretext that the Commission's findings had shown the difficulties of the poorest to be 'not financial but moral', the authority settled for a policy of providing for 'classes of the population a little above the very lowest'.[16]

A main motive for mounting a building project at the outset was often little more than desire to stem losses resulting from cleared sites no one else would take off their hands. The site of Liverpool's Nash Grove flats had been vacant since 1878, that of Birmingham's Ryder Street cottages since 1883. Glasgow's Saltmarket tenements were undertaken to 'bring back life and business' to a quarter that had been a wasteland since clearances going back over more than ten years.[17]

And yet, as with the LCC at Boundary Street (see Figures 2.1 and 2.2), where the challenge was more squarely seen to be producing better working-class housing, enormous thought went into the design of all these first schemes. Boundary Street, housing over 5,000 people in a radial plan of five-storey flats round a garden, rich in Arts and Crafts movement detailing, was to bring visitors from the world over. The design for Liverpool's Gothic quadrangle at Nash Grove, housing over 1,500 people at a similar high density, was awarded the diploma of honour at an International Health exhibition.[18]

The problem authorities had to square with their consciences was that these were not cheap buildings. The resulting rents were very little different from those of the model dwellings companies, if for more distinguished housing. At Boundary Street the aim of achieving an average rent per room of 3s. was largely achieved. But only 2 per cent of the flats did consist of one room; 50 per cent had two rooms, and the remainder more. Households paying the 3s.10d.

Figure 2.1   The first London County Council estate at Boundary Street, Bethnal Green

for a single room which the Commission had established as the average in the districts it studied, because that was all they could afford to spend on housing, found small help here.

The Ryder Street cottages ran from 5s. a week to 7s.6d. in an area where an average working-class rent was 3s.6d. The Nash Grove flats ran from 2s.3d. to 5s.3d. in an area where the average was 1s.9d.[19]

The search for answers

A reappraisal followed the first schemes in every city. Baillie Chisholm, in Glasgow, rebutted the assertion that 'we have no right to erect anything but houses for the poor'. The city's remunerative neo-classical flats in and around the Saltmarket, of which there were over 1,000 by 1893, supplied, he thought, 'a higher standard of comfort and a lower rental than others can'. But he authorised a search for ways of housing a poorer class. Liverpool had taken a decision to do the same as early as 1886. Manchester was to follow in 1896, Birmingham in 1898.

'We should provide for the 3s.6d. class', argued the chairman of Birmingham's Health Committee, Alderman William Cook. The closures and clearances resulting from his own committee's work under Part II of the 1890 Act were increasing shortage in the poorest areas. The city, he thought, had a

Figure 2.2   Boundary Street: Arts and Crafts Movement detail

responsibility here. Manchester's equivalent committee felt inhibited about putting further pressure on the landlords of Ancoats and Hulme until there was more housing for people likely to be displaced.[20]

The search was to become a six-stage voyage of discovery occupying the whole period until the legislation was replaced in 1919. Salisbury's first

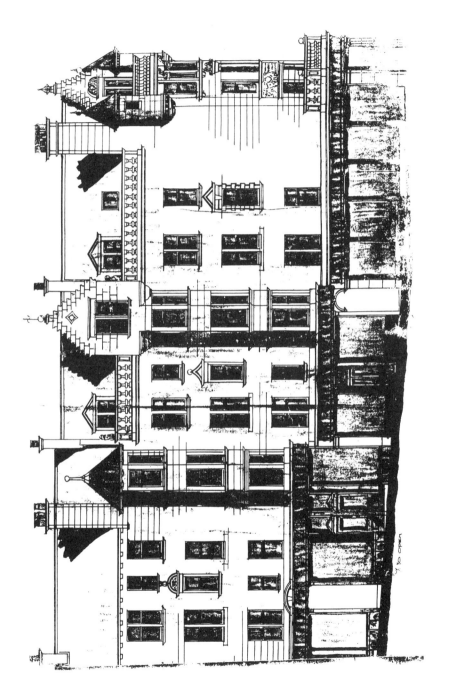

Figure 2.3   Ornate early flats in Glasgow

Figure 2.4   Tenements for labourers at Haghill

challenge, to build 'cheaper than Peabody', was soon to be replaced by his second, to build 'without loss'. But authorities were to learn this only by trial and error.

The first experiment was to try and cut the cost by building the most minimal housing possible. Of them all, this was perhaps the most rapidly abandoned. Glasgow, Liverpool and Birmingham all tried a scheme so spartan and devoid of amenity that it came close to breaking their own new building regulations. Glasgow's was a 'back house' in a court behind the Saltmarket, surfaced in hose-down tiles, in which two households shared a room separated by a corrugated-iron partition.[21]

Such housing evoked public comment. It was liable to attract a transient population and could end up, as with the Birmingham Milk Street scheme, actually running at a loss because of consistently high void levels.[22]

A second course was to forget about 'housing' for the poorest and instead provide common lodging houses. LCC had seen a place for these from the outset for London's single working population and was to provide some 1,800 beds. In Manchester, 'models' for families, charging 4d. a night, were to be seriously proposed in 1896. Though rejected here (the committee insisted on 'cottages') Glasgow was to go on to include accommodation for families in its own large hostel-building programme, which by 1914 was accommodating close on 2,000 people per night.[23]

The third course, fairly generally adopted in the later 1890s, was to build at cheaper sites a little way from the centre but still within reach for those who

Figure 2.5 Glasgow's 'garden suburb' at Kennyhill

worked there. Glasgow, Manchester and Sheffield particularly explored the scope of this. It enabled Glasgow to offer a simple one-room tenement flat at Haghill for 1s.9d., in contrast to the 3s. charged in the Saltmarket area (see Figures 2.3 and 2.4).[24]

But a reaction was now beginning to set in against this constant cut-price operation. It produced mean-looking housing and did nothing for the under-lying problem that too many, still, lived in densely occupied inner areas. Tramway systems were being developed apace in every city by this time. If site cost were the key to that affordable rent, then why not start using the cheapest land of all, at the end of the tramway lines, and use the saving to provide a better standard of housing?

Glasgow had been paying £15 a square yard in the Saltmarket, £5 a square yard in inner working-class suburbs. In 1899 the city bought Kennyhill estate on the outskirts for £1 a square yard and prepared to build larger, more comfortable flats, set in open space (see Figure 2.5).

This fourth answer was to sweep the country. Within the year, LCC was to buy Totterdown Fields near Tooting, followed by other large suburban estates in Tottenham, Norbury and Hammersmith, for the development of cottages with gardens (see Figure 2.6). Manchester bought an estate at Blackley for the same purpose, as did Birmingham at Bordesley Green and Sheffield at High Wincobank.[25]

The strategy was prompted to a very large extent by new thinking about the development of cities, later to produce the Housing, Town Planning, etc. Act

Figure 2.6   LCC cottages at White Hart Lane

of 1909, and by the Garden Suburb movement, which had just produced Bournville and Port Sunlight. It was to rekindle the creative well-springs of the architects and produce some very attractive housing, models for the more widespread cottage building to follow after 1919.

Manchester acquired its first city architect, Henry Price, for Blackley. He scrapped the dreary by-law terraces first proposed and designed Tudor cottages with porches and half-timbered gables.[26]

The question was, however, how many such schemes could help, whatever the cost. The Glasgow scheme was attacked from the outset as small use to those who perforce had to live near the shipyards. It was some years before there was proof that they attracted residents already in outer areas, sometimes even from beyond the city. For example a third of those in LCC cottage estates in 1912 were found to have come from the outlying area itself. But the connection with working-class housing need seemed tenuous.

Also, once again, they were not cheap. LCC accommodation at Totterdown Fields might begin at 6s.6d. for two rooms. But the typical building was a cottage of three to five rooms, costing from 9s. to 13s.6d. There would also be fares to be met for anyone attempting to commute.[27]

By this point, finally, the limits of self-financing were beginning to be reached, despite loan term extensions which allowed up to sixty years after 1903 and were to allow up to eighty years after 1909. The new schemes involved large capital investment and, outside London, were slow to let. The occasional losses picked up by the rates before began to look like the unavoidable price of development.

A division of opinion

The positive side of the fifth stage was a general attempt to do more for those who continued to live in the old slums, untouched as yet by any of the experiments. The trend-setting initiative here came from Birmingham, following John Nettlefold's appointment as chairman of the Housing Committee in 1901. Using the 1890 Act's Part II powers, he began a rate-funded programme of work to thin out densities, improve sanitation and encourage landlords to upgrade their property. By 1913, some 2,700 Birmingham houses had been 'reconditioned' in this way.[28]

Authorities were now to divide on the question of whether this obviated any further need to build. The background, by 1905, was a ten-year private building boom during which construction ran consistently at twice the level of 1890. Houses with a rateable value below £20, deemed 'working-class' housing, formed 66 per cent of the total. The enquiries which preceded clearances now regularly showed vacancies available. Rents of some older properties fell. Leeds noted in 1906, for example, that one could now obtain an old house entered directly off the street for 2s.3d. a week. Vacancies showed up in less attractive municipal schemes in Leeds, Sheffield, Birmingham and Manchester, causing losses on account.[29] Had Salisbury been right? Had the model offered by the local authorities now served its purpose? Journals and conferences debated this very seriously for a period of years. The debate carried into the council chambers.

In 1905 Nettlefold killed the plan to build a 'second Bournville' at Bordesley Green. The land was sold on to the Ideal Benefit Society. The city's task was to plan, he said, but leave development to other undertakers. Leeds was already doing so. Manchester was shortly to follow Birmingham's example and end its own building programme.[30]

Building was to continue for a range of reasons in London, Glasgow, Sheffield and Liverpool. There was everywhere a sense that objectives required to be clarified, but none the less that a purpose was being served. LCC was even to be joined at this point by several of the new metropolitan boroughs created in London in 1899 in its efforts to try to reach down to a lower class. Glasgow, with 75,000 still estimated to be crowded into one-room tenements, considered the need to set a higher standard as great as ever.

Liverpool had perhaps the plainest sense of purpose of them all. From the beginning this city had been trying to reach a particular group, the dock workers and others tied to the port in the congested old streets of the Scotland Road and the Dingle. Others still relied to some extent on 'filtering' to help their target groups. That is, they would ultimately find better housing when others better placed had moved. This city sought to help them directly, by this point actually restricting access to its schemes to those displaced by improvements in these areas.

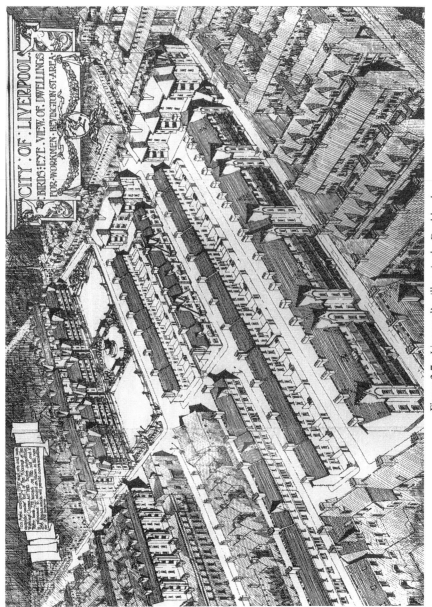

Figure 2.7 Liverpool's village in the Docklands

Figure 2.8 (Detail) Cottages in 'garden suburb' style

Liverpool had seen no point in suburban development. But the new thinking was reflected in higher standards of amenity and design. Tudor detailing and landscaped open space began to appear in its dockside developments (see Figures 2.7, 2.8 and 2.9). The two policies inevitably opened up a cost gap. The city was prepared to charge this to the rates. It mounted steadily to some 2½d. in the pound by 1913, a total of £56 per Liverpool ratepayer on account of some 3,000 homes.[31]

Towards subsidy

The debate was to be closed by a second house-building slump which took construction down, by 1910, below the level even of 1890. Even then, it continued to fall. This time the cheaper houses fell quite disproportionately, to some extent as a consequence of yet further tightening of building regulations. Damp-proof courses and internal sanitation were now generally required.

Just 46,000 houses with a value of under £20 were begun in England and Wales in 1912–13 as against 100,000 in 1904–5. Liverpool was to note, when virtually all building came to a halt during the war, that in the previous four years only the authority had built any houses in the city with a value of less than £18.[32]

As the slump took effect, gradually reducing vacancies and increasing overcrowding, the Local Government Board began to urge councils to build.

Figure 2.9   (Detail) A flatted scheme built just before the War

Since 1909 they had been expected to report on 'need' in their areas. They should not hold back, the Board said, because they could not see themselves thereby helping the poorest.

An illustration of what 'filtering' could achieve was provided in the Board's report for 1913–14. A farm worker's family in Hemel Hempstead had recently moved to a new council tenancy at 4s.6d. per week. The old cottage previously rented was repaired and let for 2s.9d. to an elderly woman. The family of a very poor labourer then moved into her even older cottage, freeing unfit accommodation which could now be demolished.

Authorities were indeed to respond by building. Over the next five years applications for consent reaching the Board rose from a total of just 78 houses in 1909–10 to 484, 1,021, 1,880, 3,387 and 4,408 houses respectively. Close on 5,000 further houses were in proposals to hand when loans were discontinued during the war. By that time a total of 316 councils had built under Part III.[33]

But if one built to meet a defined need and to an adequate standard, charging only the rent people usually paid in the area for such property, then it almost certainly now meant putting in a subsidy, as in Liverpool. This was the sixth step to be taken. Land costs had always been a difficulty. Since 1900 the cost of borrowing had risen from a prevailing 2.5 per cent to 4 per cent. So had building costs. The LCC cottage which could be built for £256 in 1900, site costs excluded, now cost £294.

Projects proposed and turned down in Birmingham and Manchester during this period showed high recurring deficits for years ahead. In one Manchester example, of outgoings of £1,500, £500 would have had to be carried by the rates.[34]

Birmingham resisted to the last. A special enquiry under Neville Chamberlain found that house building had dropped by half across the city in three years to under 4,000 starts by 1913. Reconditioning was itself generating shortage by now. Owners were demolishing rather than repairing. Chamberlain proposed only that two further estates on the lines of Bordesley Green be acquired and offered to private undertakers. There were to be no takers, this time. But it was too late by then to restart the programme.[35]

Manchester ended six years of inactivity in 1914. Two inner urban estates of cottage flats and a second stage of development at Blackley were decisively sanctioned. The decision we are told, even evoked the support of the leading advocate of reconditioning, the veteran Alderman, Sir Edward Holt. 'I have always opposed housing by the Council', he is reported to have said. 'But my opinions are changing.' He could accept now that the priority was 'to meet the necessities of the poorest of the working classes, whether it raised the rates or not'.[36]

He seems not to have been alone. By the middle of the war, when the Local Government Board, with an eye to the future, was becoming interested in the cost of local authority housing, it emerged that no less than a quarter of all running costs were being met by rate fund contributions. In 1916–17, rents were meeting just £750,000 of outgoings. The remaining £250,000 came from the rates.[37]

But by then the question was not whether subsidy was justified; it was whether the local rate fund should be providing it.

The achievement

By 1917 authorities had built perhaps 25,000 homes in England and Wales, 3,000 more in Scotland. Only in the final years before the war did they account for a significant percentage of all houses built, in 1914 possibly reaching 10 per cent of the under £20 category. This compares with perhaps 50,000 homes produced by trusts and model dwellings companies.[38]

By this point, authorities seem to have been trying to charge what would be regarded as a 'normal' rent for their properties, regardless of actual cost, actually glancing sideways at Peabody or the charitable model suburbs on occasion for comparables. The range of 4s.–13s.6d. recorded by the LGB in 1914 for new schemes therefore shows no especial virtue. Before subsidy became general, however, rents in the two sectors ran at much the same level. There were even instances where a trust charged less than the authority for its area. The Guinness Trust, for example, charged less for its inner-area flats than the LCC.[39]

At these rents, neither was reaching groups who were really poor. Liverpool is alone here. A Local Government Board survey of council tenants in 1914 found that labourers accounted for just 601 out of 3,422 tenants covered by the enquiry in urban areas, even in rural areas for just 264 out of 783 tenants. Policemen and postal workers were strikingly represented. The remainder belonged to a range of relatively skilled trades, and included many miners. Among the LCC's 8,608 tenants by 1912, just 549 were found to be labourers.[40]

Yet it was to authorities, from as early as 1914, that the Government was looking for a crash building programme to produce some 120,000 additional houses. The notion predates the war, predates any decision on subsidy, and had the support of both main political parties. Walter Long, the Conservative local government spokesman, was already thinking of a way to subsidise the programme.[41]

Where did their edge lie? Looking at their achievement by the war, one can see three possible explanations. The first is the sheer quality of council house-building, at its best by this time. There is nothing in the voluntary sector to compare, for example, with the homes designed by the LCC architect's department. These had been subsidised, but to a government prepared to consider subsidy, they were an indication of what it could buy.

Secondly, authorities offered a greater certainty of provision. In London, heartland of the philanthropists, there was by then a choice of provider. But the voluntary sector was not well represented outside London. No other agency had shown much interest in the Liverpool docklands, in developing garden suburbs for those on modest incomes in Manchester or Sheffield or, in hard times, even in developing them for well-paid Birmingham. Even rural district councils, by 1914, were responding to need as they became aware of it.

By the war, finally, authorities were organised and ready. They had teams of officers in place and had demonstrated an ability to deliver. Even as the war halted further consents, somehow they managed to complete up to 2,000 further homes before it ended, with whatever materials and labour were left under wartime conditions. To a government desperate for production by the end of the war, there must have seemed no need to look further for a reliable agent.

Notes

1. Housing of the Working Classes Act, 1890, Part III, Section 53.
2. See, for example, the evidence of Lord Shaftesbury, Royal Commission on the Housing of the Working Classes, 1884–5, *Evidence*, pp. 1–14.
3. Salisbury Memorandum, Ibid., *Report*, p. 61.
4. Ibid., *Report*, pp. 14–16.
5. Charles Booth, *Life and Labour*, London, Vol. II, 1887, pp. 25–9.
6. John Burnett, *A Social History of Housing, 1815–1970* David and Charles, 1978, p. 196; Royal Commission, *Report*, pp. 16–21.
7. W V Hole and M V Pountney, *Trends in population. Housing and Occupancy Rates, 1861–1961*, HMSO, 1971, pp. 29–30. From a peak of 4.7 per 1,000 population in 1876, completions throughout Great Britain dropped to 2.4 in 1886, 2.3 in 1890, and rose again to 4.4 only in 1898.
8. Royal Commission, *Report*, pp. 37–55.
9. Ibid.

10. Royal Commission, *Evidence*, pp. 434–43, 493–99.
11. Ibid., *Evidence*, pp. 1–14; *Report*, p. 41.
12. *Hansard*, Lords, 21 July 1885; Royal Commission, *Report*, pp. 60–1; *Hansard*, Commons, 12 August 1885.
13. Housing of the Working Classes (Metropolis) Bill, *Public Bills*, 1890. p. 459; *Hansard*, Lords and Commons, 11 and 12 February 1890.
14. Housing of the Working Classes Act, 1890: Part I, Sections 11, 12; Part III, Section 63; Sections 54–60.
15. Royal Commission, *Report*, pp. 37–40; Housing of the Working Classes Act, 1890, Part III, Section 67.
16. *Housing of the Working Classes, 1855–1912*, London County Council, 1913, p. 27.
17. *Proceedings*: Liverpool Health Committee, 30 October 1878, Birmingham Improvement Committee, 2 July 1889; Baillie Gray, reported in *Glasgow Herald*, 1 September 1887.
18. Susan Beattie, *A Revolution in London Housing: LCC Housing Architects and their Work, 1893–1914*, Architectural Press, London, 1980, p. 32; *Proceedings*, Liverpool Insanitary Property Committee, 10 November 1884.
19. *Proceedings*: Birmingham Improvement Committee, 2 June 1885, Liverpool Insanitary Property Committee, 15 April 1885.
20. Paper by Samuel Chisholm to the Philosophical Society of Glasgow, 4 December 1895; *Proceedings*: Liverpool Insanitary Property Committee, 13 October 1886; Manchester Sanitary Committee, 16 March 1896; Birmingham Improvement Committee, 5 January 1897; Manchester Sanitary Committee, 27 August 1896.
21. *Report on the Operations of the Improvements Department for 1894*, Corporation of Glasgow.
22. See for example *Birmingham Post*, 30 July 1898; Accounts for the Milk Street scheme, 1901–2 — 1913–14, given in C A Vince, *History of the Corporation of Birmingham*, Vol. IV, Birmingham Corporation, 1923, p. 183.
23. See account and comment in *Manchester Guardian*, 29 October 1896; *Municipal Glasgow, 1914*, Corporation of Glasgow, pp. 50–6.
24. *Evidence* of William Menzies, Manager of the Improvements Department, to the Glasgow Municipal Commission on the Housing of the Poor, 1902–3.
25. *Housing of the Working Classes, 1855–1912*, London County Council, p. 70; *Proceedings*: Manchester Sanitary Committee, 12 December 1899, Birmingham Health Committee, 31 July 1900; *History of the Corporation Housing Schemes*, City of Sheffield, 1959, p. 4.
26. See plans and description appended to *Proceedings*, Manchester Sanitary Committee, 4 February 1903.
27. Beattie, *Revolution in London Housing*, pp. 89–101.
28. *Proceedings*: Birmingham Housing Committee, 4 March 1902, 27 October 1914.
29. *Housing Improvement: A Summary of Ten Years' Work in Leeds*, by F M Lupton, Chairman of the Unhealthy Dwellings Committee, Leeds City Council, 1906, p. 3; see, for example, *Report* of the Manchester Sanitary Committee for 1907.
30. *Proceedings*: Birmingham Housing Committee, 4 April 1905, 15 January 1907; Lupton, *Housing Improvement*, p. 7; *Proceedings*: Manchester Sanitary Committee, 8 January 1908, 6 May 1908.
31. *Proceedings*: Liverpool Insanitary Property Committee, 4 February 1902, Liverpool Housing Comittee, 7 July 1909; *Report of the Housing Department, 1914–15*, Liverpool City Council.
32. Local Government Board (1918) *Report of the Committee on Building Construction in England and Wales* (the Tudor Waters Report); *Report of the Housing Department, 1916–17*, Liverpool City Council.

33. Local Government Board, *Annual Reports*, 1909–10 – 1915–16.
34. Local Government Board, Correspondence with the Reconstruction Committee, Memorandum from Sir Noel Kershaw, 23 August, 1916; *Proceedings*: Manchester Housing Committee, 9 July 1911.
35. *Report of the Special Housing Enquiry* and *Proceedings*, Birmingham Housing Committee, 27 October 1914.
36. *Report of the Enquiry into Housing Conditions in Manchester* and *Proceedings*, Manchester Housing Committee, 20 October 1918.
37. Ministry of Health, *Annual Report*, 1919–20. Appendix on Local Financial Statistics, pp. 136–137.
38. It is difficult to be precise. The Local Government Board estimates 20,000 already by 1913 in its *Report* for 1913–14 and construction continued into the war years. The Local Financial Statistics (note 37), suggest no fewer, given an average rent of 6s.6d.; and rates around 2s.6d. Over 25,000 trust and other homes were identified by 1901 by Dr John Sykes in the survey reported in the *Journal of the Royal Statistical Society*, June 1901. A S Wohl, drawing on LCC statistics, estimates 100,000 rooms in London alone by 1914, most of which would be in two-room tenements, 'The housing of the working classes in London, 1815–1914', in S D Chapman (ed) *The History of Working Class Housing* David and Charles, 1971, p. 39.
39. Sykes (note 38) is the most comprehensive source; see also, C H Denyer, 'Recent progress in the housing of the poor', *Economic Journal*, 1897, pp. 487–502.
40. Kershaw Memorandum, 23 August 1916; *Housing of the Working Classes, 1855–1912*, pp. 158–9.
41. He was considering splitting their deficits 3:1 with authorities to get the programme off the ground; LGB *Annual Report* of 1913–14, Kershaw Memorandum, 23 August 1916.

3 The origins and development of local authority housing in Nottingham 1890–1960

Roger Smith and Paul Whysall

Local authority housing is a key theme in any synoptic history of the modern British industrial city. How did the urban local authority respond to the sequence of national housing legislation following the 1890 Act? The aim here is to offer a partial answer by drawing on the case of Nottingham to 1960.

Housing issues prior to 1908

Nottingham ended the nineteenth century with a legacy of some 5,400 inadequate and predominantly back-to-back working-class dwellings built between 1780 and 1850. These represented some of the country's worst housing environments. This was the result of a land shortage within the boundaries of old Nottingham (Chambers, 1945): they embraced about 2,000 acres, but some two-thirds were undevelopable commons or commonable lands. This led to excessively high residential densities at a time of rapid economic and demographic growth. These commons and commonable lands were released for building through the 1845 General Enclosure Act. As a result higher-quality working-class terraced houses and middle-class villas came to surround the older built-up area, and this growth continued, engulfing outlying industrial villages with their share of inadequate housing. There were major boundary changes in Nottingham in 1877 to accommodate this growth and by 1901 the city's population was a quarter of a million.

Despite the national increase of borrowing by local authorities to improve working-class housing following the 1890 Housing Act, Nottingham failed to take advantage of this new legislation (Wilson, 1970, p. 233). The Corporation was even more cautious in intervening in the housing market than it had been in the 1870s, despite a worsening housing situation. In his report for 1906, the city's Medical Officer of Health wrote that over the previous three decades, while 'some thousands of poor houses have been cleared away . . . by railway and tram extensions, by street improvements, and by the condemnation of one area and of many individual dwellings . . . the conditions of the poorest slum districts as regards house accommodation has probably not changed at all for the better'. Such actions tended to exaggerate the problem 'by driving the poor people closer together in any neighbouring slum districts which remain'. Modest efforts by the Corporation were met with procedural difficulties: a closure order on thirty-seven houses in the Poplar district had been defeated after legal appeals in the 1890s, and when a similar order was finally confirmed in 1906, the adverse effects on the owners, portrayed as poor people who had bought property in good faith, resulted in this approach being rejected.

This in turn resulted in more frequent calls for greater Corporation activity in housing. Corporation minutes record pleas from 'a large meeting of the clergy' in 1901, the Nottingham and District Trades Council in 1902, a meeting of 'working men' in 1903 and the Southwell Diocesan Housing Committee in 1904. The controlling liberal councillors were unmoved. The council was becoming more centralised and old and self-confident lace and hosiery manufacturers were giving way to a new breed of councillor—professionals and small traders—which was more responsive to the ratepayers, property owners and builders (Wilson, 1970, p. 224). Thus the Nottingham and Midland Merchants and Traders' Association petitioned the Corporation in 1901 to take a cautious approach, and be mindful of the implications for the rates.

Until the early 1920s the ratepayers feared that housing reform would increase the rates. The property owners feared that their properties would be demolished with inadequate compensation and that lower local authority rents would rob them of tenants. The builders feared that direct labour forces would take work from them.

The establishment of a housing policy 1908–22

A more enlightened view of working-class housing came in 1908 when the Conservatives achieved power in Nottingham, and by 1922 those Conservative councillors, often working cautiously, mindful of the powerful vested interests opposing them, and anxious to take advantage of national legislation, had changed the ideological objections in Nottingham against interventionist housing policy. Of course, irrespective of local attitudes, Nottingham would have built council houses under the 1919 and subsequent Housing Acts and would have undertaken slum clearance programmes in the 1930s. But without this new local commitment those activities would have been undertaken on a smaller scale. Catherine Bauer, the American housing analyst, argued in 1935 that local authority housing in Nottingham was as good as any to be found in England, an opinion repeated throughout the 1930s (Bauer, 1935, p. 315; Richards, 1938, p. 52). After 1945 Nottingham came to build, at Clifton, the largest local authority estate in the country. The foundation for those achievements was grounded in attitudes struck between 1908 and 1922.

By 1900 the Medical Officer of Health for Nottingham, Dr P Boobbyer, had become concerned about the squalid living conditions of the city's working class. He was an autocrat, opposed to the self-help and voluntary programmes advocated by national housing reformers such as Octovia Hill—local authorities must intervene in housing in order to wrest those social residuals from lives of idleness and vice, rearing more children to transmit this life-style of sin and indolence to future generations.

The new Conservative Council of 1908 was impressed by Boobbyer's quantitative research (Smith et al., 1986, pp. 404–39). A housing committee was formed in January 1909 and its first chairman, Dr Milner, announced his intention, 'to rehouse the people because one of the main . . . causes of physical and moral degeneration of the people of Nottingham . . . was the neglect to seriously tackle the question of the houses in which they lived'. Despite these brave words, Milner and his committee worked cautiously. An experimental and small scheme was undertaken in Radford, one of the engulfed industrial villages. Only the worst houses were pulled down (without replacement) and the rest were improved.

It was not until 1910 that plans were announced for a clearance scheme of 599 dwellings at the heart of Nottingham in the Carter Gate area. The debate was whether the area should be redeveloped for commercial purposes and the inhabitants dispersed (a more profitable policy) or whether the cleared site should be redeveloped with houses. The result was a compromise, but it mattered little as the outbreak of the First World War blocked the implementation (Ministry of Health, 1920, p. 5). The work had been retarded because of the vested interests and especially the Nottingham and District Property and Ratepayers' Association.

Positively, much had been learned of the nature of the opposition, and the war provided the opportunity to rethink housing policy. Nottingham was mirroring the work of the reconstruction committees of central government. By 1917 central government announced that it would give short-term financial assistance to local authorities to enable them to build working-class houses, because the private sector would not be able to provide new dwellings at affordable rents. Slum clearance was not a consideration. None the less in Nottingham new build and clearance policies were fused. The survey work that was undertaken locally, prior to a request for a national subsidy, revealed that Nottingham contained around 7,000 inadequate working-class houses ripe for immediate clearance. The survey also showed that whilst the population of Nottingham had grown from 259,000 in 1911 to 270,000 in 1917 only 439 working-class dwellings had been built during that period by the private sector. There was undoubtedly a housing shortage in the city.

Meanwhile a Housing Sub-Committee was sent from Nottingham to examine housing conditions in Birkenhead, Liverpool, Glasgow, Rosyth, Edinburgh, Newcastle and London. The conclusion was that 'A comparison of the slums of Nottingham with those of other towns visited shows that the need for housing reform is as great here as in any of those places and far greater than in most of them.' The committee was also impressed by the products of some of the more progressive housing schemes.

The Local Government Board in 1917 wanted to deal more narrowly with an immediate post-war housing shortage. Nottingham presented a more wide-ranging housing policy. Cleared slum sites in the core of the city would be disposed of profitably for commercial or industrial purposes. Low-cost and rapid municipal transport would enable the former slum dwellers and newly formed households to live on well planned, low-density, suburban estates where land was cheap.

These were not novel ideas. Much of this thinking was developed by those working on the Tudor Walters Report which was published in 1918, the practical experience of settlements like Rosyth, and much contemporary planning thought. The significance is that the Nottingham Corporation, which only a decade earlier had opposed interventionist housing policy, now embraced a comprehensive housing 'blueprint'.

Over the next forty-five years Nottingham attempted to implement that blueprint partly by utilising to the full what national legislation was available. Of course practical expediency, dictated by government subsidy, inevitably meant that there had to be trimming, compromise and shifting short-term priorities. But the vision was there as a base upon which the inter-war and early post-1945 reputation of Nottingham's housing achievements was to be based.

Immediately after Armistice Day and before the Housing and Town Planning Bill was published, the Nottingham Housing Committee announced plans to build 1,000 working-class dwellings. From this point forward developments seem straightforward. In July 1919 the Housing and Town Planning Act was passed. For the first time a central government subsidy was available to local authorities to offset the costs of providing working-class housing. For their part, local authorities were required to satisfy high design standards and contribute the yield of a penny rate.

Nottingham acquired by agreement with the owners two large sites (Stockhill Lane and Sherwood) and a number of smaller sites abutting the built-up area of the city (Butler, 1949, p. 11; see Figure 3.1). The Corporation built or started 1,476 houses between 1919 and 1922 (the time period of the Act). This was no mean achievement because Nottingham, like most local authorities, had had so little experience in housing provision. None the less it still managed to provide as many working-class houses between 1919 and 1923 as the private sector of the city had between 1912 and 1916. Furthermore in October 1919 the Corporation concluded that there was a shortfall of some 3,700 working-class dwellings in Nottingham. By providing 1,476 of them under the 1919 Act Nottingham did better, pro rata, than the country as a whole; while Lloyd George had proclaimed a need for England and Wales for 500,000 working-class dwellings, nationally only 155,000 were built under the Act.

The Nottingham story was not, however, as straightforward as that. Up to 1921 opponents within and outside the Corporation were attempting to reduce the size of the housing programme and limit the acquisition of land. Ultimately they failed, but they did retard initial implementation.

Three factors broke that opposition. First there was the commitment of the Housing Committee, now under the energic chairmanship of Alderman Crane, a local builder. Second was the increasing realisation of the scale of the housing shortage that could not be met by the private sector. Third was the dent to civic pride following the refusal by the Ministry of Health in 1920 to grant Nottingham major boundary extensions, partly because of the poor state of the city's housing. Could an authority which had failed to tackle that problem

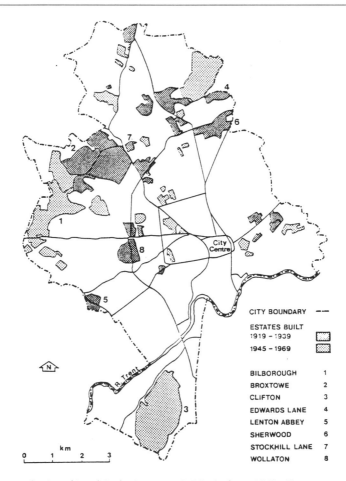

CITY BOUNDARY — —

ESTATES BUILT
1919 - 1939
1945 - 1969

BILBOROUGH 1
BROXTOWE 2
CLIFTON 3
EDWARDS LANE 4
LENTON ABBEY 5
SHERWOOD 6
STOCKHILL LANE 7
WOLLATON 8

Figure 3.1 Distribution of Local Authority estates in Nottingham, 1919–69

be trusted to administer a much more extensive area? Clearly there was no direct relationship between that point and the housing activities under the 1919 Act, but there was an indirect relationship. The need to heal wounded civic pride was greater than any adherence to *laissez-faire* housing economics.

The paradox was that the more unified approach to local authority housing provision in Nottingham came at a time when the national government was experiencing financial difficulties in supporting its housing policy. Thus, in 1922, when that government fell to be replaced by a Conservative administration, Nottingham was anxious to get on with the job of providing more dwellings in the face of a house waiting list of 2,500.

Apart from the number of local authority houses built or started in Nottingham between 1919 and 1922, a psychological barrier had been crossed. The Corporation now knew that it could build and manage large-scale housing schemes successfully, was aware of the size of the housing problem and had a determination to face up to the task.

Implementing policy 1923–39

The 1923 Housing Act was not helpful as far as Nottingham was concerned. Chamberlain, the new Minister of Health, was anxious to return to a free market in housing but believed that in the short term this was impossible. A new housing subsidy was devised (a maximum of £6 per year for each dwelling built under the scheme, which was to last until 1925, for twenty years). The administration was to be in the hands of the local authorities, which would work through the private sector (Bowley, 1945, pp. 36–7).

Nottingham held a conference with the Nottingham and District Association of Building Traders Employers and the Nottingham and District House Builders Association. The Corporation agreed to give each builder £100 per approved dwelling. At the current rate of interest the government subsidy represented a lump sum of only £75. The additional £25 would thus come from the rates. The commitment of the Corporation to ensure a supply of new working-class dwellings is evident. In the event the contribution of private builders was inadequate, as was the national experience, and the local authority again reverted to providing houses directly. In all 2,356 dwellings were provided in Nottingham under the provisions of the 1923 Act.

A minority Labour government came into power in 1924, and was replaced by another Conservative administration until 1929. It is difficult to summarise the complexity of housing policy between 1924 and 1929 (Burnett, 1978, pp. 227–8). All that needs to be noted here is that the period for the subsidy was extended to 1939; the subsidy itself was increased to a maximum of £9 per annum payable over a forty-year period; local authorities were once again the main vehicle for providing subsidised housing, and rates could be used to reduce rents. The Nottingham Corporation thus found sufficient practical encouragement from central government to build 7,490 council houses by 1932 under the provisions of Labour's 1924 Housing (Financial Provision) Act and the subsequent modifying and amending legislation of the 1924–9 Conservative Government.

Given the scale of house-building undertaken by the Nottingham Corporation between 1922 and 1932 it was inevitable that it should take place on the periphery of the city. Necessity coincided with one of the constituent elements of the 1917 housing blueprint. By 1925 the land that had been purchased to satisfy the requirements of the 1919 Act had been utilised. The Corporation began to search for other, larger sites.

Lying on the periphery of Nottingham were a number of extensive landed estates, some of which had been assembled by religious houses in the Middle Ages. These estates fell into secular hands following the Reformation. By the inter-war period they were being broken up for various reasons, including the need to pay death duties. The bottom had fallen from the agricultural land market, and private builders of the time operated at too small a scale for them to contemplate large land purchases. Only the Corporation, with its governmental housing subsidies, could afford to acquire extensive land holdings (Thomas, 1971, p. 121). So it was that Nottingham was able to acquire by negotiation on the open market the Wollaton Park estate (93 acres of which was to be devoted to housing), the Lenton Abbey estate (61 acres), the Windmill Lane estate and the Colwick estate (Butler, 1949, p. 11).

Initially the Wollaton Park estate was used to provide housing under the terms of the 1923 Act, and, because of the inability of the private sector to satisfy the need for housing, the Corporation built 500 dwellings for sale there. By 1939, 391 had been sold. A further 500 dwellings were subsequently built by the local authority for renting. As the legislation proceeded to facilitate the return of local authorities into a more direct role in housing supply so the lands on the other newly acquired sites began to be utilised. The exception was Colwick, which was subject to occasional flooding by the river Trent. It was not until the early 1930s, when that problem was overcome, that houses were built there.

As the 1920s drew to a close the Corporation had to adopt compulsory purchase procedures for land (Thomas, 1971, p. 121). This continued into the 1930s. Those lands tended to be to the north and west of the city. In 1932 Nottingham obtained a boundary extension increasing its area from 10,935 acres to 16,166 acres, absorbing all the lands which had been developed for council housing but which lay beyond the 1877 boundaries, as well as some undeveloped lands (Edwards, 1966, p. 374).

In 1917 the Corporation had linked slum clearance policies with new house provision, and there had been every expectation that once peace returned the proposed demolition of the Carter Gate area would proceed as a prelude to more extensive schemes. In the event central government concentrated simply on ensuring that new dwellings were provided to meet a general need. This policy and the local situation compelled Nottingham to follow suit.

As a result of the 1923 Housing Act it appeared that local authorities would have a diminished direct role to play in housing provision. Nottingham therefore redirected its concerns toward slum clearance (Gray, 1973, p. 97). The powers to do this under the 1890 and 1909 Acts were still on the statute books. For various reasons the 1912 Carter Gate Clearance Order had to go to the Ministry of Health for amendment. During that process the Corporation found, because of changing national legislation, that it was once more able to involve itself directly in housing supply. Given that the housing waiting list in 1924 stood at 6,184, and was rising at the rate of twenty-five per week, slum clearance policies were once again postponed and energies were concentrated on simply providing new dwellings. Nottingham did not return to slum clearance until it was prompted to do so by central government.

The second minority Labour Government of 1929 to 1931 passed the 1930 Housing Act which provided a subsidy of £2 5s. over a forty-year period for each *person* displaced and rehoused following clearance activity (Burnett, 1978, p. 237). The succeeding National Government passed the 1933 Housing Act, which attempted to speed up the slum clearance programmes by imposing a five-year time limit. In response Nottingham declared twenty-nine clearance areas (some of which were coterminous), including the Carter Gate area, in a ring around the central core of the city and containing 2,200 dwellings (Gray,

1973, p. 100). By 1933 that figure had been increased to 3,123, following a survey required by the Ministry of Health. Nottingham was the first large city in England to send in a completed five-year plan for clearance and the first large city to receive approval (Richards, 1938, p. 51). By November 1940, 3,062 new dwellings had been completed under the programme, an indication of the extent to which clearance had been effective.

Subsidies continued to be paid for houses built to satisfy a general housing need until 1933, when the Housing Act of that year removed them. In Nottingham that programme had been halted in 1931 to concentrate on building for families displaced through slum clearance programmes. Families on the general housing waiting list had to be content with vacancies in the existing stock. By 1933, however, the waiting list stood at well over 3,000 and was growing. The Corporation responded by being one of the first to build houses without the aid of central government subsidy (Richards, 1938, p. 51). These dwellings were built more cheaply to ensure that rents covered full costs.

The 1935 Housing Act required local authorities to survey overcrowding and to prepare housing plans to alleviate it within five years. Of the 66,835 dwellings visited in Nottingham as a part of the survey only 1,015 were statutorily overcrowded, although many families outside that category had to use living rooms as bedrooms. Because overcrowding was a growing problem in Nottingham 1,560 dwellings had been completed under the Act by June 1939.

Between 1920 and 1939 17,095 houses were built by the Nottingham Corporation, over two-thirds of which were built after 1929, predominantly in the northern and western part of the city (Thomas, 1966, pp. 88–90) (see Figure 3.1). The larger estates which were developed in the 1930s, like Broxtowe and Edwards Lane, were increasingly remote from the central parts of Nottingham where the employment was. This forced the Corporation, against its better judgement, to build a limited number of flats and some dwellings on the sites released through slum clearance in an attempt to contain the outward growth of the city (Gray, 1973, p. 101).

Despite these needs to compromise on estate design and housing location, Nottingham prided itself on the high quality of its schemes. From the first they demonstrated a sensitivity towards the grouping of dwellings, the importance of vistas, the careful use of crescents, circuses and central points, the nature of the terrain, and the conservation of trees (Howitt, 1921, pp. 5–13). This tradition continued during the 1920s (Howitt, 1928) and, indeed, throughout the inter-war period. In 1928 Raymond Unwin saw in Nottingham how much could be achieved in housing layout, 'by the steady and consistent exercise of careful thought and imagination'; so much so that 'The City which gave the opportunity and the architect who made such good use of it are alike to be congratulated on the result of their collaboration' (Unwin, 1928, pp. iv–v).

Wartime policy, post-war implementation

The period of the Second World War proved to be an important and formative one for Nottingham's housing policy, as had been the case during the First

World War. The Reconstruction Committee, which was set up in May 1942, argued that the housing issue would be the most urgent problem for Nottingham. The Committee's report of 1943 identified land within the city boundaries capable of accommodating some 5,000 dwellings, but this had to be set against an estimate of total need over a twenty-year period for 18,000 new houses. Thus an additional 1,500 acres of land was required, and a boundary extension to the south and east was advocated.

The Corporation had made a case for a major boundary extension in 1942, but the Nottinghamshire County Council was unwilling to offer support. None the less, in 1945 the Corporation sought the compulsory purchase of 936 acres of land at Clifton, beyond the city boundary to the south-west and on the opposite side of the river Trent. By 1949 the County Council agreed to a boundary extension, which became effective in 1952 (City of Nottingham, 1953, p. 7).

In October 1945 the Corporation's Finance and General Purposes Committee identified an immediate shortage of over 8,000 dwellings. Three sites were acquired which, together with some existing land holdings, were used for the building of 1,000 temporary bungalows. But a more coherent and concerted policy was needed, and this was provided by an expanded and revised policy of decentralisation and peripheral growth. Between 1946 and 1949 (taking advantage of the 1946 Housing Act) 1,600 houses were built in seven separate developments, and a start was made on the Bilborough estate where, by 1952, 2,881 dwellings had been built.

Turning to slum clearance, a report of a survey under the 1947 Town and Country Planning Act, published in 1952, now categorised 11,232 dwellings as unsatisfactory, a far larger figure than the 2,875 slum dwellings said to be in need of replacement by the Reconstruction Committee in 1943 (City of Nottingham 1952, p. 17). Yet such was the need for general housing that the decision was made to postpone all but the most limited of slum clearance schemes until the 1960s. This was despite the 1954 Housing Repairs and Rent Act, which modified central government subsidies to make it more financially advantageous to build for clearance purposes.

The culmination of the city's post-war housing strategy came with the building of the Clifton estate (Edwards, 1966, p. 376; see Figure 3.1). Between 1951 and 1959, 6,860 dwellings were built there, housing 28,000 persons. Yet, as the scale of the city's housing projects had increased, and the commitment to decentralisation if anything strengthened, the policy came increasingly to be a focus for criticism. General standards of urban design had fallen, as quantity rather than quality became dominant. In 1958 an ITV television documentary about the Clifton estate described it as 'a concrete wilderness, a soulless, heartless dormitory' being 'devoid of social life — a graveyard with lights'. Addressing the 1962 Summer School of the Town Planning Institute, Professor K C Edwards noted that 'While we may sense a lack of inspiration and social vision in the planning of Clifton, the Corporation can at least claim that compared with only a few decades ago its ratepayers are decently housed. Yet, I submit, it takes more than mass-produced housing to make a desert blossom' (Edwards, 1962, p. 9). This was to be but an early skirmish in the debate to come between the proponents of 'sound' urban design and those whose first priority would be the effective delivery of dwelling units in volume.

Conclusions

This study has been presented to offer a brief examination of how one local authority responded to changing patterns of housing legislation between 1890 and 1960, gradually finding itself a provider of mass housing. It could be argued that the history of mass housing was determined by central government policy, legislation and finance (in broad terms the supply of council houses and its impact on urban structure exhibited a similarity in all the provincial industrial cities), but it is important to recognise that those city authorities were not simply passive implementers of central government policy. They had to learn how to do the job, they had to be fired with commitment, and there were areas for local manoeuvrability.

The 1890 Act had virtually no impact on working-class conditions or housing supply in Nottingham. The period from 1908 to about 1922 was one in which the authority developed an eagerness to engage in slum clearance and provide houses on well planned peripheral estates. Once established, that commitment was translated into action, sometimes anticipating national policy, sometimes vigorously applying it, sometimes operating without national financial support.

Yet despite that policy framework the dominant concern in Nottingham to 1960 and beyond was with volume building for a general need. This explains why slum clearance took a subordinate role, apart from during the 1930s. More sustainable during the inter-war period was the policy of high-quality estate design, although that too was compromised in the 1950s to facilitate high output.

Professor Roger Smith was tragically killed on 14 January 1991. His co-authors wish this chapter to stand as a tribute to his memory.

References

Bauer, C (1935) *Modern Housing*, Allen and Unwin, London.

Bowley, M (1945) *Housing and the State*, Allen and Unwin, London.

Burnett, J (1978) *A Social History of Housing 1815–1970*, David and Charles, Newton Abbot.

Butler, W S (1949) *Nottingham and District Factual Survey*, Report No. 8, Book I, Association for Planning and Regional Reconstruction, Nottingham.

Chambers, J D (1945) *The Making of Modern Nottingham*, Nottingham Journal, Nottingham.

City of Nottingham (1952) *Town and Country Planning Act, 1947, Report of the Survey*, City of Nottingham, Nottingham.

City of Nottingham (1953) *Town and Country Planning Act, 1947, Report of the Survey (Part II)*, City of Nottingham, Nottingham.

Edwards, K C (1962) 'Nottingham: the planners' legacy', in Proceedings, *Town and Country Planning Summer School, University of Nottingham*, Town Planning Institute, London, pp. 1–10.

Edwards, K C (1966) 'The geographical development of Nottingham', in K C Edwards (ed) *Nottingham and its Region*, British Association for the Advancement of Science, Nottingham.

Gray, D (1973) *Settlement to City*, E.P. Publishing, Wakefield.

Howitt, T C (1921) *A Review of the First Two Years' Progress of the Housing Schemes in Nottingham under Part III of the Housing and Town Planning Act 1919*, Nottingham Corporation, Nottingham.

Howitt, T C (1928) *A Review of the Progress of the Housing Schemes in Nottingham under the Various Housing and Town Planning Acts*, Nottingham Corporation, Nottingham.

Ministry of Health (1920) *City of Nottingham: Proposed Alteration of Boundary: Minutes of Proceedings*, HMSO, London.

Richards, J E (1938) 'Municipal life in Nottingham', in A J Bates (ed) *The Book of Nottingham*, Elkin, Matthews and Merrot, London.

Smith, R, Whysall, P and Beuvrin, C (1986) 'Local authority inertia in housing improvement 1890–1914', *Town Planning Review* 57 (4): 404–39.

Thomas, C J (1966) 'Some geographical aspects of council housing in Nottingham', *The East Midlands Geographer* 4 (2): 88–98.

Thomas, C J (1971) 'The growth of Nottingham's residential area since 1919', *The East Midlands Geographer* 5 (3): 119–32.

Unwin, R (1928) Introduction, to Howitt (1928), pp. iv–v.

Wilson, L F (1970) 'The state and the housing of the English working class with special reference to Nottingham 1845–1914', Ph.D. thesis, University of California, Berkeley.

4 From solution to problem? Council housing and the development of national housing policy

Peter Kemp

Introduction

Over the past century the role and image of council housing have undergone considerable change. The introduction of Exchequer subsidies for council housing in 1919 was obviously an important turning point and helped transform it from a minor but growing sector of housing provision into the most important source of new housing to rent. Since then the precise role which central governments have encouraged local authority housing to play has changed over time. The emphasis has generally varied from one aimed at meeting 'general' housing needs to one focused on slum clearance rehousing and meeting 'special' needs such as housing for the elderly.

While it is perhaps inevitable that the spirit and purpose of council housing should have changed over time, it now appears to have reached a critical point in its development. For since the mid-1980s the role of local authorities as housing landlords has been seriously questioned for the first time since they became major housing providers in the early 1920s. Several councils have even divested themselves completely of their housing stock, which they have transferred to newly set up housing associations.

With the publication of the White Paper on housing in 1987 and subsequent legislation, the Conservative Government has made it clear that it wishes to end the role of local authorities as providers of *new* housing. Instead of themselves providing new housing to let, local authorities should see their role as one of enabling others to do so (DoE, 1987). Local authorities are thus no longer viewed by the Government as the appropriate vehicle for solving the shortage of rented housing. Further, the Government wishes to transfer as much as possible of the *existing* council housing stock to alternative landlords. As Malpass (1990) has pointed out, this represents a significant departure from the previous widely accepted consensus that local authorities had an important and perhaps inevitable role to play as landlords and as providers of new housing to let. Indeed, far from being regarded as part of the solution to the housing problem, council housing is now being presented by the Government as part of the very problem itself (Kemp, 1989a; Malpass, 1990).

This chapter examines why it is that council housing, which was once seen as a solution to housing problems, should have come to be viewed as part of the problem. The first section looks at why council housing originally became established as an important sector of housing provision after the First World War. The second section then looks at the post-war years up until 1979, for most of which period council housing was regarded as the normal mode of provision of new rented housing. The chapter then looks at national policy under the Thatcher governments, during which time council housing has increasingly been presented as an aberration, out of touch with consumer demands and out of time with modern society.

The origins of council housing

Most accounts of the origins of council housing see the Housing and Town Planning etc. Act 1919 as the key milestone (e.g. Swenarton, 1981).[1] This Act was significant because it introduced Exchequer subsidies for council house building and was the first to place a duty on local authorities to survey the housing needs of their district and to submit plans for the provision of houses to remedy shortages.

Although a few local authorities had begun to build unsubsidised rented housing towards the end of the nineteenth century, by 1914 only about 24,000 dwellings had been constructed, mostly by the large city councils (Merrett, 1979). But immediately after the First World War, the Government exhorted local authorities to build as many 'homes fit for heroes' as they could manage. By 1939, aided by Exchequer subsidies, they had built a million homes, accounting for 10 per cent of the total stock, and had become firmly established as housing providers (Bowley, 1945).

Thus the 1919 Act was certainly an important turning point in the history of council housing. But why did this change of direction occur? As with so many other areas of our history, this is under dispute; but it is an important debate, for the conclusions one can draw from it are relevant to current debates about who should provide rented housing.

Some historians have seen the origins of council housing in the Victorian public health reform 'movement', believing it to be a natural and logical progression from that early legislation to do with sanitation, building standards, overcrowding and slum clearance (e.g. Wohl, 1977). Council housing was thus one more step on the way to a more enlightened and humane social policy, a product of the growing awareness of bad housing conditions and, ultimately, a recognition of the need to provide decent, subsidised housing to rent for the poor. In this view, local authorities were the obvious candidates for the task of providing housing, since they were already responsible for public health and building regulations.

This 'Whig' interpretation of history usually focuses on major Acts of Parliament and on key individuals (usually male, often wealthy) whose foresight and humanity allowed them to be prime movers behind legislation enacted for the benefit of the poor. Indeed, the legislation is often referred to after these 'great men'. Thus the 1919 Act is often called the Addison Act after the Minister responsible for piloting it through Parliament.

In recent years this view of the inevitability of (subsidised) council housing has been challenged by accounts that focus less on the good deeds of key individuals and more on social forces and conflicts. And instead of being regarded as passive recipients, ordinary women and men are often seen as having had a pivotal role (e.g. Melling, 1980). Moreover, it is argued that there was nothing inevitable about the introduction of Exchequer subsidies for council housing, rather that it needs to be explained and not simply assumed (Daunton, 1987).

At the risk of oversimplification, two competing explanations of the origins of subsidised council housing can be identified. Within each can be identified numerous variations, qualifications and subtleties, but there is insufficient space to consider them here. In brief, the first explanation sees council housing as a *response* to the failure of the private market. The other says the market failed *because* of state interference and that far from being a solution, council housing was part of the problem.

The first view, then, sees the introduction of subsidised council housing as a response to the failure of the private landlord to provide decent-quality housing at rents that working people could afford. Some authors focus on the long-term failure of the private landlord (Merrett, 1979), while others also argue that there was a permanent, structural pre-war collapse of investment in private housing to rent which forced the state to intervene in housing provision (Ball, 1983).

Prior to 1914, perhaps 90 per cent of housing was provided by private landlords, while rents were set by the interaction of supply and demand. Many poor people lived in appalling slum conditions, largely because that was all they could afford. While the introduction of minimum building standards and public health legislation did improve the quality of new construction, it also raised building costs and hence rents. Essentially the problem was that many people's income was simply too low for them to afford decent housing (Merrett, 1979).

It was to show that private enterprise really could provide decent housing at affordable rents that the 'model dwelling companies' were set up in the late nineteenth century. As Richard Best shows in Chapter 10, these forerunners of the housing association movement, such as Peabody and Guinness, constructed blocks of dwellings and aimed to give a 5 per cent return to their investors, compared with the 8 per cent often secured on rented housing at that time. Yet their rents were usually still too high for the poorest households and the dwellings were often let to the better-off working class.

This was also true of the—unsubsidised—housing built by local authorities before 1914: it was generally beyond the means of the poorest households. Moreover, like the model dwellings companies' housing, it was often aimed at those considered to be the 'deserving poor' anyway, not those whom we would now regard as being most in need (Wohl, 1977). Prior to 1914 a debate did emerge about whether local authorities should get more involved in providing rented housing (Daunton, 1987). But even many of those in favour of subsidies for council housing saw local authorities as taking second place to the private sector, perhaps filling gaps in provision and providing a model for the market to compete with.

Some versions of the market failure explanation claim there was a collapse of investment in rented housing before 1914, which signalled an end to private landlordism (Ball, 1983; Offer, 1981). Hence the introduction of subsidies for council housing was a necessary consequence of this crisis. On this view, the war merely influenced the timing of the introduction of subsidies, while rent controls were only another nail in the private landlord's coffin rather than the fatal blow (Dickens, 1978).

An alternative explanation sees council housing as a consequence of the First World War. On this view, the pre-war slump of investment in rented housing construction was essentially a cyclical downturn rather than a permanent collapse, one from which it would have recovered had it not been for the introduction of rent controls in 1915 following the rent strikes which took place in Glasgow and elsewhere (see Daunton, 1983).

The introduction of Exchequer subsidies in 1919 is seen, in this view, as a direct consequence of rent controls (Damer, 1980). Politically, the housing shortage made it imperative that building took place after the war, yet it also made it impossible to remove rent controls. And unless rent controls were removed, private landlords would not build any houses, especially as building costs and interest rates had increased greatly during the war. Hence an emergency programme of subsidised council house building had to be introduced to remove the shortage, thus making it possible to end rent controls and get the building of housing to rent back on to a commercial footing (Daunton, 1984).

The subsequent failure to decontrol rents, according to this view, meant that private investment in rented housing never returned and council housing has remained with us ever since. For some, this transformation amounted to the 'sacrifice' of the private landlord (Daunton, 1987), but for others it represented a victory for working-class struggle (Damer, 1980).

In trying to make sense of these competing explanations it is helpful to distinguish between two separate, though related, questions. Firstly, why did the Government introduce housing subsidies in 1919 when previously it had been most reluctant to do so? Second, why were local authorities given the subsidies and entrusted with responsibility for the housing programme? For in other countries, as the Milner Holland report pointed out in 1964, subsidies were focused on private landlords and housing associations, while municipal housing was given a relatively minor role.

Separating these issues makes it easier to understand why subsidies were introduced. In brief, the failure of the private sector to provide decent-quality housing for the poorest households created growing pressures on government to do something about the housing question. The pre-war decade did see a major, though not a complete, collapse of investment in rented housing and this made some kind of state intervention very likely (Kemp, 1984). Wilding

(1972) has suggested that the war actually *delayed* the introduction of Exchequer subsidies. But even if that view is correct, the precise form and scale that such subsidies would have taken in the absence of the war is still very much an open question (Kemp, 1984).

In the event, the war transformed the whole way in which the housing question was debated. First, the severe housing shortage that developed during the war, and the social unrest this threatened, made it urgent that the state deal with it when war ended (Merrett, 1979; Swenarton, 1981). The short-term increase in building costs and interest rates meant that, unaided, the private sector could not be relied upon to meet the shortage. Some kind of subsidy, therefore, was even more necessary to ensure that building took place in the immediate post-war period than it had been before 1914 (Kemp, 1984).

Second, the war had a significant effect on the way in which assistance was provided, with the result that local authorities emerged as the obvious candidates to carry out the post-war building programme. The wartime rent strikes and profiteering by some private landlords meant that, politically, it was not possible to give subsidies to private landlords. Though never popular, private landlords became widely reviled during and after the war, and this effectively precluded them from receiving handouts from the state (Kemp, 1984). However, an additional Housing Act passed towards the end of 1919 did provide grants to private house-builders (Bowley, 1945; Merrett, 1982).

Housing associations (or 'public utility societies' as they were known) were considered for the job of meeting the post-war housing shortage, but they were not felt able to cope with the scale of the problem (Kemp, 1984). Even so, the Addison Act of 1919 did make subsidies available to them on a similar basis to local authority building. The societies eventually constructed 4,545 dwellings under the Act, compared with 170,090 by local authorities, in England and Wales (Bowley, 1945).

It was also considered whether central government itself should carry out the programme, but this course was rejected because the Ministry of Works did not have the necessary local knowledge. Local authorities, on the other hand, did have knowledge of local housing market conditions, land supply and building costs. And unlike the public utility societies they collectively covered the whole country (Kemp, 1984). Moreover, local councils already had building and other housing powers under pre-war legislation and hence some relevant experience. State housing was a demand of several groups representing working people at this time, while a number of official reports—including the Royal Commission on Scottish housing, which was set up before the war but reported in 1917—recommended that subsidies for municipal housing be introduced (Merrett, 1979; Damer, 1980; Swenarton, 1981).

Yet many local authorities were initially reluctant to get involved in providing housing, especially if it meant a charge on the rates. This was partly why the 1919 Act subsidy was so generous: all their deficits above the product of a penny rate (three-quarters of one penny in Scotland) were met by the Exchequer. Despite this open-ended subsidy, the rents charged on 1919 Act houses were too expensive for many working-class tenants and they were often let to better-off and lower middle-class households (Bowley, 1945). Some councils even had to advertise their larger houses outside the district in order to find tenants for them (Dickens and Gilbert, 1981).

During 1919–20 the Ministry of Health urged authorities to build as many houses as they could and gave advice on design as well as construction materials and methods, to hasten the implementation of the programme. Yet in 1921 the subsidies were prematurely axed. This is used by Swenarton (1981) to justify his argument that the 'homes fit for heroes' campaign was designed as an insurance against revolution, aimed at buying off social unrest. Once the threat of revolution had receded, the insurance policy was no longer needed and could be terminated, especially in view of its high cost (see also Merrett, 1979).

Cabinet minutes show that fear of revolution was certainly a significant factor behind the post-war housing programme. But Swenarton's argument seems overdrawn. In any case, it does not explain why subsidies were reintroduced, for private and municipal house-building, by the Conservative Government in 1923. By this date there was even less prospect of social upheaval than there was when the Addison programme was axed. In fact, the Conservatives suffered several spectacular by-election defeats in what were considered safe Tory seats during March 1923, largely on their failure to tackle the housing shortage and on their proposal to decontrol private sector rents (Kemp, 1984).

The Labour Government which came briefly to power in 1924 also introduced a housing subsidy programme—for municipal and private rental construction —which resulted in half a million council houses being built, compared with 75,000 under the less generous 1923 Act. It was the 1924 Act rather than the 1919 one which really established council housing as a long-term feature of the housing market. It had little to do with slogans about 'homes for heroes', however, and instead reflected the collapse of private rental construction. Criticised in a Commons debate for interfering with private housing investment, Labour's Minister of Health, John Wheatley, pointed out that there was no investment in working-class homes. 'Are we to remain without houses', he replied, 'merely because people who have money . . . refuse to invest that money directly in working-class houses?' (quoted in Kemp, 1984, pp. 246–7).

When the Conservatives returned to power in late 1924, they retained Labour's subsidy along with their own of 1923. While their legislation of 1923 gave council housing only a residual role, Labour's 1924 Act orientated them towards meeting general needs: the Conservatives reluctantly assisted the growth of this tenure, largely because investment in privately rented construction had dried up and alternatives had to be found; but Labour favoured municipal provision.

Some have argued that the lack of investment in private rented building after the war was due to the failure to decontrol rents. But rent control applied only to pre-1919 dwellings, not to new building. Economic factors were more important, especially the dramatic increase in building costs at the end of the war and the—correct—expectation that they would eventually fall. Hence investing in rented housing would have meant making a capital loss. At the same time interest rates were high and alternative investment outlets developed which proved more attractive than housing to let (Kemp, 1984).

In the 1930s, when housing market conditions improved, a revival of building for private rental, averaging over 66,000 units a year in 1933–9, did occur (Kemp, 1980). This return of private rental construction was, however, only part of a much larger private sector house-building boom that was largely geared towards the owner-occupier. In 1933 the 'National' Government took the opportunity to bring the general needs Wheatley subsidy to an end but kept in place the slum clearance rehousing subsidy that the second minority Labour Government had introduced in the Housing Act 1930 (Bowley, 1945). As Merrett (1979) has pointed out, even in the extremely favourable economic climate for private house-building that existed in the 1930s, slum clearance and rehousing was not a profitable way to invest capital. Thus in the 1930s council housing was refocused towards a residual role, providing accommodation for households whose needs the private sector could not meet. In fact, local authority house-building averaged only 65,000 units a year in 1933–9, a little less than was built in the private rental sector.

Nevertheless, by 1939 local authorities had built one million dwellings or more than a quarter of all new construction during the inter-war years (Bowley, 1945). The result was that in 1939 they accounted for one in every ten houses in England and Wales and had become firmly established as major suppliers of new housing to rent, an outcome that few would have foreseen in 1914.

The age of mass council house-building

Council housing under Labour 1945–51

The period after the Second World War was also crucial in the development of council housing. Malpass (1990) points out that in the ten years after 1945 the local authority sector doubled in size with the construction of 1.6 million new homes. That amounted to 50 per cent more than was produced between the wars and more than in any other decade either before or since.

As in 1919, after the Second World War there was a considerable housing shortage and a corresponding political imperative to develop an emergency programme to tackle it. Thus in 1945 opinion polls showed that housing was the most pressing social issue that the new Labour Government had to face, more urgent even than full employment (Campbell, 1987). The caretaker Conservative Administration had estimated in May 1945 that 750,000 new houses were required immediately to clear the shortage and provide every family with a separate home. Yet the construction industry had virtually to be rebuilt from scratch, while the severe economic crisis meant that the competing demands for the nation's resources were great (Merrett, 1979).

The question of which agency or agencies should be chosen to provide the houses was a hotly debated issue (Foot, 1975). It was not taken for granted that local authorities would necessarily be the only or even the main agency to receive Exchequer subsidies for house-building.

Once the Labour Government had decided in August 1945 that house-building during the immediate housing shortage should primarily be for letting, the Minister of Health, Aneurin Bevan, set about developing the emergency housing programme. He successfully proposed that local authorities should take the main burden and that private enterprise, whether for rent or for sale, should be restricted to no more than 20 per cent of the total houses built. This contrasted with the Conservative approach, for in their 1945 election manifesto they had promised a programme of subsidies for both local authority and private sector building. But Bevan axed plans drawn up by the civil servants for giving subsidies to the private sector. When criticised for this decision Bevan derided the Conservatives' remedy which, he said, consisted of allowing the private sector 'to suck at the teats of the state' (quoted in Foot, 1975, p. 71).

But Bevan was also criticised in the Labour Cabinet. For example, Morrison argued that greater freedom should be given to private builders, while Ernest Bevin made out a case for using the Ministry of Works (Campbell, 1987). Others suggested that a separate Ministry of Housing should be created which would directly provide the houses itself (Foot, 1975). And Douglas Jay persistently argued that local authority building should be supplemented by housing associations, directly funded by central government, along the lines of the Scottish Special Housing Association (Campbell, 1987). Thus it was by no means inevitable that council housing was chosen in 1945 not only as the main supplier of new housing to rent but also as the dominant supplier of all new housing.

Bevan, however, was an enthusiastic believer in local authority provision on the grounds that, unlike the Ministry of Works or Jay's proposed Housing Corporation, local authorities were directly democratically accountable to their local electorate. And whereas the private sector would provide first for the better off, only through local authority provision could houses be supplied to those in greatest need. At the same time, the urgency of the housing problem in the post-war reconstruction period provided a practical reason why local authorities rather than private enterprise should be relied upon to supply the houses: there was a need for planning and 'the speculative builder, by his very nature, is not a plannable instrument' (quoted in Foot, 1975, p. 71).

Bevan also chose to sacrifice short-term political popularity to his ideals, by insisting in the face of some opposition from his colleagues, including Chancellor Dalton, that local authorities should build houses of a very high standard, thus holding back quantity for the sake of quality. This related to his idealistic conception of municipal housing. According to his most recent biographer, Bevan hoped

that council houses would be built in a range of sizes to suit every income, so as to encourage a healthy social mix and dispel the stigma of living in council accommodation. His vision was that council housing should become a universally provided social service like the National Health Service, and equally widely accepted. (Campbell, 1987, p. 164)

The fact that local authorities were made the main instrument for providing new, subsidised construction was thus greatly affected not only by the great urgency of the housing shortage and the outcome of the 1945 general election, but also by the fact that Attlee—knowingly—chose as his Minister of Health (who had responsibility for housing) Aneurin Bevan, a politician committed to local authority provision. Of course, local authorities would probably have been an important provider of new houses after the war whoever had won the election and whoever had been made Minister in charge of the housing programme. But it is unlikely that they would have had so dominant a role, for both the private sector and directly funded housing associations might well have been key agencies in the programme too if a different Minister or party had been in power. In the event, under the post-war Labour Governments (1945–51) local authorities were responsible for almost a million house-building starts and accounted for four out of every five houses completed (Merrett, 1979). This represented the first major impetus to council housing since the Wheatley Housing Act of 1924 (Campbell, 1987).

Council housing under the Conservatives, 1951–64

When the Conservatives came to power after the October 1951 general election they were commited to getting housing construction up to 300,000 a year: the housing shortage was still an urgent political issue. They pursued an explicitly dual strategy, involving a preference for owner occupation combined with an acceptance of the need to provide sufficient houses for those who wished, or had, to rent (MHLG, 1953). But in the private rental sector, both existing lettings and new construction were still subject to rent control. Since the Conservatives felt that the housing shortage prevented them from decontrolling rents, it was inevitable that private sector output would predominantly be for sale rather than for rent. At the same time, unlike many countries in Western Europe (Wendt, 1962) they chose not to provide subsidies or tax incentives for private sector rental house-building. In these circumstances and with local authorities geared up to a relatively high level of output, it was almost inevitable that they would have a key role in the renewed housing drive despite the Conservatives' preference for private sector provision. Having got above 100,000 units by 1948, local authority building did not fall to below that level again until 1973 (Malpass, 1990). This was the age of mass housing provision by local authorities (Dunleavy, 1981).

Yet while post-war Conservative governments, until recently, have accepted that local authorities would play a major role in housing provision, they have always been fairly 'reluctant collectivists', as Hamnett (1987) has pointed out. This can be seen most clearly with the restructuring of housing policy that took place between 1954 and 1957. In brief (see Merrett, 1979, Holmans, 1987, and Malpass, 1990, for details) the Conservative Government reaffirmed its faith in owner occupation as the most desirable tenure and attempted to engineer a revival of private renting while seeking to circumscribe the role of local authorities in new construction.

As Peter Malpass shows in Chapter 5, subsidies for local authority building for general housing needs were brought to an end in 1956 and were instead confined to slum clearance rehousing and one-bedroom flats for the elderly. Other housing needs were to be met by the private sector, thus leaving local authorities in a residual role. They were to provide accommodation only for those households whose needs the private sector could not meet. At the same time, an attempt was made to restore profitability to private rental provision via a combination of decontrol and raising rents of dwellings which remained controlled. Merrett (1979, p. 246) refers to this reformulation of housing policy as a return to the 'philosophy of Chamberlain'. Harold Macmillan, then Minister of Health, summed it up like this: 'Local authorities . . . alone can clear and rehouse the slums, while the general housing need can be met, as it was to a great extent before the war, by private enterprise' (quoted in Forrest and Murie, 1988, p. 26).

Yet by 1961 the Government was forced to reconsider its strategy for rented housing. Local authority house-building declined as planned but private rental housing construction did not revive. The Conservatives appear to have believed that 'freeing the market' from rent restrictions would induce a resurgence of investment in private sector housing to let (Cullingworth, 1979). But in fact the existing stock of privately rented dwellings continued to decline and new building for private letting remained negligible. Decontrol thus proved to be a necessary, but not a sufficient, condition for the return of the private investor in rented housing. Thus while the private sector was able to meet the growing demand for owner-occupied housing it continued to prove unable to supply general needs, new housing to let.

In the face of growing concern about housing shortages, the Conservatives published a White Paper on housing in 1961. While expressing the hope that as incomes rose an increasing number of households would have their needs, whether for rent or sale, met by private enterprise, the White Paper acknowledged that there was a need for local authority provision (MHLG, 1961). The Housing Act that followed later in the year introduced a new system of subsidies for council house-building, as a result of which starts increased from the post-war low to which they had fallen (Merrett, 1979).

However, in order to demonstrate to the private investor that rented housing could be profitable, the 1961 Housing Act also made a loan fund of £25 million available for the setting up of cost rent housing societies. In 1964 this fund was increased to £100 million and was extended to include co-ownership societies. According to Cullingworth (1979), as it had by then become apparent that the private investor was not going to return on a significant scale, the objective shifted towards providing an alternative form of non-profit housing to council housing.

Council housing in the 1960s and 1970s

Housing was an important issue in the 1964 general election. The newly elected Labour Government under Harold Wilson consequently felt it had to give house-building a high priority and expected local authorities to make a major contribution to this goal. Even so, Labour's 1965 housing White Paper presented a different view of council housing from that of Bevan after the war:

once the country has overcome its huge social problem of slumdom and obsolescence, and met the need . . . for more houses let at moderate rents, the programme of subsidised council housing should decrease. The expansion of the public programme now proposed is to meet exceptional needs; it is born partly of a short-term necessity, partly of the conditions inherent in modern urban life. The expansion of building for owner-occupation on the other hand is normal; it reflects a long-term social advance which should gradually pervade every region. (quoted in Merrett, 1979, p. 25)

Many people have interpreted this as a shift in Labour's approach to housing tenure, bringing it closer to that of the Conservatives (Merrett, 1979; Clapham et al., 1990). It certainly paints a picture of council housing as a second-class tenure when compared with owner occupation. But this interpretation requires qualification.

In the first place, Labour has always been favourably disposed to owner occupation, though they have never pursued it with quite the vigour that the Conservatives have. Even in 1945, when Labour opted for heavy reliance on council house-building, the Cabinet sub-committee which took the decision stated that this would be only for the period of the immediate housing shortage and 'entirely without prejudice to the ultimate principle of the owner occupier' (quoted in Campbell, 1987, p. 157).

Second, while Labour in the 1960s may have begun to see council house-building in a more residual role than previously, they were not opposed to the principle of council housing; they were not reluctant collectivists like the Conservatives who would really have preferred a private sector route to providing housing to let. Indeed, the two main political parties have always differed most sharply over privately rented housing, for Labour has generally been antagonistic towards this form of provision whereas the Conservatives have keenly espoused it. By contrast, housing associations, as Richard Best points out in Chapter 10, have provided a compromise tenure for the two main political parties: they have tended to be regarded as a replacement for private landlords by Labour and as an alternative to council housing by the Conservatives.

In fact, throughout the 1960s and 1970s council house-building provided for general family as well as for special housing needs. By the early 1960s the proportion of the dwelling stock owned by local authorities finally overtook the share owned by private landlords. Local authorities had dominated the provision of new rental construction since the Second World War, while the privately rented sector continued to decline in both relative and absolute terms.

However, this period also saw a significant turning point in the development of council housing. Under Labour's 1965 'national housing plan', local authority house-building rapidly increased to a level not seen since the mid-1950s, with completions peaking at over 180,000 in Great Britain in 1967. But in January 1968 output was cut back as part of public expenditure reductions following the devaluation of the pound in November 1967 (Merrett, 1979). By 1973 completions had fallen to only 88,000, a post-war low (1946 excepted). Although output increased again to 129,000 in both 1975 and 1976, it has fallen almost continuously since then. The age of mass council house-building was over.

Thus in some respects 1968 was an important turning point (Holmans, 1987). The immediate cause of the fall in output was the perceived need to cut back on public expenditure plans. But a number of other, related developments occurred in the late 1960s and the 1970s which seemed to reduce the need for large-scale municipal house-building.

First, in 1968 the White Paper *Old Houses into New Homes* was published, which signalled the end of large-scale slum clearance and rehousing (MHLG, 1968). Henceforth the emphasis of housing renewal was to switch to rehabilitation of the existing stock (Merrett, 1979; Thomas, 1986). As Merrett (1979) has pointed out, housing renewal in Britain has been effectively partitioned along tenure lines. Thus whereas slum clearance has generally involved the replacement of private housing by new local authority dwellings, rehabilitation has usually involved the retention of the existing stock within the private sector or, after 1974, its transfer to housing associations. Hence the switch to rehabilitation removed a significant part of the demand for new local authority housing.

Second, Holmans (1987) has argued that the late 1960s and early 1970s also saw a slackening of the demand from households for council housing. This may have reflected both the increasing preference for home ownership and the end to large-scale housing shortages. Since 1971 there has been a crude housing surplus in the sense that the absolute number of dwellings has exceeded the enumerated total of households. Of course, once various adjustments are made to the figures to reflect second homes, dwellings undergoing repair and vacant units, the surplus turns into a deficit (Malpass, 1986). But it is also true that the scale of the housing shortage in the 1970s was significantly less than it was in the 1950s. The emergence of difficult to let housing to some extent reflects this changed balance of supply and demand (Holmans, 1987).

Third, the political imperative to produce a high number of completions each year was no longer as pressing as it had once been. At any rate, the Labour Government's 1977 Housing Policy Review Green Paper argued that there was no longer a national housing problem but rather a series of local ones (DoE, 1977). With the end to a large-scale housing shortage and hence an end to mass house-building, the need for construction by local housing authorities was perhaps reduced. If the housing shortage was only localised and small in scale, then it was much more feasible for smaller, non-statutory agencies such as housing associations or the private sector to provide the bulk of new housing.

Fourth, there was at the same time a growing disillusion with mass housing, and in particular with high-rise building, as a solution to the housing shortage that remained. This partly reflected a growing recognition of the design and construction faults associated with industrialised and systems-built estates. It also reflected increasing community resistance to living 'in the shadow of the bulldozer' (Dennis, 1970), the emergence of difficult to let council dwellings and the growing management and maintenance problems on run-down and unpopular estates. As Dunleavy (1981) has pointed out, although high rise accounts for only a relatively small minority of local authority housing, the image and the reality of this built form has helped to delegitimise council housing as a mode of provision.

Since 1976 local authority house-building has declined very considerably and is now at its lowest peacetime level since Exchequer subsidies were first introduced. These cuts were initiated by a Labour Government as a result of the need to cut back on public expenditure as part of the IMF loan agreement

(Merrett, 1979). Some commentators have pointed out that the Conservative governments since 1979 have only continued a trend that commenced under Labour, though others have noted that what Labour began reluctantly the Conservatives continued enthusiastically (Malpass, 1990).

Yet while Labour's commitment to council housing may have lessened, it is apparent from their 1977 Housing Policy Review Green Paper that they still believed it had a valuable and inevitable role to play. While acknowledging that mistakes had been made, the Review argued that 'no one should forget the horrors of the Victorian slums which the local authorities have now banished from most of our cities. The public sector has made a notable contribution towards raising the general level of housing conditions across the country' (DoE, 1977, p. 75). Local authorities, together with other public sector agencies—among whom they included housing associations—were still seen by Labour as having an important role in new housing provision (DoE, 1977).

Housing under the Conservatives: 1979–90

The election of the first Thatcher Government in 1979 marked a new phase in the development of central government policy on council housing. But it is also important to acknowledge that this new phase has to be seen in the context of the historical development of the housing market and, in particular, the polarisation of housing provision between owner occupation and council housing (Kemp, 1989b; Malpass, 1990).

On the one hand, the long-term decline of private renting has contributed to the increasing dominance of council housing in the supply of housing to let and also lies behind the Conservatives' search for alternatives to it. On the other hand, the increasing polarisation between owner occupation and local authority renting has thrown into sharp relief the differences between these two tenures—to the apparent disadvantage of the latter—in respect of resident control and opportunities for capital accumulation.

The relative attractions of home ownership, combined with both the design and construction faults of part of the council stock and the management and maintenance difficulties that exist on some estates, has provided the evidence to support the Conservatives' critique of public sector provision. As I have pointed out elsewhere (Kemp, 1989a, pp. 172–3), by mining a seam of discontent among council tenants about paternalistic and inefficient council housing management, the Thatcher Administration has been able to present the problem as the very existence of municipal landlordism.

Two overlapping phases of policy towards council housing can be discerned during the Conservative governments under Mrs Thatcher. In the first phase, which lasted from 1979 until about 1986, the Conservatives pursued a more vigorous version of their previous policy of reluctant collectivism. The role of council housing was more sharply defined as being about providing for those 'special' housing needs that the private sector was unable to meet. Restrictions on capital spending meant that local authority house-building was greatly reduced. However, the main focus of housing policy during this period was on the extension of home ownership, which was implemented principally by giving council tenants the right to buy their houses and to do so at significant discounts on the market value. With sales exceeding completions in 1982, the council sector began to decrease in both absolute and relative terms for the first time in its history.

The second phase was heralded by the publication of the White Paper *Housing: the Government's Proposals* in 1987 (DoE, 1987) and given legislative force by the 1988 Housing Act and the 1989 Local Government and Housing Act. The White Paper signalled a move towards an anti-collectivist approach to housing provision. The Conservatives had been publicly moving towards this position since 1986 and this second phase in many respects represented a logical next step from the first one (Kemp, 1990).

Although promoting home ownership was still an important objective, government attention shifted towards extending the privatisation drive into the provision of rented housing. In 1987 the then Minister for Housing, William Waldegrave, claimed to see 'no arguments for generalised new build by councils, now or in the future' (Waldegrave, 1987, p. 8). What was so different about this new phase, however, was not merely that the Government wished to bring to an end all production of new housing by local authorities. It is even more the fact that it wanted to demunicipalise the existing stock as well (Kemp, 1989b). As the then Minister for Housing put it shortly after the 1987 general election, 'the next big push after the right to buy should be to get rid of the state as a big landlord' (Waldegrave, 1987, p. 8).

The critique of local authority provision presented in the 1987 White Paper very much reflected the New Right, market ideology of the Thatcher Government. Local authorities were criticised as inefficient, paternalistic and excessively large landlords. We should 'get rid of these monoliths', said one housing minister, and transfer council estates to agencies 'who will be closer in touch with the needs and aspirations of individual tenants' (Patten, 1987). Again, the 1987 White Paper said that local authority housing allocation methods 'can all too easily result in inefficiencies and bureaucracy, producing queuing and lack of choice for the tenant' (DoE, 1987, p. 3). In contrast, private provision was presented in the White Paper as both efficient and responsive to consumer demands, held back only by restrictive state legislation such as rent controls.

Following the 1987 general election, the Conservative Administration under Mrs Thatcher thus commenced an attempt to engineer a major restructuring of rental housing provision (see Kemp, 1989b, 1990, for details). In respect of new construction, the government sought to revive investment in privately rented housing, largely through the deregulation of new lettings and the tax incentive provided by the Business Expansion Scheme (Kemp, 1988; Whitehead and Kleinman, 1989); and it also attempted to expand the output of housing association dwellings, as described by Richard Best in Chapter 10.

In respect of the existing council stock, the new Tenants' Choice scheme was aimed at hiving off individual estates and dwellings to alternative landlords. Housing action trusts were also an instrument of demunicipalisation but one which at the same time was intended to 'turn around' run-down estates. In contrast to much housing renewal, therefore, they were meant to involve the transfer of public housing into the private sector whereas previously housing renewal had involved the reverse process. So the rationale behind housing action trusts was that council housing was a problem to which the private sector could provide the solution.

At the time of writing it is not clear how successful this reprivatisation process is going to be. So far it appears unlikely that private rental and housing association output will get anywhere near the levels achieved by local authorities prior to 1976. Yet homelessness is increasing not only for families and others accepted under the Housing Act 1985 but also among young single people and childless couples (Clapham et al., 1990).

The housing action trust programme appears to have ground to a halt in the face of tenant opposition, notwithstanding the 'carrot' provided by the cash earmarked for improving the proposed estates. Similarly, Tenants' Choice has attracted little interest among either tenants or alternative landlords. It is possible that the new financial regime for local authority housing revenue accounts, described by Peter Malpass in Chapter 5, may provide council tenants with a greater incentive than at present to accept an alternative landlord. But there is apparently no latent demand among council tenants for renting from a private landlord or to be 'helped out into the market' as one housing minister expressed it (quoted in Kemp, 1989b), while housing associations appear to be an unknown quantity to many of them.

If a large-scale demunicipalisation of the existing stock does occur this is not likely to be by means of Tenants' Choice or housing action trusts, but rather via the route of wholesale stock transfers (Kemp, 1989b). Ironically, while the former two schemes were introduced by the Government in the 1988 Housing Act, the latter was an initiative that has come from local authorities, though the climate that has stimulated them has been in part constructed by government policies. So far, five district councils have transferred their entire stock and in a further six the tenants have voted to accept a transfer. In ten local authorities the tenants have voted to reject transfer proposals put to them by their council.

Conclusion

We have seen that one of the reasons for the introduction of subsidised council house-building after the First World War was the failure of the private sector to provide decent housing at rents working people could afford. To this extent it was a response to market failure rather than a cause of it. More recently, council housing has come to be regarded by the government as a problem in need of a private sector solution.

While this view of council housing does not appear to be especially widely held, there seems little doubt that there is no longer the confidence that there once was that council housing is both inevitable and desirable. The growing interest in wholesale stock transfers is to some extent a reflection of this partial delegitimation. Even the Labour Party has been careful to present council housing as simply one way of providing housing, albeit an important one. Thus in a recent speech to the Association of District Councils, the Shadow Environment Secretary said that, under Labour, local authorities would be the most important contributor to meeting the need for social housing. However, this was 'not because there is any intrinsic superiority in local authorities or in the public rented sector, but because it remains the most effective means in pragmatic terms of meeting that need' (quoted in Travis, 1990, p. 5).

Council housing, then, has reached a turning point in its development, though the direction in which it is now going is not yet fully apparent. It seems likely that there will be significant variation throughout the country, as is currently happening with the most significant development, 'voluntary' stock transfers. Whatever the advantages and disadvantages—and for whom—of such transfers, it is important to note that the impetus behind them has not come from the tenants, but rather from officers and councillors (Kemp, 1990). The long-term implications of stock transfers are not yet clear—nor do they appear to have been thought through by those authorities who have opted for this route—but they are likely to be significant. Like high rise, therefore, wholesale stock transfers may prove to be an insufficiently thought out response, which has important long-term consequences, to what is an immediate problem. Now, more than at any time since the Second World War, there is a need for strategic thinking, not only about what needs council housing is best equipped to meet and how it should meet them, but also about how this form of provision fits in with the wider housing system.

Notes

1. This part of the chapter was first published in *Roof* and is based on my D.Phil thesis (Kemp, 1984).

References

Ball, M (1983) *Housing Policy and Economic Power*, Methuen, London.

Bowley, M (1945) *Housing and the State 1919–44*, Allen and Unwin, London.

Campbell, J (1987) *Nye Bevan and the mirage of british socialism*, Weidenfeld and Nicolson, London.

Clapham, D, Kemp, P A and Smith, S J (1990) *Housing and Social Policy*, Macmillan, London.

Cullingworth, J B (1979) *Essays on Housing Policy*, Allen and Unwin, London.

Damer, S (1980) 'State, class and housing: Glasgow 1885–1919', in J Melling (ed) *Housing, Social Policy and the State*, Croom Helm, London, pp. 73–112.

Daunton, M J (1983) 'Conclusion. The "housing crisis" of the early twentieth century', in Daunton, *House and Home in the Victorian City: Working-class Housing, 1850–1914*, Arnold, London, pp. 286–307.

Daunton, M J (1984) 'Introduction', in Daunton (ed) *Councillors and Tenants: Local Authority Housing in English Cities, 1919–1939*, Leicester University Press, Leicester, pp. 1–38.

Daunton, M J (1987) *A Property-owning Democracy?*, Faber, London.

Dennis, N (1970) *People and Planning*, Faber, London.

DoE (Department of the Environment) (1977) *Housing Policy: a Consultative Document*, HMSO, London.

DoE (Department of the Environment) (1987) *Housing Policy: the Government's Proposals*, HMSO, London.

Dickens, P (1978) 'Social change, housing and the state: some aspects of class fragmentation and incorporation 1915–1946', in M Harloe (ed) *Urban Change and Conflict*, Centre for Environmental Studies, London, pp. 336–96.

Dickens, P and Gilbert, P (1981) 'Inter-war housing policy: a study of Brighton', *Southern History* 3, pp. 201–31.

Dunleavy, P (1981) *The Politics of Mass Housing in Britain 1945–1975*, Clarendon, Oxford.

Foot, M (1975) *Aneurin Bevan, Volume 2, 1945–1960*, Granada, London.

Forrest, R and Murie, A (1988) *Selling the Welfare State: the Privatisation of Public Housing*, Routledge, London.

Hamnett, C (1987) 'Conservative government housing policy in Britain, 1979–85: economics or ideology?', in W van Vliet (ed) *Housing Markets and Policies under Fiscal Austerity*, Greenwood Press, Westport, USA, pp. 203–20.

Holmans, A E (1987) *Housing Policy in Britain*, Croom Helm, London.

Kemp, P A (1980) 'Housing production and the decline of the privately rented sector', Urban and Regional Studies working paper 20, University of Sussex, Brighton.

Kemp, P A (1984) 'The transformation of the urban housing market in Britain, 1885 to 1939', D.Phil. thesis, University of Sussex, Brighton.

Kemp, P A (1988) *The future of private renting*, University of Salford, Salford.

Kemp, P A (1989a) 'The housing question', in D T Herbert and D Smith (eds) *Social Problems and the City* 2nd ed, Oxford University Press, Oxford, pp. 159–75.

Kemp, P A (1989b) 'The demunicipalisation of rented housing', in M Brenton and C Ungerson (eds) *Social Policy Review 1988–9*, Longman, London, pp. 46–66.

Kemp, P A (1990) 'Shifting the balance between state and market: the reprivatisation of rental housing provision in Britain', *Environment and Planning A* 22 (6), pp. 793–810.

Malpass, P (1986) 'From complacency to crisis', in Malpass (ed) *The Housing Crisis*, Croom Helm, London, pp. 1–23.

Malpass, P (1990) *Reshaping Housing Policy: Subsidies, Rents and Residualisation*, Routledge, London.

Melling, J (ed) (1980) *Housing, Social Policy and the State*, Croom Helm, London.

Merrett, S (1979) *State Housing in Britain*, Routledge and Kegan Paul, London.

Merrett, S with Gray, F (1982) *Owner Occupation in Britain*, Routledge and Kegan Paul, London.

MHLG (Ministry of Housing and Local Government) (1953) *Houses: the Next Step*, HMSO, London.

MHLG (Ministry of Housing and Local Government) (1961) *Housing in England and Wales*, HMSO, London.

MHLG (1968) *Old houses into new homes*, HMSO, London.

Milner Holland Committee (1964) *Report of the Committee of Inquiry on Housing in Greater London*, HMSO, London.

Offer, A (1981) *Property and Politics 1870–1914*, Cambridge University Press, Cambridge.

Patten, J (1987) 'Housing—room for a new view', *The Guardian*, 30 January, p. 23.

Swenarton, M (1981) *Homes Fit for Heroes*, Heinemann, London.

Thomas, A D (1986) *Housing and Urban Renewal*, Allen and Unwin, London.

Travis, A (1990) 'Gould pledges housing boost', *The Guardian*, 30 June, p. 5.

Waldegrave, W (1987) *Some Reflections on Housing Policy*, Conservative News Service, London.

Waldegrave, W (1988) 'A third force enters the market', *The Guardian*, 29 February, p. 36.

Wendt, P F (1962) *Housing Policy: the Search for Solutions*, University of California Press, Berkeley and Los Angeles.

Whitehead C M E and Kleinman M (1989) 'The private rented sector and the Housing Act 1988' in M Brenton and C Ungerson (eds) *Social policy review* 1988–89, Longman, Harlow, pp. 67–84.

Wilding, P (1972) 'Towards Exchequer subsidies for housing 1906–14', *Social Policy and Administration* 6 (1), pp. 3–18.

Wohl, A S (1977) *The Eternal Slum: Housing and Social Policy in Victorian London*, Edward Arnold, London.

5 The financing of public housing

Peter Malpass

The architects of the Housing of the Working Classes Act 1890, displayed what Enid Gauldie has described as, 'wilful ignorance of the problems of housing finance' (Gauldie, 1974, p. 294). It was almost another thirty years before the particular circumstances at the end of the First World War brought about the injection of Exchequer subsidy which was necessary to stimulate a significant level of investment in house-building by local authorities. Since that time there has been an Act of Parliament affecting council house subsidies on average every three and a half years (Malpass and Murie, 1990). However, a century after the 1890 Act there is still no sign of an equitable, efficient and durable solution to the financial questions raised by council housing. These questions are concerned with issues of capital expenditure, rents and subsidies, and the relationship between central and local government in determining the particular patterns of income and expenditure in different localities.

The purpose of this chapter is to provide an assessment of the new financial regime for the 1990s in the light of past experience. The intention is to identify the continuities in housing finance as well as the major changes, and to establish a coherent overview which will provide a basis for evaluating the prospects for the new century of social housing.

The centrality of finance

Housing finance is widely seen as a difficult subject, inherently complex and constantly changing. However, this reputation is not fully justified: above a certain level of detail it is possible to perceive the essential elements and the broad shape of housing finance, and it is necessary to do so because the subject is too important to be left as a virtual black box in housing studies, accessible only to a small coterie of specialists.

The basic issue is the relationship between housing costs and consumer incomes. In market-based societies where housing is produced as a commodity there is an inherent tension in the relationship between builders and consumers. Housing is unavoidably expensive to produce: even the most minimal dwelling occupies land and requires relatively large amounts of materials and labour for its production. In order to produce houses a builder brings together land, labour and materials, often using borrowed money to finance the process (Ball, 1988). At the end of the construction period the builder needs to realise, or convert into money, the capital invested in the completed dwellings so as to finance the next site, and so on. The builder's profitability depends on the rate at which capital circulates from the money form into the built form and back again (Boddy, 1976). As this highly simplified model of the construction process indicates, builders have a strong interest in rapid circulation of capital.

Consumers, on the other hand, are generally in a very different position. The high cost of housing means that most people (especially in their early adult lives) cannot afford to pay the full cost of suitable accommodation from income or savings (Holmans, 1987, p. 7), but neither can they postpone their consumption until they can afford to buy outright. The high cost of housing in relation to incomes means that consumers require some method of spreading that cost over a long time. Renting and mortgaged house purchase represent different ways of solving the consumer's dilemma, whilst at the same time meeting the builder's need to realise capital in the short term. In other words, landlords (whether public or private) and mortgage lenders constitute essential parts of the housing system, standing between builders and consumers and facilitating the fulfilment of their differing needs. Historically it was private renting which provided the standard method of cost spreading. Landlords would typically invest their own or borrowed money in houses produced by speculative builders, and they would then draw an income in the form of rents paid by tenants. This form of provision came to dominate the housing market in nineteenth-century Britain, but it was a system which was never capable of producing enough housing to meet demand, or of guaranteeing that the poor could occupy housing of a satisfactory standard. There remained a significant gap between the price of decent accommodation and the rent that could be afforded by a large proportion of the working class (DoE, 1977, p. 7).

One of the main arguments for council housing has always been that public intervention was necessary to provide suitable housing for those on the lowest incomes. In practice, of course, large-scale subsidised council house building began in the aftermath of the First World War, when the private sector could not provide enough houses to meet shortages affecting a wide range of income groups, and at that time council housing was clearly not targeted on the least well off. Indeed, although council housing in Britain has always remained a working-class tenure, it has continued to accommodate people from income groups well above the poorest. The debate about the proper role of the public sector has persisted for a hundred years, and changes in housing finance arrangements have to be seen in the context of the shifting balance of arguments. In times of acute shortage authorities have been given incentives to build relatively high-quality dwellings, to be let at subsidised rents, but without much emphasis on ensuring that these rents are affordable by the poorest. At other times the emphasis has swung away from production incentives and general subsidy towards lower levels of new building and greater concentration on means-tested assistance for the least well off. Finance, therefore, is central to questions of both how much council housing has been produced at different times and at whom that housing has been targeted.

Policy issues and responses in the financing of public housing

As the previous section has indicated, finance is at the heart of the housing problem. In terms of the finance of public housing there were three particular issues which became apparent during the First World War, and which have continued to pose difficulties for policy makers and local authorities through-out the intervening decades. The first of these issues was how to secure a level of output in line with policy objectives. The second was how to set rents in a subsidised public sector where market forces did not apply. And the third was how to apportion subsidy between the Exchequer and local rates. To these early problems were added two further distributional issues: how to distribute subsidy within and amongst local authorities. In the present period new problems have emerged, but consideration of these is postponed until a later section. Underlying the whole question of public sector housing finance is the issue of central–local relations and the fact that while local authorities build, own and manage council housing, they do so within the scope of central government policy and with financial support from the Exchequer.

In considering policy responses to these various issues it is not appropriate to describe the entire history of the financing of public housing. Table 5.1 summarises the key events since 1919 and provides a basis for discussing the main features of policy in that period.

It is necessary to recognise the continuities in policy and the persistence of policy instruments, and to avoid a view of history as just one piece of legislation after another. Local authority housing finance has developed within a particular framework of accounting conventions, subsidy and pricing arrangements and central–local relations. This framework has not remained constant, of course; it has been subject to change in response to a range of factors, most notably changes in housing policy, the changing nature of council housing itself, and the impact of inflation. The perspective offered here suggests that certain important elements of policy, developed in the early years of large-scale council housing, remained in place for many years, and some have persisted into the present period. On this view, 1916–35 is seen as a formative period, followed by a long spell of stability in the policy framework, until major changes in 1972. Since the early 1970s there have been three attempts to establish a legislative basis for a new orthodoxy, combining new policies and methods with established conventions.

There are seven important and enduring features of the financial structure of council housing which had their origins in the period 1919–35.

First, from the start local authorities acted as developer landlords, initiating the construction of new housing and retaining long-term ownership of the finished product. In this role they represented an interface between private sector supply and public sector consumption of housing. In other words, local authorities typically developed their housing stock by raising loans from private investors to acquire land from private owners at market prices and then

Table 5.1   Key events in local authority housing finance, 1919–89

1919	*Housing and Town Planning Act:* introduced Exchequer subsidy and established the tripartite structure of income from rents, subsidy and rate fund contributions.
1923	*Housing Act:* introduced Exchequer subsidy as fixed cash sum per dwelling per year, an approach that survived until 1972.
1930	*Housing Act:* introduced subsidy targeted on slum clearance and facilitated rent rebate schemes.
1935	*Housing Act:* introduced single housing revenue account (HRA) for each local authority and established the principle of 'reasonable' rents.
1955	Adoption of rent pooling as government policy.
1956	*Housing Subsidies Act:* made rate fund contributions voluntary.
1963	*White Paper:* signalled intention to review and possibly phase out existing subsidies.
1972	*Housing Finance Act:* introduced 'fair' rents in an attempt to switch to current value pricing; rent rebate scheme made mandatory; existing investment subsidies replaced by deficit subsidy based on state of housing revenue account.
1975	*Housing Rents and Subsidies Act:* repealed most of 1972 Act, but retained mandatory rent rebate scheme and associated subsidy.
1977–8	Introduction of housing investment programmes.
1980	*Housing Act:* introduced new deficit subsidy system based on notional housing revenue accounts; permitted HRA surpluses to be transferred into general rate fund.
1989	*Local Government and Housing Act:* introduced new financial regime based on ring-fenced HRA, single HRA subsidy and rent increases related to right-to-buy valuations.

to commission private builders to erect houses using labour and materials also purchased at market prices. To this extent the development process was essentially very similar to the way in which private sector housing was produced. The importance of this point is twofold: it shows first that the production of council housing remained firmly tied to the private sector, with only the consumption aspects being removed from the market, and second that the consumption costs of council housing were, nevertheless, heavily influenced by the market-based production process. Because the cost of production was largely determined by the markets for loan capital, land, labour and materials, there was a knock-on effect in terms of the loan charges to be met during the life of the dwelling.

Second, however, the financing of the consumption of local authority housing has been characterised by distinctively non-market arrangements. Whereas private landlords and property companies base their accounts on the current value of their assets, local authorities have never been required to do so. Instead, local authority housing has always been based on historic cost accounting, which in this context means that the income needed to balance the account is determined by the cost of servicing historic loans, plus management and maintenance charges. This approach has very important implications for rents and subsidies in an era of general inflation: a house built for, say, £10,000 in the early 1970s might have a current market value of up to £100,000 in the early 1990s. Clearly, if authorities were required to show a commercial rate of return on the current capital value of their properties then rents and/or subsidies would be very much higher than under historic cost accounting.

Third, associated with the historic cost accounting approach is the next significant feature of British public housing finance: the cash flow definition of subsidy which has been used in council housing since 1919. In the context of historic cost accounting the income to be generated is the amount which balances expenditure, and subsidy has always been defined and measured in terms of the cash amounts actually transferred into the account in order to achieve a balance. The alternative definition of subsidy, favoured by most economists (Merrett and Sykes, 1965, pp. 48–51; Goss and Lansley, 1981, pp. 6–7; Ermisch, 1984, p. 39), holds that the level of subsidy is represented by the difference between the price which is actually paid and the price that would be paid in a free market. On this view, therefore, council tenants could be said to be subsidised if their rents were below market rent levels, even though the housing revenue account balanced without any injection of external assistance. However, throughout most of the period since the First World War the great majority of local authorities have been entitled to, and in need of, subsidy as defined in cash terms, and policy has been framed accordingly. Public debate has correspondingly focused on the cash value of subsidies, with little attention paid to the more esoteric issue of economic subsidy. This partly reflects the precise, tangible nature of cash subsidy, compared with the more theoretical and debatable value of economic subsidy.

Fourth, the Housing and Town Planning Act of 1919 established the principle that the cost of providing council houses should be met from three main sources: rents, Exchequer subsidy and rate fund contribution (RFC). From the start of large-scale council housing authorities were required to maintain housing accounts which were separate from the general rate fund, but payments from the general rate fund in support of housing were required by all Housing Acts from 1919 to 1956 (except the 1923 Act). In addition, authorities had discretion to top up statutory RFC with further contributions, and some councils established a tradition of very substantial voluntary RFCs.

In the three years of negotiations which preceded the 1919 Act one of the main issues was the balance of subsidy contributions as between central and local government. The outcome was that in the particular circumstances prevailing at that time the local authorities were able to secure a deal which was highly advantageous to local ratepayers. Under the 1919 Act local authority liability was limited to the product of a penny rate, and Exchequer liability was much more open-ended. This arrangement was obviously unsatisfactory from the Treasury point of view, and the situation was soon reversed.

This brings up the fifth enduring feature of public housing finance to be established in the early period. From the 1923 Act there was a period of virtually fifty years (until the Housing Finance Act 1972) when Exchequer subsidies were set in terms of fixed cash sums per dwelling per year for a prescribed number of years. Treasury liability was therefore highly predictable and controllable, depending only on the numbers of houses built each year. It was independent of short-term changes in costs and was unaffected by the efficiency of local authorities. In other words, by fixing subsidies in this way the Treasury shifted to the local level the responsibility for containing costs and for covering expenditure increases from councils' own resources of rents and/or rates.

Another aspect of this approach is that the mode of Exchequer assistance established in the 1920s can be seen as investment subsidy. That is, authorities were given a guarantee of subsidy for every approved house that they built, irrespective of the need for financial assistance. The subsidy system was used as a device for influencing the level of local authority house building. Merrett (1979, pp. 43–6) has referred to the 'butterfly valve' effect in which higher subsidies generated higher levels of building, and vice versa. In relation to the question of how to secure desired levels of housing production it is important to note that the subsidy system was the main source of central government influence from 1919 until the late 1970s. Throughout that period there were no explicit limits on capital expenditure by individual local authorities. As time passed, however, it became clear that while investment subsidies had been very effective in generating high levels of new building, their impact on rents was increasingly inequitable and hard to justify.

The sixth and seventh housing finance legacies from the inter-war period are the housing revenue account (HRA) and the concept of 'reasonable rent', and they are best considered together. Before 1935 there were attempts to relate council rents to levels prevailing in the private sector, but there were major problems of comparability given that virtually all private rented housing had been built before 1914 whereas virtually all council housing was new and built to different standards and specifications. The relatively high cost of council housing and continuation of rent control in the private sector, especially amongst working-class housing, added to the difficulties. The 1924 Act, for instance, specified that council rents should relate to the average rent charged for pre-1914 working-class houses in the area, but in practice costs made this virtually impossible in most areas (Jarmain, 1948, p. 85; Holmans, 1987, pp. 306–7).

At first authorities were required to keep separate accounts for houses built under the different Housing Acts from 1919 to 1930. This was administratively cumbersome, and led to differences in rents for very similar houses which happened to have been built at different times. The solution to both problems was introduced in the Housing Act 1935. From 1936 local authorities were required to maintain a single housing revenue account, into which all rent income, Exchequer subsidies and RFC had to be paid, and from which all expenditure on loan charges, management and maintenance had to be met. The pooling of rents and subsidies within a single HRA was to become a characteristic feature of British council housing, along with a system of pricing based on reasonable rents. The terms reasonable rent was not defined in the 1935 Act, nor subsequently, and authorities were in practice given wide discretion to set rents and to devise rebate schemes, although they were required to have regard to private sector rents paid by working-class tenants in the locality. The meaning of reasonable was never successfully challenged in the courts (Parker, 1967; see also Chapter 6) and in practice reasonable rents came to mean the rents set by local authorities, taking into account local political and financial circumstances and the impact of central government policy.

The considerable autonomy enjoyed by local housing authorities between the wars (Bowley, 1945, p. 258) arguably constitutes an eighth characteristic which endured for many years in matters of capital expenditure and rents.

In the period 1919–35 a distinctive framework of public sector housing finance arrangements was established, in which the role of central government was essentially that of an enabling agency. The centre established statutory powers for local authorities to build houses, and provided financial support, but how many houses were built and what rents were charged were issues to be determined locally. At the same time, however, the centre sought to influence, if not to prescribe, the volume of building and the level of rents (see Peter Kemp, Chapter 4 in this volume). The autonomy enjoyed by local authorities naturally led to variation from place to place, and this eventually became an important part of the problem of local authority housing finance, at least from the central government point of view.

Towards current value pricing

The framework established in 1919–35 survived without major change until 1972 because it had three distinctly advantageous attributes. It was effective in terms of housing production, especially in the period 1945–68 when all governments pursued high output policies, it combined a reasonable balance between central and local government and it was flexible, permitting changes of policy without major structural alterations. To press home this point, it is clear that on the one hand the succession of Housing Acts from 1923 to 1967 (apart from aspects of the 1935 Act referred to earlier) were essentially concerned with changing the level of subsidy in line with changes in the value of money and shifting priorities between building for general needs and slum clearance, rather than effecting major changes to the policy framework. On the other hand, significant policy change was accommodated without recourse to legislation. It was in 1955 that the Government made the decision to adopt rent and subsidy pooling as a device which would both help to raise the rents of older, cheaper houses, and contain the growth of Exchequer subsidies (Malpass, 1990, Ch. 5). This meant that the amount of subsidy paid on new houses in the future would be set at a level acknowledged to be lower than was required to produce affordable rents on those houses. Local authorities were thus given an incentive to raise rents on their older houses and, in effect, to transfer the subsidy to the new ones. At the same time the Government began to urge councils to introduce rent rebate schemes, and over the next fifteen years there developed what Merrett (1979, p. 184) has described as a crescendo of advice, demands and exhortations to local authorities to adopt the rebating principle to protect poorer tenants from rising rents. Rebates were financed from existing subsidies, a fact which illustrates the flexibility within the system: authorities were given subsidies on the basis of investment costs but they could redistribute the money as income-related rebates. The 1955 decision to pursue rent pooling and to encourage rebating not only demonstrated flexibility in the housing finance system; it also marked the beginning of a trend which has continued until the present—a trend away from general subsidy towards means-tested benefits for the least well off as the main form of assistance with housing costs.

Rent pooling was broadly effective for some years after 1955 as a way of responding to inflation and nudging council rents upwards in a context of improving living standards and rising rents in the private sector. The impact of the new policy was such that between 1955–6 and 1970–1 average rents rose in real terms by between 85 and 90 per cent (Holmans, 1987, p. 340) and rebate schemes spread, although fewer than 10 per cent of tenants were receiving rebates in 1969, and less than 15 per cent of Exchequer subsidy was being devoted to rebate provision (Malpass, 1990, p. 111). But an important aspect of the implementation of rent pooling was that its impact varied from place to place. Authorities with a high proportion of old houses and low levels of new building were subject to much less leverage than those which had low levels of older houses and high rates of building.

As a means of raising rents, rent pooling had limitations which became increasingly apparent towards the end of the 1960s. Critics of the existing framework built their case around four main points: (1) that the gradual spread of fair rents in the private sector was beginning to invert the long-standing relationship between public and private rents, giving renewed strength to claims that council rents were 'too low'; (2) that council rents varied considerably from one authority to another in a way which bore little or no relation to variations in the quality or popularity of dwellings in different places; (3) that subsidies were inequitably distributed amongst local authorities, with some receiving more than they needed in order to charge rents which were reasonable in relation to current wages and prices, while others received too little; and (4) that subsidy was inequitably distributed amongst tenants — that the use of subsidy to provide general rent reductions meant that some rather well-off tenants received help that they did not need, while others who were less well off received inadequate assistance.

It was argued that existing methods of financing the development of public housing, by means of fixed-value annual subsidies in the form of contributions to loan charges, had permitted rents to rise as inflation continued, but that the time had come to move to a system specifically designed to set rents in relation to current wages and prices. According to this view (Macey, 1967) rent fixing was currently approached from the wrong direction; since subsidies were fixed, the total amount to be raised in rents was calculated from the difference between expenditure and subsidy. The alternative was to fix rents first, in relation to what dwellings were currently worth, and to derive subsidy, if any, from the relationship between expenditure and total rent income.

This approach could not be contained within the existing framework. Indeed, in the form that change was introduced in the Housing Finance Act 1972, the transition to fair rents in the public sector breached four basic rules or conventions. First, existing subsidies, pledged by Act of Parliament, were phased out; no previous government had attempted such a move. Second, general subsidy, where applicable, was paid in relation to the deficit on the HRA, and a new rent rebate subsidy was introduced. Third, rent fixing ceased to be a local authority responsibility; current value pricing implied that market criteria rather than political ideology should determine rents, and the role of councillors was further eroded by the introduction of a mandatory rebate scheme. And, fourth, the 'no profit' rule which had always applied to the HRA was abandoned; in future rent income could exceed expenditure, and transfers out of the account would be permitted.

The 1972 Act was too controversial and too flawed to survive, but it stands as a major landmark in the development of public sector housing finance. In the period since the early 1970s a degree of political consensus has been established around a new set of principles: (1) that rents should be set in relation to the current value of money, reflecting current wages and prices generally; (2) that general subsidy should be calculated on a deficit basis, reflecting any shortfall in HRA income as a whole, after rents have been set in accordance with the first principle, and (3) that a system of means-tested assistance should be available on a standard basis in all areas. In relation to the historic problems of financing public housing identified earlier in this chapter these principles have some advantages over the old system. For instance, they give greater priority to issues of pricing and subsidy distribution, both amongst authorities with different financial circumstances and tenants with different incomes. The separation of general assistance from rebate assistance represented a definite step towards greater clarity and equity. In practice the shift away from investment-based subsidy has coincided with a long-term decline in new building by local authorities, and it is arguably more appropriate in such circumstances to have a subsidy system which is more sensitive to pricing issues. However, an inevitable feature of deficit subsidy systems (as demonstrated long ago by the 1919 Act) is that they involve central government in closer scrutiny of local decisions and reduce local autonomy. If the Exchequer is committed to funding HRA deficits then clearly it has an interest in the levels of income and expenditure which produce those deficits. There are both technical and political aspects here. It can be argued that the level of maintenance expenditure quite properly varies from place to place, for reasons to do with a whole variety of factors ranging from the age and composition of the stock to the weather, and that therefore the technical specialists in each locality are better qualified judges of what is required than are DoE civil servants in London. Similarly, it can be argued that in a housing market which is heavily distorted by tax incentives, property values are artificially inflated and therefore provide no valid basis for rent setting in the public sector; in this situation judgements made by democratically elected local councillors may be seen as the best available way of setting council rents.

The 1972 Act represented an attempt to move to a full-blown current value pricing system, in which each dwelling would have a registered fair rent and local authorities had no role in rent fixing. Subsequent developments have been rather more subtle, less provocative, and have contained an important element of compromise between the interests of central and local government. This is perhaps a surprising conclusion to reach about Thatcherite housing legislation, but none the less it is clear that the Housing Act 1980 indicated a retreat by central government, to the extent that local authorities remained free to set individual rents. Whereas the 1972 Act was openly concerned to raise rents to fair rent levels, in the 1980s ministers were careful not to be prescriptive about rents. Instead attention focused on subsidy levels, based on notional changes in income and expenditure at local level.

Although the 1972 Act marked the end of the old system dating from the inter-war formative years, it did not establish a sustainable framework for the latter part of the century. In this sense the 1980 Act can be seen as marking a new era in housing finance, to the extent that it remained in force for a decade and provided the basis on which the 1989 Act was built. Before 1980 council housing was characterised by relatively high levels of new building, low levels of sales, proportionately fewer poor tenants and rents influenced by the no-profit rule (apart from 1972–4). In that situation all authorities continued to receive general subsidy in amounts which in aggregate exceeded rent rebate subsidy. Since 1980 the situation has changed considerably: there has been very little new building, sales have consistently exceeded completion of new homes, the proportion of poor tenants has increased and HRAs have been permitted to move into surplus. This has been accompanied by a major reduction in general subsidy and a large increase in the proportion of HRA income derived from rent rebate subsidy. An important aspect of this last point is that rent rebates (housing benefit) are financed and administered by the Department of Social Security, a rationalisation dating from the introduction of the housing benefit system in 1982–3. (Malpass, 1984; Kemp, 1985). The significance of this lies in the way it identifies and reinforces the separation of housing subsidy from housing benefit: the social security system and the DSS have replaced housing subsidy and the DoE as the main central government financial supporters of council housing.

What has happened since 1980 is that the politics of housing finance have left behind the period when growth and subsidies were key issues. 1980 marked the beginning of an era of decline and HRA surpluses—which can be seen as largely funded by rent rebate subsidy. Both central government and local authorities have sought to obtain control and use of HRA surpluses. In the 1980s the struggle was won by the local authorities. The 1980 system contained provision for the centre to push rents up, thereby generating surpluses, and for those surpluses to be recouped by reductions in subsidy and/ or block grant, (Malpass, 1990, pp. 142–4) but local opposition prevented the system working as planned after 1981–2. In one sense the new financial regime introduced in the Local Government and Housing Act 1989 represents another attempt to gain control of rents and surpluses.

The new financial regime and the prospects for the future

Space does not permit a full account of the new financial regime for local authority housing (Malpass 1990, Ch. 8; Malpass and Murie, 1990, Ch. 7). However, it is important to acknowledge that the system which came into operation in April 1990 embraces both capital and revenue finance. It was mentioned earlier that throughout most of the century housing capital expenditure by individual local authorities was not directly controlled, and that central government sought to exercise influence via the subsidy system. In the late 1970s the introduction of housing investment programmes (HIPs) placed an annual limit on borrowing for capital projects, and in the 1980s limits were placed on the use of capital receipts from sales of land and houses. As sales exceeded new building so receipts came to prominence in the capital side of local authority housing. The new financial regime for the 1990s represents an attempt to tighten central government's control of local authority capital spending in general, and of particular importance in housing is the rule that reduces authorities' ability to spend capital receipts from council house sales. Whereas in the 1980s authorities could gradually spend 100 per cent of capital receipts, under the 1989 Act 75 per cent of receipts from the sale of houses (50 per cent in the case of non-housing receipts) must be used to repay existing debts.

On the revenue side the new regime is essentially a modified version of the 1980 system, but incorporating three important changes, all of which represent a tightening of central government control. The first change to be considered is the introduction of the ring-fenced HRA, a concept which means that authorities have lost their long-established right to subsidise council housing from the rates (now the poll tax). They have also lost the freedom to make surpluses on the HRA and to transfer those surpluses into the general fund. The Government's determination to restrict local authorities in this way stems from the perception that in the 1980s, on the one hand RFC had become the major form of 'indiscriminate' (i.e. non-means-tested) subsidy, and on the other hand, up to a quarter of authorities were transferring surpluses into the rates fund yet were also receiving rent rebate subsidy (and in some cases general subsidy as well).

The second major innovation in the 1989 Act was the amalgamation of general subsidy and rent rebate subsidy into one HRA subsidy, which replaces three pre-existing forms of assistance: Housing Act subsidy, rent rebate subsidy and RFC. In most authorities this means that HRA subsidy has taken over from rent rebate subsidy alone (since the majority had lost entitlement to Housing Act subsidy and chose not to draw on the rates to support housing). However, whereas under the previous arrangements rent rebate subsidy was calculated from the aggregate entitlement of *all* housing benefit claimants in HRA dwellings, the new subsidy is paid only to the extent necessary to balance the notional HRA.

This is in fact much more significant than the ring fence in most areas because of the way in which virtually all authorities' HRAs are once more regarded as being in substantial notional deficit. The easiest way to understand this is to recognise that under the 1980 system the deficit to be met by subsidy was the gap between notional expenditure and notional income from rents (including rebates) plus any RFC and other income. In effect the new definition of HRA deficit is expanded to include rebates and RFC. Without increasing public expenditure at all the new system massively expands the definition of HRA deficit, by a factor of six on a national level. The importance of this is that the amount of leverage which central government can exert on rents is directly related to the magnitude of the deficit. Thus, by the late 1980s only a quarter of authorities were susceptible to leverage on rents through subsidy withdrawal, but for the foreseeable future virtually all authorities will be in that position.

The third important change introduced in April 1990 was the Government's commitment to adopt a more sophisticated approach to the calculation of subsidy by differentiating assumed changes in income and expenditure.

Throughout the 1980s the subsidy system involved the issue of annual 'determinations' of assumed changes, in which all authorities were treated the same, irrespective of their actual circumstances. The removal of local councils' right to subsidise the HRA from their own resources only added to the case for a more sensitive system. However, finding a satisfactory way of differentiating determinations proved very difficult because of the degree of variation in circumstances and the lack of adequate data. On the issue of rents the Government's position is that it is not pursuing a policy of market rents in the public sector and has no particular target for council rents. The official line is that, 'Rents should generally not exceed levels within reach of people in low paid employment, and in practice they will frequently be below market levels' (DoE, 1988). Local authorities retain the freedom to set individual rents, but it is clearly government policy to move towards a situation in which rents reflect current values. The approach which has been adopted is to relate assumed rent *increases* to the capital values in each locality, using right-to-buy valuations as a guide to values and the subsidy system as a way of putting leverage on rents. In the fullness of time this method would tend to generate a pattern of variation in rents across the country reflecting price and rent variations in the private sector.

However, when the data were first run through the DoE computers in 1989 it quickly emerged that some form of damping mechanism would be needed in order to prevent very large increases in some London and south-eastern authorities, and large *reductions* in some northern authorities. In practice the guideline rent increases for 1990–1 were calculated on the basis of local capital values, plus a real increase of 5 per cent and a further 5 per cent for inflation, but then damped so that, for subsidy purposes, no authority was assumed to raise its rents by less than 95p per week and none by more than £4.50 per week.

In the case of management and maintenance expenditure (m & m), it proved impossible to find a satisfactory basis for differentiating increases in assumed spending, and the new regime began in 1990–1 by rolling forward from the old system on the assumption that inflation was 5 per cent and expenditure would increase by 3 per cent in real terms. The assumption that m & m expenditure would rise by less than rent income is important, for it is a necessary part of the way leverage is exerted on rents.

What, then, are the prospects for the future? And how should the new regime be understood in relation to past experience? A main theme of this chapter has been to draw out the continuities in the development of public sector housing finance, and to show how over a long period policy has moved towards a form of current value pricing, with means-tested assistance becoming more significant. The new regime is consistent with that broad policy trend. It is also consistent with past legislation to the extent that it combines aspects of long- and short-term thinking. Governments have to consider short-term feasibility as well as longer-term strategy, and the 1989 Act provides a good example of the centre's readiness to sacrifice principles to feasibility.

In terms of the historic problems of financing council housing the new regime represents a clear position: it will produce very low levels of new building, in line with Conservative Government policy objectives; it takes a line on rent setting which combines local autonomy to fix individual rents with powerful leverage from the centre on overall increases; responsibility for subsidy is no longer divided between central and local taxes; subsidy distribution amongst authorities is more sensitive to local circumstances than in the past, and the distribution of subsidy amongst tenants is also more sensitive to need than in the past.

However, as a contribution to the reform of housing finance the new regime leaves a lot to be desired. As an approach to the financing of public housing it is grounded in a particular ideological perspective on the future role of council housing and local government. The stated aims of the new regime were that it should be simpler, fairer and more effective. Unfortunately these are not easily compatible objectives. Given the past level of local autonomy in relation to new building and rents policies, the Government faces a highly varied set of local circumstances. This means that a set of simple policy inputs will be very likely to generate highly uneven effects across the country. Thus fair and effective policy outputs require complex policy inputs. In the first year of operation it is already clear that the implementation of the new system is extremely complex, and the outcomes in terms of rent increases and spending levels are widely divergent from the Government's assumptions.

The main criticism of the new regime has to be that it represents an unprincipled sleight of hand in which rent rebates are combined with housing subsidy. Rebates are properly regarded as a form of social security, a fact that has been acknowledged in the public expenditure accounts and ministerial responsibilities since 1982–3. From the point of view of council tenants it will appear that the cost of rebates is increasingly falling on the better-off tenants themselves rather than on the taxpayer. This will undoubtedly reinforce right-to-buy sales and the further residualisation of council housing.

From the point of view of local councils, the capping of HRA subsidy represents the latest attempt by the centre to cream off the benefits of rising rents and growing surpluses. Central government has equipped itself with a powerful device to keep council rents rising in real terms, and the prospects for the 1990s appear to indicate a continuing series of significant increases.

However, the potency of the system lies in the relationship between the determination for rents and management and maintenance expenditure. The power to keep rents rising requires asymmetrical determinations, in which the assumed rent increase is greater than the assumed m & m increase. The larger the difference the greater the pressure on authorities to raise rents. But the impact on tenants will be that they will not receive improvements in housing services that reflect increases in rents. From their point of view the new regime represents very poor value for money, and is therefore likely to lead to yet more right-to-buy decisions, and it may be the trigger for the 'tenants' choice' provisions in the Housing Act 1988 to assume belated significance and appeal.

However it is viewed, the new financial regime is clearly a centralising measure produced by a government which is deeply opposed to local government in general and council housing in particular. As a result the housing outlook for the least well off continues to be bleak indeed. A change of government must surely lead to new legislation concerned with the problem of reviving the supply of affordable housing in the public sector.

References

Ball, M (1988) *Rebuilding Construction* London, Routledge.

Boddy, M (1976) 'Building societies and owner occupation', in *Housing and Class in Britain* London, Political Economy of Housing Workshop.

Bowley, M (1945) *Housing and the State* Allen and Unwin, London.

DoE (1977) *Housing Policy Technical Volume, part I* London, HMSO.

DoE (1988) *New financial regime for local authority housing in England and Wales: A consultation paper*, July.

Ermisch, J (1984) *Housing Finance: Who Gains?* London, Policy Studies Institute.

Gauldie, E (1974) *Cruel Habitations: a History of Working Class Housing, 1780–1918* London, Allen and Unwin.

Goss, S and Lansley, S (1981) *What Price Housing?* London, SHAC.

Holmans, A (1987) *Housing Policy in Britain* London, Croom Helm.

Jarmain, J R (1948) *Housing Subsidies and Rents* London, Stevens.

Kemp, P (1985) 'The Housing Benefit Scheme', in M Brenton and C Jones (eds) *The Yearbook of Social Policy in Britain, 1984–5* London, Routledge and Kegan Paul.

Macey, J (1967) 'Housing policy and its implications, with particular reference to economic rents', *Housing* 3 (1) May.

Malpass, P (1984) 'Housing benefits in perspective', in C Jones and J Stevenson (eds) *The Yearbook of Social Policy in Britain, 1983* London, Routledge and Kegan Paul.

Malpass, P (1990) *Reshaping Housing Policy* London, Routledge.

Malpass, P and Murie, A (1990) *Housing Policy and Practice* 3rd edn, London, Macmillan.

Merrett, A J and Sykes, A (1965) *Housing Finance and Development* London, Longman.

Merrett, S (1979) *State Housing in Britain* London, Routledge and Kegan Paul.

Parker, R (1967) *The Rents of Council Houses* London, Bell.

6 Rents and income: a legal overview

Trevor Buck

Introduction

Policies to determine rent levels in social housing and to determine appropriate levels of income-related assistance for individuals to meet their housing costs, have, in Britain, been framed largely as a corollary to other major policy issues. Frequently, such policy as exists in relation to rents and incomes is a product of reaction to a complex interaction of central and local government and, on the macro level, a response to the general structural alterations in the balance between three main forms of housing tenure; social housing, owner occupation and the private rented sector. From the 'consumer' point of view though, the cost of housing and the ability to pay are of primary importance in determining access to housing. This chapter does not chart the complete history of rent fixing in social housing. There are various existing sources which provide such accounts (Parker, 1967). Nor does it provide a comprehensive account of the development of rent and rebate schemes (see Deacon and Bradshaw, 1983 and Malpass, 1990). The focus of this chapter is the role of the law. What specific contribution does the legal framework make to such policies? There are other perspectives which it could be claimed, with good reason, have greater explanatory power. For example, some commentators regard central–local government relations as an enlightening theme to apply in the housing field. Others would regard rent policy as unintelligible without recourse to detailed discussion of the housing subsidy system (Malpass, 1990). Still others would prefer economic interpretations (Hills, 1988).

The concentration on the *legal* nature of powers and duties in this area does have some significant advantages. First, the legal framework reflects certain policy concerns; studying specific legal materials will often demonstrate, in some detail, the problems of *implementing* policy options. As regards the housing field it has been shown in the past that aspects of implementation at local level have frequently been overlooked. Secondly, a study of the incidence of legal technique often puts into relief areas of activity where the chosen controls are purely extra-legal, for example, fiscal or political. This will naturally provoke questions about choice and mix of regulatory techniques.

Finally, law does not of course always act to 'regulate' in a compulsory sense; it also enables the establishment of social programmes. It has to be conceded that the 'legal environment' of rent policy and income-related assistance is not so conspicuous compared with, for example, tenants' rights' (see Chapter 7). But the importance of the legal context in this and other areas of housing policy is undoubtedly increasing and will continue to be of greater significance in the twenty-first century.

Background

A historical analysis of rent fixing by local authorities shows quite clearly the importance of appreciating the central–local government relationship to understand the particular legal framework chosen. For example, under the Housing and Town Planning & etc. Act 1919 (the 'Addison Act') local authorities were under a duty to survey their area's housing needs and undertake the necessary plans to provide housing. Before the Local Government Board (Ministry of Health from June 1919) could approve a scheme the local authority had to provide estimates of costs including 'rents expected to be derived from the houses under the scheme' (s. 1(4)). Local authority liability was restricted to the product of a penny rate, consequently the potential open-ended commitment by central government to subsidise authorities was met by the appointment of (eleven) regional commissioners to monitor implementation at the local level. Rents were generally fixed in line with controlled rents of similar (privately) rented pre-war houses and tenants' ability to pay (English, 1982).

From time to time setting rent levels can also achieve immense political significance. For example, the 'controlled rents' just referred to had been introduced in the private sector by the Increase of Rent and Mortgage Interest (War Restrictions) Act 1915; rents were frozen at levels charged on 3 August 1914. This Act was passed primarily to stave off political unrest, such as the Glasgow rent strikes of 1915, which were becoming increasingly 'revolutionary' in character and threatening the war effort (Melling, 1980).

The nature of the subsidy system is crucial in explaining rent-fixing practices. For example, under the Housing Act 1923 (the 'Chamberlain' Act) fixed-rate subsidies (£6 p.a. for twenty years for each house built) were introduced. This innovation of the fixed-rate subsidy was continued in the Housing (Financial Provisions) Act 1924 (the 'Wheatley' Act) but on more generous terms, (£9 p.a. per house for forty years). There was also a statutory rate-fund contribution fixed at a maximum of £4.50 for forty years. Rents would thus be fixed at a level which would prevent any greater loss than £13.50 p.a. The Act provided, again, the yardstick of controlled rents in the private sector (s. 3(2)(e), (3)). This subsidy system was convenient for the Government in that its commitment was no longer open ended as it had been under the Addison Act. Consequently, central government was less likely to interfere with the local authorities' view of the correct balance between rents and subsidy.

However, the fixed subsidy systems had certain disadvantages too. The loan charge debt payable on the various housing programmes might quickly become out of step with the original amount of subsidy. During inflationary periods such 'historic' costs would fall, allowing greater local freedom to set rents lower. The equivalent debts on costs of newer housing programmes could be much higher, thus leading to higher rents for such properties. Quite startling disparities between rents could occur not only between different authorities but also within one local authority in relation to property of a similar type. Partly in response to this situation, and also as a general instrument to facilitate the withdrawal of 'general needs' subsidy, the device of 'rent pooling' was adopted.

Finally, taking a broader view of the historical development of policy, it is arguable that a dominating theme in the twentieth century will always be the impact of two world wars. The similarities between the development of post-First World War and post-Second World War housing policy has been noted several times in the literature. In particular, the imposition of rent control and subsequent deregulation of rents after both world wars in the private sector has been well documented (Doling and Davies, 1984). Another persistent similarity is that after each war initially generous 'general needs' subsidies were eventually cut back and converted into special needs subsidies for rehousing slum dwellers, and/or other special category housing groups, for example, the elderly.

Rent pooling

Under the Housing Act 1935 local authorities were required to set up a single 'housing revenue account' bringing together all the separate accounts of their previous housing programmes. They were also empowered in law to set 'reasonable rents' for their housing stock. In addition to pooling subsidies authorities were also permitted to pool rents. This enabled them to adjust rents to the differences between dwellings in terms of their 'use-value'. However, the intention at the time was not only to introduce a measure of equity between households; the primary purpose was to enable subsidy to be channelled towards the low-income tenants cleared from the slums after the Housing Act 1930 (Merrett, 1979). With rising financial and construction costs, rent pooling came to serve a different purpose. Inflation and real growth in earnings meant that the 'historic' cost of older properties fell as a proportion of income, partly offset by management and repair costs. Rent pooling enabled authorities to raise rents on older properties above their historic costs and any surplus was effectively transferred to newer stock, thereby reducing the levels of rent required on newer properties. From the point of view of central government rent pooling helped to influence authorities to charge higher rents for older properties and thus facilitated a reduction in current subsidy. As well as financing the cost of new council houses, the pool was also seen as a source of payment for rent rebates. As a mechanism for controlling rent levels, rent pooling was probably proving too weak an instrument by the late 1960s. This was especially so in relation to authorities who managed without much or any subsidy. Once such subsidy had gone central government had effectively lost an important point of leverage. It has also been suggested that the significance of rent pooling in terms of central government control is to some extent curtailed by the addition of the principle of 'relative desirability' in the Housing Act 1985, section 24(3) and (4); see below and see Hoath (1989). On occasion it has been mooted that a *national* rent pooling system should be devised so that transfers can be made from one authority to another (Housing Centre Trust, 1975; Kelly, 1986). However, official responses, so far, have been negative (Green Paper, 1977).

Housing Finance Act 1972: 'fair rents' in the public sector

In contrast to fixed subsidy systems, deficit subsidisation, introduced after 1972, emphasises current rather than historic costs; the level of subsidy is calculated by reference to the gap between expenditure and income. As Malpass (1990, p. 71) points out 'the adoption of the deficit subsidy principle involved a departure from the idea that rent fixing was a local matter, and gave central government a much more direct interest in rent fixing'. Deficit subsidisation therefore ran in parallel with the notion that council rents should reflect current money values and earnings accompanied by income-related assistance for those less well off.

The 1972 Act was an important landmark. It departed from previous practice in that rather than using the familiar *fiscal* methods of influencing local authority policy on rent levels (see Chapter 5), the chosen policy instrument was an *administrative-legal* one. The avowed aim of the Act was to raise council rents in stages to the (then) higher levels of 'fair rents' via determinations by rent officers similar to those in the private sector with review performed by 'Rent Scrutiny Boards'. Such 'fair rents' were generally much higher than council rents. But many factors conspired to defeat this policy, not the least of which was the resistance presented in a highly publicised manner by the Clay Cross councillors (Skinner and Langdon, 1974). However, the rent rebate schemes, increasingly developed by local authorities since the 1950s, were substituted by a national mandatory scheme, though there was a considerable amount of discretion built into the scheme to enable authorities to adapt it to local conditions if they wished. Nevertheless, the eventual failure to regulate local authority rent levels resulted in a return to the concept of 'reasonable rents' in law in 1974. Of course the practice of influencing authorities' rent fixing continued through refinements to the subsidy system itself. Although the Act had attempted to establish some comparability between local authority rents and 'fair rents' in the private sector it became increasingly clear that the tenant's primary comparator had become the owner-occupier rather than the private sector tenant. This reflected the general shift to owner occupation as the preferred tenure. The shift also prompted a 'residualisation' of council housing accompanied by a policy preference for social housing to be performed by non-municipal agencies.

Reasonable rents

The legal requirement for local authorities to set 'reasonable' rents dates back, as we have seen, to the 1930s. The current provision states that '[a] local authority may make such reasonable charges as they may determine for the tenancy or occupation of their houses' (Housing Act 1985, s. 24(1)). The local authority is also under a duty to review rents and make appropriate changes 'as circumstances may require' (s. 24(2)). There has also been a significant addition of two new subsections to Section 24, (see p. 81). There is a well developed case law which, generally speaking, supports the local authorities' autonomy in determining what is 'reasonable' for these purposes. There is only one occasion where judicial review of the exercise of this discretion has succeeded in defeating local discretion, *Backhouse v. London Borough of Lambeth* (1972) 116 Solicitors' Journal 802, concerning a professed device to avoid certain provisions in the Housing Finance Act 1972. The cases have arisen either as a direct challenge in judicial review proceedings or by way of a ratepayer's challenge to the district auditor's approval of local authority accounts (Local Government Finance Act 1982, s. 19); see for example *Hemsted v. Lees and Norwich City Council* 18 Housing Law Reports 424. It has also been held that a defendant, facing an action for possession by a local authority for rent arrears, can raise the lawfulness of an authority's rent decision as a defence *London Borough of Wandsworth v. Winder* [1985] Appeal Cases 461. However, the cases demonstrate that a balance must be struck between the interests of tenants as a whole and the ratepayers generally *Belcher v. Reading Corporation* [1959] 1 Chancery 380. Lord Justice Diplock stated in *Luby v. Newcastle-under-Lyme Corporation* [1964] 2 Queens Bench 64 that

In determining the rent structure to be applied to houses provided by a local authority the local authority is applying what is, in effect, a social policy upon which reasonable men may hold different views. Since any deficit in the housing revenue account has to be made good from the general rate fund, the choice of rent structure involves weighing the interests of the tenants as a whole and of individual impoverished tenants against those of the general body of ratepayers.

Other cases have also emphasised that the courts are not willing to intervene in such a *social policy* area. In the absence of an authority acting in a way in which no reasonable local authority would act (i.e. *Wednesbury* unreasonableness, see *Associated Provincial Picture Houses Ltd v. Wednesbury Corporation* [1948] 1 Kings Bench 223), the discretion of an authority remains unimpeachable. The wide ambit allowed by the law to local authorities is well demonstrated in *R. v. Secretary of State for Health and Social Services, ex parte Sheffield City Council* (1985) 18 Housing Law Reports 6 where the council established a scheme whereby tenants could pay a lower rent if they undertook responsibility for certain repairs, but tenants on housing benefit (HB) were excluded from the scheme. The result was that tenants receiving housing benefit would be paying higher rents, paid for by government subsidy to the local authority for HB expenditure. The scheme was thought to be a device to inflate the local authority's funds by effectively raising rents of tenants on HB.

If the exercise of discretion is supported by the courts even in such circumstances where the motive was somewhat dubious then, *a fortiori*, such discretion is likely to be upheld by the courts in a wide range of circumstances. In a recent case for example, it was held not to be unreasonable for an authority to increase its rents by 37 per cent (inflation was running at 10.5 per cent) and simultaneously arrange a significant reduction in the rate fund contribution to the housing revenue account. The relative means of council tenants and ratepayers generally was not a compulsory factor to be taken into account. Furthermore, it was reasonable to disregard the rents legislation that applied in the private sector; see *London Borough of Wandsworth v. Winder (No 2)* (1987 19 Housing Law Reports 205, (High Court), (1988) 20 Housing Law Reports 400, (Court of Appeal).

However, the precedent value of some of these authorities will have to be reviewed in the light of the recent addition of two further sub-sections to section 24. It is now provided that 'In exercising their functions [under s. 24], a local housing authority shall have regard in particular to the principle that the rents of houses of any class or description should bear broadly the same proportion to private sector rents as the rents of houses of any other class or description' (Housing Act 1985, s. 24(3)), as inserted by Local Government and Housing Act 1989, s. 162. The term 'private sector rents' in this context means those relating to lettings on assured tenancies within the meaning of the Housing Act 1988.

It should be noted that the words 'in particular' make the consideration of this principle a significant and potent factor for local authorities to have regard to. It will mean that if under an assured tenancy a house with a garden would fetch twice as much as a purpose-built flat with the same number of rooms then the authority must acknowledge that its rents in relation to such classes of housing should also be (broadly) twice as much for the former category as for the latter. This should be so even if each rent is substantially more (or less) than in the private sector. The amendment, therefore, introduces a principle of 'relative desirability'.

The DoE Consultation Paper (1988) stated that 'The Government will also consider whether more should be done to encourage authorities to reflect the value or popularity of different dwellings in establishing rent differentials between properties in the same area' (para 18). But the significance of the amendment should not be overstated. The question of reasonableness is still at the core of the discretion. The principle of 'relative desirability' has to be a factor to which 'in particular' the authority must have regard. If there are other factors, which a local authority considers override the application of this principle, then there seems no reason, in law at least, why such a determination should be impugned. The interesting point arising from the amendment is that it does open up possibilities for the future for further legal regulation in this area. However, given the more important influence that is exerted on rent-fixing practices through the subsidy system, one may question why recasting the legal provisions should be thought appropriate. Presumably, the new legal 'structuring' of the rent-fixing discretion was intended to reinforce such fiscal influences. However, such barely disguised attempts to reduce local autonomy in this area have in the past met with resistance at local level (broadly) in proportion to how directly those attempts were presented to local government.

The difficulties of legally challenging a municipal reasonable rent are well documented elsewhere (Hughes, 1987; Hoath, 1989). It has been suggested that where the defect lies with the authorities' internal decision-making procedure the chances of successful challenge are higher than a judicial review case (Hoath, 1989). There have been numerous practical difficulties, not least of which is obtaining legal aid. It might also be thought that such a procedure ought to go ahead by way of a 'representative action', but English law has traditionally been inimical to adopting the format of 'class actions' used in the United States. In principle, the 'local inquiry' format might provide an appropriate model of dispute resolution. Indeed under Housing Act 1957 (ss 171–6, 181) the Minister had the power to hold a local inquiry into a council's rents, but this provision was removed by the Local Government Act 1972.

Rent increases

Direct intervention in the authorities' powers to *increase* rents has occurred from time to time. A good example was the attempt to restrict increases by the Labour Government of 1964–70 as part of its wider counter-inflation policy at the time. Following a report on local authority rents National Board for Prices and Incomes (NBPI, 1968) powers to restrict increases were taken in the Prices and Incomes Act 1968. It became illegal to raise rents without ministerial consent and subsequent guidance by the department stated that average increases of more than 37½p would not obtain approval nor would individual increases of more than 50p. The policy was continued under the Rent (Control of Increases) Act 1969, but the evidence shows that, irrespective of these controls, rents rose faster than gross earnings and faster than retail prices (Malpass, 1990). The policy was terminated when the Conservatives were elected in June 1970. Currently, the legal regulations relating to *increases* of local authority rents are concerned largely with formalities, for example the notice requirements applying to non-secure tenants (Housing Act 1985, s. 25; see also ss. 102, 103). There is a basic duty to 'review' rent levels under Housing Act 1985, s. 24(2) and there is also a reserve power to restrict or prevent rent increases under the Landlord and Tenant Act 1985, s. 31. However, in relation to this latter provision, it should be noted that, firstly, no orders have yet been made under the provision, and secondly, they can only be made 'generally or in relation to any specified description of dwelling', i.e. such an order could not apply to an individual council or council house (Hoath, 1989). An authority is also precluded from making a rent increase on account of tenants' improvements (Housing Act 1985, s. 101).

The more significant extra-legal regulation of rent increases is achieved through the subsidy mechanisms. From 1980–9 the subsidy received by an authority depended on central government assumptions about changes in the costs and incomes of the local authority. Each year the Secretary of State assumed a rate of change for both rents and management and maintenance costs for calculating subsidy for the following year. In setting a rent increase he was to 'have regard, among other things, to past and expected movements in incomes, costs and prices' (Housing Act 1980, s. 100).

Affordable rents

Government policy in relation to non-council social housing is reflected in the changes achieved by the Housing Act 1988 which, generally, seeks to make housing associations more reliant on private finance and provides for transfers of property out of council housing through 'Tenants' Choice' and housing action trusts. New lettings by housing associations were taken out of the 'fair rent' assessment scheme. Up to this point most housing association property fell under the 'fair rent' procedure because most such properties would have had a registered rent as a condition of receiving housing association grant (Hughes, 1987). Setting rent levels is now at the discretion of the association in the context of the subsidies it receives. However, the Housing Corporation and Housing for Wales (the 'Corporations') have wide powers to issue guidance to associations and one of the matters specifically mentioned in Housing Associations Act 1985, s. 36A is 'the terms of tenancies and the principles on which the levels of rent should be determined'. If an association decided to refuse to comply with such guidance its registered status (and eligibility to government money) could be in question (Housing Association Act 1985, ss. 5 & 6).

Such rents have become known as 'affordable rents'. Indeed the National Federation of Housing Associations argued for a simple guideline for setting assured tenancy rents at an 'affordable' level not exceeding 20 per cent of the net incomes of households for whom the accommodation is intended. Currently new lettings monitored by the National Federation of Housing Associations are running at approximately 2,700 per month (NFHA, 1990). The greater penetration of non-council social housing by market principles has certain implications for rent levels. Wilmott and Murie (1988) point out, for example, that if rents of housing associations were to become much higher than council rents then low-income families would be excluded and a new form of polarisation would then occur between council housing and other social housing. They are concerned at the dangers of such diversity. It is argued that there is a need for some type of 'framework' to ensure that the balance struck is reasonable; local authorities should have powers to step in where there are clearly gaps in the various types of social housing available. Wilmot and Murie (1988) have suggested the creation of a Housing Inspectorate to undertake these tasks.

Rent rebates and allowances

Rent-fixing practices have certain consequences for the issue of tenants' access to housing. Under the Housing Act 1930 (the 'Greenwood' Act), for example, legislative expression was given to an increasing campaign for slum clearance for which this Act provided a new subsidy. It was clear that rehoused slum-dwellers would not be able to afford the relatively high rents charged for existing council houses. To meet this problem the Act provided that the authority 'may charge in respect of any house such rent as they may think fit, and may grant to the tenant of any house such rebates from rent, subject to such terms and conditions as they may think fit' (s. 27(c)). Authorities were thus free to adopt any scheme of rebates or differential renting scheme they chose provided that rents were what tenants 'could reasonably be expected to pay' (s. 27(c)). The provisions were extended in the Housing Act 1936 to all tenants but did not become a significant part of housing policy until at least the late 1950s. In 1955–6 only 15 per cent of authorities operated rebate schemes, while in 1963–4 nearly 40 per cent did (Malpass, 1990). But progress was by no means uniform; some authorities were also abandoning or restricting the scope of their schemes. In 1956, however, because of reductions in subsidies councils tended to raise rent levels.

But it should not be assumed that the implementation of rebate schemes acted as an extra cost overall; the intention was to raise average rents. The existence of a rebate scheme meant that there were less scruples in raising 'reasonable rents' as those unable to pay would receive some assistance. Generally, during this period, rental income increased as an item in the housing revenue account. By 1970 over 60 per cent of local authorities operated a rebate scheme (Deacon and Bradshaw, 1983).

The next step was the circulation by government of a 'model' local scheme. As the regime envisaged under the Housing Finance Act 1972 assumed public sector rents would rise, a mandatory scheme of rent and rate rebates became irresistible. Reflecting a concern, fundamentally, of social security, (rather than housing) policy, i.e. to achieve equity as between householders, the scheme also included rent allowances for private and housing association tenants. Several discretionary elements remained in the scheme. In particular, an authority could operate a 'high rent' scheme. Where the average rents in the area exceeded the national average by 30 per cent or more, the figure of 60 per cent of 'eligible rent' used in the initial calculation of the rent allowance could be increased to 80 or 90 per cent, subject to the approval of the Secretary of State. A local authority could, at its own expense, increase expenditure on 'standard' cases by up to 10 per cent by paying more to certain classes of persons (e.g. war pensioners) or to individuals in 'exceptional circumstances'.

One of the problems of introducing rent rebates and allowances was that it overlapped with existing social security provision. Rent had been an established element in determining needs under the unemployment assistance scheme and was continued in the national assistance scheme proposed by Beveridge (Beveridge, 1942), and renamed 'supplementary benefit' in 1966. Eventually, the 'better-off' problem, i.e. the difficulty of assessing whether a person not in full-time work should claim supplementary benefit or rent rebate, fuelled reform and a unified housing benefit scheme was devised (though relief for owner-occupiers' mortgage relief still fell within the provenance of supplementary benefit: SB) (Social Security and Housing Benefits Act 1982). But the new scheme, effectively a mass means-tested benefit, phased in over the following year was to be administered by the authorities themselves and not the DHSS. There was much administrative difficulty in the initial stages of implementation (Hill, 1984; Kemp, 1984). Further anomalies were created as between 'certificated' cases, (claimants in receipt of SB who received all their eligible housing costs), and 'standard' cases (claimants not entitled to SB, in which case there was a set-off between a 'needs allowance' and gross income). Sixty per cent of rent and rates were met where income was less than the notional allowance. Where income exceeded the allowance, deductions were made from the 60 per cent amount according to a system of 'tapers'. 'Housing Benefit Supplement' (HBS) was quickly invented to patch up the embarrassment caused to the government of having 'standard' case claimants on low incomes actually worse off than 'certificated' cases in certain circumstances. HBS was arguably one of the most complex, least known, and administratively disastrous social security benefits ever devised in Britain. Despite the difficulties of the first HB scheme, benefit expenditure increased, partly because local authority rents were increasing and also because unemployment rates rose. The various tapers proved to be a useful instrument to regulate public expenditure in this field, but it was clear that more significant reforms would have to be made.

In conjunction with the 'Fowler Reviews' of social security provision a review of the housing benefit scheme expressed concern that the scheme had not succeeded in removing inequities between households with similar needs and income (Housing Benefit Review, 1985). The general rules for assessing income were harmonised as much as possible for all the 'income-related benefits' under the Social Security Act 1986 (i.e. income support, family credit, and housing benefit). The new scheme came into effect in April 1988 and contained just two tapers (for rent and rates); these would be applied to 'net' rather than 'gross' income, thus avoiding some of the previous 'poverty trap' effects arising from the withdrawal of benefit as income increased (see generally Ogus and Barendt, 1988, Ch. 13).

Housing benefit and the new role of the rent officer

The legal structure of the HB scheme is extremely complex. For the purposes of analysing rent-fixing policies, the important area to focus on is housing benefit subsidy and the new role of the rent officer in relation to this system.

Under the Housing Act 1988, s. 120, provision is made for the reorganisation of the rent officer service in the light of the expected contraction in the service due to the fact that the main tenancy created under that Act, the 'assured' tenancy, is not to be included in the 'fair rent' assessment scheme. Rent officers have been allocated additional functions in relation to determining rents for the purpose of setting limits to housing benefit subsidy that an authority is entitled to. From April 1989, rent officers determined a 'market rent' for properties which the authority are under a duty to refer to the service (mainly tenancies established by the 1988 Act; see Housing Act 1988, s. 121, and the Rent Officers (Additional Functions) Order, SI/1990 No 428). The authority can still pay *more* in HB than the levels of rent determined by the rent officer, if they wish, but such payments will have subsidy implications providing authorities with an incentive to keep within levels determined by the rent officer.

Eventually, this system will replace the setting of 'local thresholds' by the Secretary of State which have similar implications in the housing benefit subsidy system. As well as generally acting as a brake on local authority housing benefit expenditure the rent officers's new role will also specifically encourage the use of existing powers in the Housing Benefit Regulations to withhold benefit where there has been an unreasonable rent increase and/or where the accommodation is unreasonably large or expensive (see Housing Benefit (General) Regulations 1987, regs 11 & 12, SI/1987 No 1971, as amended). In exercising such powers, the housing authority is now specifically directed to take into account a Housing Act 1988, s. 121, determination.

The main legal question that arises here is the issue of whether the authority, in resorting routinely to such 'thresholds' or the 'market rent' level set by the rent officer, will have 'fettered' its discretion, leaving it vulnerable to judicial review. Allied to this issue is the question of how far the authority can take into account its own financial situation in exercising the powers to pay benefit. In *R. v. Brent London Borough Council, ex parte Connery* ([1990] 2 All England Reports 353), it was held that the council's own financial situation was not a lawful consideration in assessing the question of whether the rent payable was unreasonably high, but once having decided a rent was unreasonably high, the council's consideration of its own financial situation was a legitimate consideration in determining how far to reduce the eligible rent. However, this was limited in that the regulations would not permit the eligible rent to be reduced below the cost of suitable alternative accommodation elsewhere.

Rent, income and 'residualisation'

The outline of the history of setting 'reasonable rents' in the public sector demonstrates a varied struggle by local authorities to achieve rent levels which enabled wider access to social housing. At times (e.g. 1919–23), because of the interaction of rising building costs and inflation, even generous subsidies gave little assistance to authorities in this task. The result was that much of this earlier housing was only within the reach of skilled or semi-skilled artisans. The recent changes in housing policy whereby local authority stock has become residualised for more specific tasks (e.g. slum clearance, housing for the elderly) rather than 'general needs' meant that it was being 'reserved for the poor'. This had several effects, some of which have historical antecedents; for example, the contraction of subsidy led to the adoption of poorer-quality building standards (for example the reduction of minimum square foot standards in the 1920s and 1930s). Likewise, the inevitable pressures to raise rents meant that rent rebate had to be given for the lower-paid groups to ensure the continuance of such a policy. Given that both major political parties have conceded that owner occupation is the primary tenure (since at least the mid-1960s) and of course the Thatcher years have seen a concerted effort to support this form of tenure, the only way to preserve local authority housing for the poor has been a proportionate increase in income-related assistance in the form of rent rebates. Many commentators argue that the significant policy development taking place in this context is the general shift from 'bricks and mortar' subsidy to income-related assistance. The implications are very clear for the encouragement of owner occupation, but the contours of the 'residual' area of public sector housing are not so apparent. The *differential* in private sector rents is now to be taken into account in setting a 'reasonable rent' (Housing Act 1985, s. 24, as amended) and an 'affordable rent' is also market-related. This 'residualises' the poorest tenants, who must be quick to claim their entitlement to housing benefit, report changes of circumstances, and generally cope with the process of being an HB claimant to ensure that their accommodation is secure. Complaints to the Local Ombudsman and instances of possession proceedings being taken against tenants who for a variety of reasons have failed to secure their full entitlement, emphasise the down-side of this new reliance on individual initiative implicit in the shift to housing benefits subsidisation (see Luba, 1989).

Conclusions

The discussion of the use of legal technique in the area of rent-fixing and the development of income-related assistance has emphasised the discretion available to local authorities in setting 'reasonable rents' and the courts' traditional reluctance to trespass in areas of 'social policy'. Nevertheless, two significant attempts to provide a tighter legal framework in 1968 and 1972, though generated from different policy concerns, both failed. The return in 1974 of 'reasonable rents' for local authority housing has recently been qualified by the addition of the principle of 'relative desirability' to the legal discretion. Given the overall trend of increasing central government monitoring of a range of local government functions, it is likely that the law will develop along similar lines as the financial imperatives for central government to concern itself with rent fixing increase. The addition to Section 24 of other 'factors' to be taken into account would, of course, be a very familiar technique available to fine-tune the 'structure' of a legal discretionary power. At present one can say that the legal discretion merely reinforces the more important influences at work in the housing finance system generally. Yet the incremental restriction of such a discretion may well yield a 'death by a thousand cuts' to such local autonomy as now exists.

The legal framework of rent rebates which survived and developed after the failure of the Housing Finance Act 1972 has, as we have seen, moved from allowing some discretion in the operation of schemes to an increasingly uniform national system of means testing. While, clearly, a complicated system of legal regulation is required to mark out the parameters of 'entitlement' to housing benefit and provide for protection against fraud and abuse, it can be argued that this aspect of the legal framework follows closely social security policy objectives rather than specific housing ones. The objectives of housing policy are now served by the developing system of housing benefit subsidy, which will take on an increasing significance for the future. However, it must also be said that the development of the HB system is already showing signs of producing unexpected outcomes; for example it would appear to be generating an element of 'consumer power'. This was epitomised by the political pressure to raise the capital limit above the threshold set for the other income-related benefits shortly after the April 1988 social security reforms.

Lastly, the control exerted over housing benefit subsidy levels by rent officers will achieve an enhanced significance in the context of the new housing subsidy regime whereby the process of 'ring-fencing' and the inclusion of rent rebate in the newly defined 'Housing revenue account subsidy' will preclude the flexibility that authorities have had in the past to make up deficits from the rate fund or other sources of income (DoE Consultation Paper, 1988). The prospect of housing benefit subsidy penalties will therefore become more influential on local authority behaviour in administering the HB scheme. The pressure will be on to avoid backdating payments and overpayments, thus precluding the opportunities that there have been in the past to write off rent arrears by such means. The evolution of the HB scheme from a relatively minor role to a major policy element in the 1990s and beyond is reflected in a recent report of the Audit Commission in which the continuing problem of rent arrears was, in part, attributed to various defects in the HB scheme (Audit Commission, 1990). In the absence of a successful campaign to secure more significant 'welfare rights' in the HB context the prospects for tenants of social housing are not good.

References

Audit Commission (1990) *Survey of Local Authority Housing Rent Arrears* London, HMSO.

Beveridge, W (1942) *Social Insurance and Allied Services* Cmd 6404, para 206, London, HMSO.

Deacon, A and Bradshaw, J (1983) *Reserved for the Poor: the Means Test in British Social Policy* Oxford, Basil Blackwell & Martin Robertson.

DoE Consultation Paper (1988) *New Financial Regime for Local Authority Housing in England and Wales* London, DoE/Welsh Office.

Doling, J and Davies, M (1984) *Public Control of Privately Rented Housing* Aldershot, Gower.

English, J (ed) (1982) *The Future of Council Housing* London, Croom Helm.

Green Paper (1977) *Housing Policy*, Cmnd 65851, p. 87.

Hill, M (1984) 'The implementation of housing benefit', *Journal of Social Policy* 13(3), pp. 297–320.

Hills, J (1988) *Twenty-First Century Housing Subsidies: Durable Rent-Fixing and Subsidy Arrangements for Social Housing*, Discussion paper, WSP/33, Welfare State Programme, London School of Economics.

Hoath, D C (1989) *Public Housing Law* London, Sweet and Maxwell.

Housing Benefit Review (1985) *Housing Benefit Review: Report of the Review Team* Cmnd 9520, London, HMSO.

Housing Centre Trust (1975) *Housing Finance Review: Evidence to the Secretary of State for the Environment* London.

Hughes D (1987) *Public Sector Housing Law* London, Butterworths.

Kelly, I (1986) *Heading for Rubble: the Political Need for Housing Finance Reform*, Catholic Housing Aid Society, London, CHAS.

Kemp, P (1984) *The cost of chaos: A survey of the housing benefit scheme* London, Shac.

Luba, J (1989) The new housing benefit scheme: one year on', *Legal Action* June 1989, p. 14.

Malpass, P (1990) *Reshaping Housing Policy* London, Routledge.

Melling, J (ed) (1980) *Housing, Social Policy and the State* London, Croom Helm.

Merrett, S (1979) *State Housing in Britain* London, Routledge.

National Board for Prices and Incomes (1968) *Increases in Rents of Local Authority Housing*, Cmnd 3604.

NFHA (1990) *New Housing Association Tenants: CORE Results Oct 1988–March 1989* London, National Federation of Housing Associations, Research Report No 6.

Ogus, A and Barendt, E (1988) *The Law of Social Security* 3rd edn, London, Butterworths.

Parker, P A (1967) *The Rents of Council Houses*, Occasional Papers in Social Administration No 22, London, Bell.

Skinner, D and Langdon, J (1974) *The Story of Clay Cross* Nottingham, Spokesman Books.

Willmott, P and Murie, A (1988) *Polarisation and Social Housing* London, Policy Studies Institute.

7 Tenants' rights

David Hughes

Read 'An Act to consolidate and amend the Acts relating to Artizans and Labourers Dwellings and the Housing of the Working Classes' passed on 18 August 1890 and better known as the Housing of the Working Classes Act 1890. Note its shortness compared with the Housing Act 1985; only 102 sections, as opposed to over 600. Even so it superseded legislation dating back to 1851. See how sparing are references to the rights of the objects of housing provision, i.e. the working classes. They are mentioned in Section 11, which granted certain rights of rehousing for persons displaced by 'improvement', i.e. slum clearance, schemes, in Section 31 which enabled 'house holders' to complain about the unhealthful condition of dwelling houses, and Section 38(2) which conferred similar powers with regard to obstructive buildings. Section 75 implied a condition into lettings of dwellings to members of the working classes that dwellings should be reasonably fit for human habitation. Section 78 granted certain tenants displaced by improvement schemes rights to removal expenses. Otherwise the Act was concerned primarily with local authority powers, the beneficiaries of which were present by implication and entirely legally passive.

In the Housing, Town Planning Act 1909 one finds the same pattern; emphasis on the powers of local authorities, though enhanced central supervisory powers to promote their more zealous action were also created (Leach and Leach, pp. xi–xiii). Section 75 of the Act of 1890 was extended by Sections 14 and 15 of the 1909 Act to imply a covenant by landlords to benefit certain tenants that their homes would be, at the start of their tenancies, reasonably fit for habitation and kept fit thereafter. Tenants were able to sue landlords under this, and other similar earlier provisions, for injury suffered as a result of defective housing conditions; see *Walker v. Hobbes* (1889) 23 Queens Bench Division 458. Section 43 prohibited the erection of back-to-back houses as working-class dwellings. But once again the Act was largely silent on tenants' rights.

Consolidation in the Housing Act 1925 repeated the established legislative pattern—a multiplicity of powers and duties entrusted to local authorities, with passing references to rights granted to tenants. Section 1 of the 1925 Act repeated landlords' obligations to make and keep certain dwelling houses reasonably fit for habitation, and Section 5 imposed an obligation for the name and address of the medical officer of health and the landlord to be inscribed in rent books given in connection with lettings to the working class. Section 17 continued the prohibition on erection of back-to-back houses, and Section 98 imposed certain rehousing obligations on local authorities in respect of those displaced by the exercise of their powers. Despite these provisions, those 'privileged' to benefit from local authority housing functions, for example as tenants of council houses, continued as primarily passive, subject to the discretionary powers of their municipal landlords.

The next 'principal' Act, in 1936, was again concerned with local authority housing functions, which had grown considerably in complexity and bulk. Part V of the Act laid down extensive requirements about providing and managing municipal housing, but *vis-à-vis* tenants, authorities were entrusted with wide discretionary powers subject to few explicit constraints. One, however, worthy of some note was that contained in Section 85(2). Authorities were placed under an obligation to ensure that in selecting tenants a 'reasonable preference' was to be given to those living in insanitary or overcrowded or otherwise unsatisfactory housing conditions, or who had large families. Constraint was more apparent than real. The 'duty' was vague and unenforceable, not being owed to specifically identifiable persons. A stricter constraint was that in Section 136, which generally required that persons rehoused should not be placed in properties other than two-storeyed houses or flats of specified sizes, with numbers of bedrooms appropriate to the size of the family concerned. The 1936 Act also empowered local authorities to promote and assist housing associations, especially with regard to the provision of working-class housing. No mention of the general rights of association tenants was made.

The amendment of the Act of 1936 by the Housing Act 1949 was, yet again, largely concerned with extending local authority functions. It also, however, extended the range of persons capable of benefiting from local housing powers by beginning the long process of removing restrictions that powers should only be used in respect of members of the working classes. Most restrictions disappeared by virtue of Section 1 and Schedule 1 of the 1949 Act, but that prohibiting provision of back-to-back houses survived until 1980, and that which determined which houses were subject to the overcrowding provisions lasted until 1985. Strangely in all this time the expression 'working class' was never statutorily defined. Litigation indicated it meant those in unskilled, poorly paid jobs (see *Guinness Trust (London Fund)* v. *Green* [1955] 2 All England Reports 871), but this did not carry over into the practice of early housing allocation by local authorities, as Stuart Lowe outlined, in Chapter 1.

The following 'principal' Act in 1957 continued 'the mixture as before', though it was the last such to pay scant attention to tenants' rights. It thus provides a pause to consider why such rights regarding municipal housing were so badly developed. The answer, from a legal view point, lies in the history of landlord and tenant law. This, the creation of common law, is essentially based on commercial notions whereby the tenant's home is the landlord's property, which the landlord lets the tenant possess for a limited period in return, usually, for payment. Throughout most of the nineteenth century it was generally assumed that landlords and tenants were equally free to make such contracts of letting as they wished, and the landlord's ultimate right of property—to end the tenant's possession of his home—should be subject only to such agreement as had been made with the tenant (Denning, 1949, pp. 69–70; Gauldie, 1974, pp. 112–22). There was strong opposition in court and Parliament to attempts to control landlords' provision and management of rented housing (Reynolds, 1974, pp. 377–98). The nub of the issue was summed up in the dictum: 'Fraud apart, there is no law against letting a tumble down house' (*Robbins* v. *Jones* (1863) 15 Common Bench New Series 221).

The encroachment on property rights represented by legislation was considered tolerable because it was a matter concerning 'public health' (Berry, 1974, pp. 9–32; Doling and Davies, 1984, pp. 13–21; Burnett, 1986, pp. 154–66).

Part of 'Public Health' was the legal classification of housing powers by some commentators well into the twentieth century (Halsbury, 1930, pp. 984–1078). When, however, the law of housing broke out of the confines of public health law, and the state, in the form of local authorities, began providing housing for rent, the old notion that by providing accommodation a landlord confers benefits on tenants, and should not in consequence be subject to overmuch legal regulation, remained deeply ingrained (Gauldie, 1974, p. 310; Berry, 1974, pp. 105–9; Housing Research Group, 1981, pp. 26–31; Swenarton, 1981, pp. 155–61; Power, 1987, pp. 3–39).

A somewhat paradoxical situation then arose. The private rented sector declined in size, but the rights of its tenants, particularly as to security of tenure, control of rents and succession, were, from 1915 onwards, increasingly enshrined in statute (Honoré, 1982, pp. 51–60). Within a few years of the first such statute Lord Justice Romer was able to declare: 'The principal object of the [Rent Acts is] to protect a person residing in a dwelling house from being turned out of his home' (*Haskins* v. *Lewis* [1931] 2 Kings Bench 1 at 18). The interesting juxtaposition there is between 'house' and 'home', indicating acceptance that, while house ownership is a recognised, legally protected property right, occupation of a home is also worthy of recognition and protection. In contrast the idea that the burgeoning municipal sector of housing provision should be subject to such regulation was alien to legal thinking; certainly to Lord Porter who, in *Shelly* v. *LCC* [1949] Appeal Cases 56 at 66, stated: 'It is to my mind one of the important duties of management that the local body should be able to pick and choose their tenants at their will. It is true that an ordinary private landlord cannot do so, but local authorities, who have wider duties laid on them, may well be expected to exercise their powers with discretion.'

Lord Porter's statements were made against a statutory background clearly supporting his arguments. The Increase of Rent and Mortgage Interest (Restrictions) Act 1920, replacing the Act of 1915, did not by virtue of Section 12(9) apply to dwelling houses erected after 2 April 1919. When the Rent and Mortgage Interest Restrictions Act 1939 was passed, which did not contain such an exclusion, specific exemption for local authority houses was made by Section 3(2)(c). The Housing, Repairs and Rents Act 1954 Section 33(1) continued this exemption and extended it to housing association and housing trust dwellings, also those of the new town development corporations. When the Housing Corporation was subsequently created its dwellings were exempted from 'Rent Act control' by Section 3(9) of the Housing Act 1964. These exemptions were consolidated in the Rent Acts of 1968 and 1977.

Legal distinctions between the private and what is now recognized as the 'social' sector in rented housing thus appeared early this century, growing as time passed. The rights of tenants of social housing fell to be decided generally by the common law. This, as has been said already, assumes that landlords and tenants freely make their own bargains, and is concerned to see that individual bargains are performed. Intervention by law was deemed necessary where one or other of the parties failed to perform his bargain, or where otherwise necessary to give the contract of letting 'business efficacy', i.e. to make it work. An example of this situation would be where the landlord had given the tenant an express, specific right which could not be enjoyed because the landlord had failed to undertake some other express obligation, with the consequence that the entire bargain between the parties would be in danger of ceasing to function, as in *Liverpool City Council* v. *Irwin* [1977] Appeal Cases 239. Here the authority owned a tower block of flats which had two lifts, and internal rubbish chutes. Vandalism and acts of neglect combined with other circumstances to make the lifts inoperable and the chutes blocked so they could not be used. The tenants claimed the authority was in breach of obligations as landlord. The House of Lords concluded the parties had not fully expressed their contract in any written document, and the court could imply a term to ensure the contract of letting was not rendered futile. They considered tenancies of the flats had to carry an implied right to use the lifts and rubbish chutes, otherwise they could not be enjoyed at all. Furthermore the landlords had to be under an implied obligation to maintain the lifts and chutes. But they also stressed that courts have no power to imply terms into a contract of letting merely because they are 'reasonable', only those truly necessary for the contract's functioning.

However, notions that periodic tenants have rights of security of tenure in their homes, or that their families should be able to enjoy rights of succession, are the product of statute, alien to the common law's thinking, and so for many years were inapplicable to tenants of social housing.

The weak tenurial position of council tenants *vis-à-vis* their landlords became the subject of adverse criticism by housing commentators (Tucker, 1966, p. 105). Then a series of legal decisions revealed how poorly protected at law a council tenancy was. While the Small Tenements Recovery Act 1838 was in force cases such as *R.* v. *Snell ex parte St Marylebone Borough Council* [1942] 2 Kings Bench 137, *St Pancras Borough Council* v. *Frey* [1963] 2 Queens Bench 586 and *Harpin* v. *St Albans Corporation* (1969) 67 Local Government Reports 479 established it was for councils to show that they needed to obtain possession of any given one of their houses in order to exercise housing powers. This obligation could, however, be discharged by showing that the house was needed for a person on the waiting list. Following the 1838 Act's repeal in 1972, even that protection was lost. *Bristol District Council* v. *Clark* ([1975] 1 Weekly Law Reports 1443) established that, despite the wording of Section 158(1) of the Housing Act 1957 that local authority possession actions should be brought to enable them 'to exercise their powers under any enactment relating to housing', the burden of proving an authority was not acting in pursuance of such powers was on the defendant. If a council tenant wished to contest a possession action it was necessary to show the authority had abused statutory powers, a task made harder by statements in *Cannock Chase District Council* v. *Kelly* [1978] 1 Weekly Law Reports 1, that the fact that the defendant was a 'good' tenant who had always observed tenancy conditions raised no presumption that the authority must have abused its powers in bringing the action (Yates, 1975, pp. 873–6; Hughes, 1977, 1067–9).

These decisions highlighted the need for enhanced legal rights for council tenants, to enshrine, and enhance, the *de facto* security and involvement in management effectively enjoyed in many places (Andrews, 1979, pp. 200–24). The 1977 Housing Policy Consultative document, Cmnd 6851, promised legislation to give council tenants security of tenure with a code of practice with regard to council tenancies, and in 1979 the Callaghan Government introduced its Housing Bill. This emerged from a wide-ranging debate on the future of council housing, where some concentrated on the lack of a legal status comparable to that under the Rent Acts suffered by council tenants, while others argued for enhanced cooperative management of council housing by its tenants (Berry, 1974, pp. 89–109; Ward, 1974, pp. 59–80). Yet others pressed, increasingly powerfully, for tenants to have the right to acquire their homes: only thus could they enjoy increasing capital values enjoyed by owner-occupiers, experience freedom of mobility, and have choice in what to do to their homes concerning decoration and improvement. Supporters of such arguments in the Conservative Party also saw the right for tenants to purchase their council houses as a potent means of advancing a desire to transfer wealth from the state to individual citizens (Tremlett, 1979, pp. 131–7, 169–71; Cooper, 1985, pp. 140–60).

The 1979 Labour Housing Bill, though not going as far as some might have wished (Cooper, 1985, pp. 148–9; Housing Research Group, 1986, pp. 1–15), however, would have introduced controls on residence qualifications, i.e. requirements about registering on housing waiting lists only those resident in an authority's area for specified periods of time, and a statutory national mobility scheme to enhance tenants' ability to move between areas. The Bill would also have introduced representative, but not responsible, democracy concerning tenant participation in housing management (Hughes, 1981, pp. 89–90, 107). The fall of Labour in 1979 brought to power those committed to the forced sale of council houses (Hughes, 1981, pp. 57–60). Though they utilised some of the framework of the lost Bill to create a new class of tenants—secure tenants—for both local authorities and housing associations, giving them whole new packages of rights, undoubtedly chief among these was the right to buy, at a discount, together with guaranteed mortgage facilities. This is a right to *cease* to be a tenant, and its extension in 1984, and exercise in relation to some one million dwellings by 1987, helped to keep the Conservatives in power throughout the 1980s (Cooper, 1985, pp. 149–52). The right to buy is also essentially an individual right belonging to an individual, in respect of an individual property, and which can benefit the individual greatly if exercised.

The other rights retained in 1980 from the previous government's Bill are likewise primarily enjoyed by individuals, reflecting the dominant housing philosophy of the decade stressing individual rights, and paying scant regard to rights to be enjoyed collectively (Forrest, 1987, pp. 67–85). This is not to say that individual rights, (security of tenure, succession, to exchange, to take lodgers and to sublet, to repair and bill the landlord, to improve) are not important. They alter the relationship previously existing between public sector landlords and their tenants, giving rise to litigation and other managerial problems unknown to authorities before 1980 (Hoath, 1989, pp. 183–210). This is particularly true with regard to housing transfers consequent on relationship breakdown. The old power of landlords to reallocate property largely at their discretion has been replaced by provisions based on the principles of the land and family law, administered by the courts (Housing Research Group, 1986, pp. 100–12; Hoath, 1989, pp. 248–69). Nevertheless there is an argument that, despite legal change in the relationship between individual tenants and their landlords, the practical effect has not been marked (Housing Research Group, 1986, pp. 231–8). Why this should be will be considered after an examination of tenants' collective rights.

Current housing legislation concentrates on giving individual rights. Collective rights are poorly represented. Six, comparatively brief, sections of the Housing Act 1985 relate to collective rights. Thus, terms of secure tenancies may be varied by landlords, tenants having the right to be consulted in relation to changes. However, an obligation to consult is not one to comply with consultees' views. Provided comments received are taken into account, no more is formally legally required. Consultation is likewise required on proposals to vary certain matters of 'housing management' relating to secure tenancies: the management, maintenance, improvement or demolition of dwellings and the provision of services or amenities in connection therewith (see Section 105 of the 1985 Act). The obligation is merely to consult, arising only in relation to matters which *in the landlord's opinion* are *new* programmes of maintenance, improvement or demolition, or changes in practice or policy, and which are likely to affect substantially a landlord's secure tenants as a whole or a distinct group of them. The obligation does not arise in relation to what is likely to be a most contentious issue of management whenever it occurs: increases in rent or service charges. Furthermore it has been further reduced in effectiveness by the courts, who have interpreted Section 105 so that the obligation to consult arises where there is a real question of *implementing* a change (see *Short* v. *Tower Hamlets LBC* (1985) 18 Housing Law Reports 171). The obligation to consult does not impose a requirement to involve tenants in policy formulation (Hoath, 1989, pp. 308–12).

Sections 104 and 106 of the 1985 Act impose duties on landlords to provide information about secure tenancies, explaining their terms, the effect of the right to buy and landlords' obligations to repair. The information must be supplied to secure tenants, who must also receive written statements of the terms of their tenancies in so far as these are not otherwise expressed in their tenancy agreements or are implied by law. Landlords must also publish summaries of selection, allocation and exchange rules, and have the full rules available for public inspection during reasonable hours at their principal offices. Section 167 of the Local Government and Housing Act 1989 also imposes on *local housing authorities* an obligation to make an annual report to those who are tenants of Housing Revenue Account dwellings: these are largely, but not entirely, those provided under general housing powers in Part II of the 1985 Act. The report must contain such information as the Secretary of State determines relating to the housing functions of the authority. This information giving requirements can hardly be seen, however, as creating a real degree of accountability to tenants on the part of landlords.

The package of rights enjoyed by secure tenants has been criticised as ineffective. The legal provisions are vague, often leaving much to the discretion of individual authorities. The implementation of tenants' rights provisions, particularly collective rights, has been accorded low priority in local government, with no speedy and economic sanctions which tenants can use to force the pace of change. Tenants collectively, of course, are unlikely to have experience of rights which are largely individualised, though the impact on landlords of individual disputes may be considerable. Finally, of course, legal rights are mere verbiage if there is lacking the wherewithal in terms of money, staff and *material* to translate them into practical action; that has certainly been the case throughout the 1980s (Housing Research Group, 1986, pp. 231–42; Centre for Housing Research, 1989, pp. 28–30, 50–8, 92–105).

Tenants' rights generally are also ineffective because, legally and administratively, they are not considered globally. This volume treats of 'a new century of social housing', and this chapter has concentrated on local authority and housing association provision, thus perpetuating the old public/private sector distinction: yet in a sense all housing is social. Nevertheless the relevant statutes, the Rent Act 1977, the Housing Acts 1985–8, together with the Local Government and Housing Act 1989 and the Landlord and Tenant Acts 1985–8, apply selectively and disjointedly throughout the rental sector. Popularly a distinction is made between 'tenants' and 'leaseholders', the former being those who have short periodic repeating interests such as weekly tenancies, and the latter being those with 'long' interests, such as 99-year leases. Legally all are 'lessees'. Ministerially and administratively, responsibility is divided between the Department of the Environment and the Lord Chancellor's Department, with the Law Commission, the Department of Social Security and the Treasury also having roles to play. Local authority tenants may additionally rely on the powers of the Commission for Local Administration (the Local Ombudsman) to investigate complaints of maladministration in housing management. Yet though not a homogeneous group, all tenants ultimately labour under the disadvantage that their homes are someone else's property, with the attendant constraints that entails. The law has sought to strike a balance between the rights of those who are party to this situation. Though it has not developed evenly across the rental sector, the law's general movement has been to grant, albeit less than effectively, greater recognition of tenants' rights.

Further enhancing effective tenants' rights is a major task for the future. Paradoxically this could be facilitated by policies which at first sight seem inimical to the notion of social housing. The 1987 Housing White Paper Cm 214 envisaged no major role for new building for rent by local authorities; that was a task for the 'Independent' sector, subsuming private landlords and housing associations. Moreover the White Paper undertook to give council tenants the right to transfer their homes to other landlords, the so-called 'Pick a Landlord' scheme. These proposals led to the Housing Act 1988. The right to choose a new landlord, however, was transmuted into the ability for certain bodies approved by the Housing Corporation to force local authorities to transfer to them areas of housing. The only *rights* enjoyed by tenants in such circumstances are the collective one to reject an 'approved body's' approach to acquire their homes, and individual rights to opt out of transfers and stay as tenants of the original landlord (Bridge, 1989, pp. 106–21; Rodgers, 1989a, pp. 127–43). It is likely that the majority of approved bodies for these purposes will be registered housing associations.

Where transfers take place the tenancies granted will be assured tenancies (as are nearly all housing association tenancies granted after 15 January 1989). Associations are, nevertheless, subject to the powers of the Housing Corporation under Section 36A of the Housing Associations Act 1985, under which the Corporation has issued 'The Tenants' Guarantee: Guidance for Registered Housing Association Housing Management Practice'. This provides, *inter alia*, guidance on meeting housing demand, allocation policies, terms and conditions of tenancies, rent and service charge determination, maintenance and repair issues and complaints and consultation procedures. The Housing Corporation has indicated that registered associations should consult tenants about proposed changes in management and maintenance policies where these are likely to affect substantial numbers or proportions of tenants, and further that tenants' views on such issues should be taken into account. More particularly the guidance indicates that every association should inform its tenants of its policies and procedures for dealing with complaints about the treatment of tenants and the service they receive, including rights of appeal should complainants not be initially satisfied. This implies that complaints policies and procedures must exist. Associations are encouraged to go further and set up arbitration schemes to settle their landlord/tenant disputes. It is also implicit in the guidance that complaints procedures are to be used in overall monitoring of the performance of associations in the management of their stock. The guidance is not specifically enforceable, but non-compliance with it may be taken into account by the Corporation when considering the exercise of its extensive powers over registered associations. The Corporation is also prepared to receive complaints from tenants who have exhausted their associations' complaints systems without satisfaction.

The 'Tenants' Guarantee', with its insistence on the provision of extensive rights, both collective and individual, by virtue of express conditions in tenancy agreements, goes further towards creating a detailed and comprehensive set of rights for tenants than other current legal provisions.

The rental sector in housing is one of shifting balances of power; balances that have steadily improved in tenants' favour for many years. From a legal point of view this is because of emphasis in legislation and case law on individual tenant rights. It is time to erect further legal structures to ensure collective rights for tenants, to provide adequate systems for receiving and dealing with tenants' complaints economically, expeditiously and effectively, and to bring about responsible democratic involvement by tenants in housing management. Having said all this, however, it must be admitted that legal structures divorced from the realities of political will, professional commitment and financial supply are little more than cosmetic. If social housing provision continues to be residualised in terms of finance and esteem so that much-needed accommodation is not built while some of that which exists declines in quality, legal rights will not matter much (Forrest, 1987, pp. 67–85; Clapham, 1987, pp. 107–43; Department of the Environment, 1988, pp. 29–40; Rodgers, 1989b, pp. 1565–76, 1603–8). Paradoxically, at the end of a century in which the law's attention has primarily focused on enhancing the powers of public landlords to provide good-quality affordable accommodation while paying scant regard to the rights of such landlords' tenants, those rights are receiving attention as the property over which they are to be exercised declines in availability, quality and affordability.

References

Andrews, C L (1979) *Tenants and Town Hall* London, HMSO.

Berry, F (1974) *Housing: the Great British Failure* London, Charles Knight.

Bridge, S (1989) *Blackstone's Guide to the Housing Act 1988* London, Blackstone Press.

Burnett, J (1986) *A Social History of Housing 1815–1985* 2nd edn, London, Methuen.

Centre for Housing Research (1989) *The Nature and Effectiveness of Housing Management in England* London, HMSO.

Clapham, D (1987) 'The new face of public housing', in D Clapham and J English, *Public Housing: Current Trends and Future Developments* London, Croom Helm.

Cooper, S (1985) *Public Housing and Private Property 1970–1984* Aldershot, Gower.

Denning, A (1949) *Freedom under the Law* London, Stevens.

Department of the Environment (1988) *English House Condition Survey 1986* London, HMSO.

Doling, J and Davies, M (1984) *Public Control of Privately Rented Housing* Aldershot, Gower.

Forrest, R (1987) 'Privatisation, marginality and council housing', in D Clapham and J English, *Public Housing: Current Trends and Future Developments* London, Croom Helm.

Gauldie, E (1974) *Cruel Habitations: a History of Working-class Housing 1780–1814* London, Allen and Unwin.

Halsbury (1930) *The Complete Statutes of England* Vol. 13, London, Butterworths.

Hoath, D (1989) *Public Housing Law* London, Sweet and Maxwell.

Honoré, T (1982) *The Quest for Security: Employees, Tenants, Wives* London, Stevens.

Housing Research Group (1981) *Could Local Authorities be Better Landlords?* London, The City University.

Housing Research Group (1986) *The 1980 Tenants' Rights in Practice* London, The City University.

Hughes, D J (1977) 'Municipal eviction', *New Law Journal* 127 (5826), pp. 1067–9.

Hughes, D J (1981) *Public Sector Housing Law* 1st edn, London, Butterworths.

Leach, C H and Leach, G H (1911) *The Housing, Town Planning Act, 1909* London, Local Government Press Company.

Power, A (1987) *Property before People* London, Allen and Unwin.

Reynolds, J I (1974) 'Statutory covenants of fitness and repair', *Modern Law Review* 37, pp. 377–98.

Rodgers, C P (1989a) *Housing: the New Law* London, Butterworths.

Rodgers, C P (1989b) 'The demise of social housing?', *New Law Journal* 139 (6432) and (6433), pp. 1565–76 and 1603–8.

Swenarton, M (1981) *Homes Fit for Heroes* London, Heinemann Educational Books.

Tremlett, G (1979) *Living Cities* London, Maurice Temple Smith.

Tucker, J (1966) *Honourable Estates* London, Gollancz.

Ward, C (1974) *Tenants Takeover* London, Architectural Press.

Yates, D (1975) 'Evicting council house tenants', *New Law Journal* 125 (5715), pp. 873–6.

8 Design for living
Patrick Nuttgens

Fundamental to all social housing are the social, political and financial policies that have often decided whether such housing appeared at all. But there is another factor just as influential—and in many cases definitive. That is the factor of *design*. It is therefore important to clarify what one means by *design* in this context and in what way it may differ from what is thought of as 'design' in its everyday meaning.

By *design* I do not mean the decoration of the exterior of a dwelling—or even of its interior—however significant that may be in making the place palatable to the occupant. What I mean by architectural design is something more fundamental—the organisation of the spaces and services in a building, the spaces and services necessary for living. It should be the result not of fashion but of a rational study of needs. The resultant building is then an expression of the satisfaction of those needs in the form of usable space. But there is a further dimension. Since housing is concerned with more than one house, the principal result of *housing design* is a number of 'housing types'. An account of the development of types of housing is therefore central to any story of housing.

Housing means something more than a collection of houses or dwellings. It is a process in which the financing, planning, construction and administration of dwellings is thought of as a whole. And that implies a width of responsibility for more than just shelter; it implies a total concept of housing as a social service. It means that at its most responsible, housing provision must mean the provision of a total environment for living.

Given time and survival it is obvious that almost any environment can become acceptable to its inhabitants, like for example many of the surviving back-to-back houses in Leeds, of which there were more than 70,000 (at least seven in ten of all houses in Leeds) at the turn of the century. But that will not suffice for the designer of new housing. There has to be (and since the nineteenth century usually has been) an element of ideology in creating something better than the houses that provoked condemnation at the height of the Industrial Revolution.

Accounts of such conditions are many and remarkably consistent. On the cellar dwellings of Manchester, for example, Peter Gaskell, in his *Manufacturing Population of England* (1833), reported that: 'These cellars are the very picture of loathsomeness . . . they speedily become disgusting receptacles of every species of vermin that can affect the human body.'

Back-to-back houses were theoretically superior to cellars, in that they were specifically designed for the working classes. They were the speculative builders' answer to mass demand. The classic description of the back-to-back was supplied by Edwin Chadwick in the famous *Report on the Sanitary Conditions of the Labouring Population* (1842): 'The walls are only half brick thick, or what the bricklayers call a brick noggin, and the whole of the materials are slight and unfit for the purpose . . . they are built back to back; without ventilation or drainage; and like a honeycomb every particle of space is occupied.'

The houses were, as their name implied, backed on to one another in a confined space, thus making the spread of disease more likely. The Committee of the Board of Health set up to research housing defects in Nottingham in 1833 found 8,000 back-to-back houses with no through ventilation and only one convenience for several dwellings. Many of the streets outside were neither paved nor drained.

What was to be done about it? Positive attempts at improvement culminated in projects by central and local government; but the improvements started with individual enthusiasts making philanthropic experiments. The philanthropists were the pioneers of improved housing, and their work preceded legislation and the work of the public authorities. They made the innovations and thus provided the components that ended as a complete vocabulary of design.

The story is an important one and it can be studied best where it started—in industrial Yorkshire. Overcrowding was at its most dense in the wool and worsted manufacturing centres of the West Riding of Yorkshire—the prodigy towns of the Industrial Revolution. The men who set out to improve them were manufacturers who hoped to create an environment in keeping with social ideals. Their motives were, of course, mixed. They involved both self-interest and benevolence: the health and well-being of the residents would encourage more efficient organisation, which would in turn ensure regularity of work. But their concern was real.

Colonel Edward Akroyd, MP for Halifax, was one of the early improvers. His first model village was Copley, built between 1844 and 1853, two miles south of Halifax. Akroyd's essay *On Improved Dwellings for the Working Classes* (1861) contains a description of Copley:

A picturesque outline was adopted in a modified Old English style, approximating to the character of many old dwellings in the neighbourhood, and also in harmony with the beautiful site. . . . In front of the cottages, facing the river are allotment gardens, flanked by a recreation ground; and on the bank is seated the village school with its separate play yards.

The major disadvantage was that Copley's houses were still of the infamous back-to-back type; many had one living room downstairs and only one bedroom upstairs. Akroyd defended himself by saying that back-to-backs were the common style and that many people only wanted one bedroom anyway.

There were no back-to-backs in Akroyd's second and more ambitious experiment, at Akroydon near the centre of Halifax. In Akroydon, started in

1861, the social purpose of the early model villages was more apparent. The houses, which were at different price levels, were deliberately arranged to promote the mixing of social classes. The houses were generally two-storey, positioned round a green, and built of stone with slate roofs. They had a large living room, a scullery or wash kitchen, a main bedroom and children's bedroom. Later houses were more spacious with a parlour and a third bedroom.

But the most celebrated and comprehensive work of the philanthropic improvers was Saltaire, north of Bradford, built between 1850 and 1863, the creation of the Bradford alpaca manufacturer, Sir Titus Salt.

In moving his works from Bradford, Sir Titus wanted not just housing, but a town that would be self-sufficient. He built his factory, whose length equalled that of St Paul's Cathedral, first, and the cottages ten years later.

The village included forty-five almshouses, an institute, a school, a church and a 14-acre park on the other side of the River Aire. The cottages were models of their kind. They had a living room, scullery and two to four bedrooms. Water and gas were supplied, and each had a private yard with privy, coal store and ashpit. None of the houses were back-to-back.

Salt had carried out a detailed survey of his employees' housing needs. He instructed his architects, Lockwood and Mawson of Bradford, that 'nothing should be spared to render the dwellings of the operatives a pattern to the country' (cited in Burnett, 1986, p. 181). At his own expense he provided amenities that included chapels, reading rooms, public baths and a gymnasium with a Turkish bath.

Salt's example was followed by other wealthy industrialists. Lord Lever founded Port Sunlight near Liverpool in 1888. He wanted to avoid urban uniformity: his model community contained a diversity of styles. The houses at Port Sunlight were therefore either semi-detached or built in groups of four to six, separated by wide, open spaces. There were low densities and large space allowances as well as a range of facilities. The Levers insisted that the annual outlay was more than compensated by high productivity and good industrial relations.

In 1879, George Cadbury decided to move his works outside Birmingham; he wanted room for expansion and cleaner conditions for food production. He went further. He built beside the factory twenty-four double tunnel-back houses, typical of Birmingham houses of the time. They reflected his philosophy that the best way to improve a man's circumstance is to raise his ideals. . . . How can a man cultivate ideals when his home is a slum and his only place of recreation the public house?

In 1885 that little settlement was expanded into the model village of Bournville. By 1912, nearly 1,000 houses had been built. The construction followed the natural contours of the land, unlike Port Sunlight which was artificially lanscaped. And Cadbury introduced an important new planning principle—that houses should not cover more than a quarter of the plot.

These were essentially cottages. There were also model settlements on a more massive scale. In London, the Peabody Trust was started in 1862 with the gift of £150,000 from an American merchant, George Peabody. It followed a different design policy. It concentrated on multi-storey blocks containing one, two and three-roomed apartments, usually with shared sinks and WCs. By 1887 the Trust had provided 5,014 dwellings.

What, however, fundamentally shaped the design of housing at the turn of the century, and provided a fully articulated vocabulary of housing types, was the Garden City movement. Its pioneer was Ebenezer Howard. In 1898 he published his seminal book *Tomorrow: A Peaceful Path to Real Reform*, reissued a few years later as *Garden Cities of Tomorrow*.

Howard had a vision of 'slumless, smokeless cities', and introduced the idea of the 'garden city'. This was to combine the advantages of both town and country with the disadvantages of neither. It was also to be an exercise in cooperative ownership.

The Garden Cities and Town Planning Association's definition of a garden city was 'a town planned for industry and healthy living; of a size that makes possible the full measure of social life, but not larger, surrounded by a belt of rural land; the whole of the land being in public ownership, or held in trust for the community'.

Carefully avoiding the utopian approach of some of the earlier reformers, Howard aimed to bring people back to the land on a sound economic basis. He suggested that garden city development companies should be formed to purchase sites and lease plots to those wishing to build. The increasing value of the land would then pass to the company, which would finance community services and municipally owned buildings. The community ownership principle was intended to avoid the paternalistic and mercenary attitudes unpopular elsewhere.

Howard looked afresh at the problem which had been troubling England since the Industrial Revolution—that of the growth and overcrowding of the cities and their fatal attraction for country people. He illustrated his idea of the existing situation and his proposals for its solution by the diagram he described as the Three Magnets. This showed the relative merits and demerits of town and country and how the strengths of each should be joined:

Neither the town magnet nor the country magnet represents the full plan and purpose of nature. Human society and the beauty of nature are meant to be enjoyed together. The two magnets must be made one. . . . Town and country must be married, and out of this joyous union will spring a new hope, a new life, a new civilisation. (Howard, 1985)

The obvious way to merge the town and country, to relieve the overcrowding pressure on the city and the unemployment pressure in rural areas, was to have a 'garden-city'—a town with all the advantages of numbers and employment but placed in the healthier and less densely populated countryside. At two garden city conferences, held at Bournville in 1901 and Port Sunlight in 1902, Howard publicly aired his scheme. It bore instant fruit in the following year (1903) when Howard's first garden city, Letchworth, was begun.

Built on virgin farmland, Letchworth was comprehensively planned to accommodate 35,000 inhabitants with four neighbourhood units, each containing public buildings, shops, schools and a recreational green. Housing density was at most 12 houses to the acre, the cottages carefully set out in short terraces and cul-de-sacs. It had an organised layout of streets, alike enough to avoid disunity, different enough for individuality.

The architect responsible for Letchworth, who worked out the physical form of Howard's first ideals, was Raymond Unwin. As a boy he had heard Ruskin lecture and had met William Morris, whom he admired both as a craftsman and a socialist.

He saw as an ideal, 'a more ordered form of society and a better planned environment for it' (Unwin, 1937), and had no doubt that practical planning on a human scale could only be generated by the satisfaction of the needs of people. Writing about town planning in 1909 he noted that 'miles and miles of ground which people, not yet elderly, can remember as open green fields, are now covered with dense masses of buildings packed together in rows along streets which have been laid out in a perfectly haphazard manner without any consideration for the common interest of the people.' (Unwin, 1937)

To understand his influence on housing, it is necessary to list the principles on which he based his ideas for garden cities and other layouts. He saw the traditional English village as a living symbol of the 'natural life' to which everyone has a right: it provided a measure of community planning. He insisted on the need to understand the past before anyone could make any appropriate plans for the future; his especial love was for the Middle Ages. He was convinced that beauty was essential to mental health:

We have forgotten that endless rows of brick boxes looking out upon dreary streets and squalid back yards, are not really homes for people and can never become such, however complete may be the drainage system, however pure the water supply. . . . Important as all these provisions are for man's material needs and sanitary existence, they do not suffice. . . . There is needed the vivifying touch of art. (Unwin, 1937)

The consciousness of tradition was thus an integral part of the creative process. But not without criticism:

Though the study of old towns and their buildings is most useful, nay, is almost essential to any due appreciation of the subject, we must not forget that we cannot, even if we would, reproduce the conditions under which they were created. . . . While therefore we study and admire it does not follow that we can copy; for we must consider what is likely to lead to the best results under modern conditions. (Unwin, 1937)

But above all, Unwin was convinced that beauty was essential to mental health. By beauty he meant not ornament, but quality and harmony of form. The architect and town planner should, he said, infuse 'the spirit of the artist' into his work because 'the artist is not content with the least that will do; his desire is for the best, the utmost he can achieve. It is the small margin which makes all the difference between a thing scamped and a thing well done . . . from this margin of welldoing beauty must spring.' He added: 'we have become so used to living among surroundings in which beauty has little or no place, that we do not realise what a remarkable and unique feature the ugliness of modern life is.' Unwin held that one of planning's chief functions was to satisfy 'the natural aesthetic hunger of mankind'.

The practical innovation specified by Unwin, confirmed in his small book *Nothing Gained by Overcrowding* (1918) and adopted by authorities after the First World War, was the rule that there should be not more than 12 houses per acre. Even in financial terms, he maintained, there was nothing to be gained by cramming more on to the land; the extra costs of roads outweighed any savings in land costs. High-density planning was only defensible where the land was excessively costly.

The first commission undertaken by Unwin and his architect partner Barry Parker was the garden village of New Earswick, three miles north of York, started in 1901 by Joseph Rowntree, though most of the development work was carried out by his son, Seebohm Rowntree.

In York there was already a surplus of housing, so the intention was not, as at Bournville, to supply desperately needed houses to those that lacked them: it was rather, as Seebohm Rowntree said, to see if housing in a congenial setting at a moderate rent was a possiblity: 'It remains to be seen,' he wrote, 'whether we can build to let at a price that people will pay.' (untraceable quotation) Later developments were to show the wisdom of these reservations.

New Earswick introduced features nowadays so familiar that they are taken for granted. They included the cul-de-sac with two-storey houses grouped around it, the elimination of useless pieces of back land, reduction in the widths of roads, places for children to play, houses with 'through' living rooms—so that they could be orientated in different ways without losing sunlight—bathrooms on the first floor, the elimination of winders on the stairs, the outside store for prams and tools. It was a beautifully planned family house, and it influenced the design of housing for years to come (see Figures 8.1, 8.2 and 8.3).

Figure 8.1   Chestnut Grove, New Earswick c. 1915

Figure 8.2 Hawthorn Terrace (South End), New Earswick *c.* 1911

Figure 8.3 Almond Grove cul-de-sac, post First World War

The character of the early houses was simple—traditional brick and tile construction. Architectural effect was achieved by varied roof lines, prominent gables and ornamental barge-boards; it was thus possible to build cheaply without monotony. There were wide-fronted houses and living rooms at the front to make the fullest use of sun and light. The whole was marked by reverence for tradition.

Raymond Unwin is a key figure in the story of housing. Artist and planner, he was a social reformer who worked with philanthropists. His influence is still apparent. It shows in picturesque housing layouts, in good landscaping and gardens, in traditional forms of houses, in the informality and common sense which characterise contemporary English design at its best. He was in the end concerned with designing a total environment. His influence was thus far wider than his own work.

To summarise what that meant in terms of the design of dwellings, Unwin established the lasting importance of the cottage rather than the terrace or tenement, the necessity of the garden not just for aesthetic reasons but for self-sufficiency and food, the importance of the grouping of houses as much as their individual design. He saw housing ultimately as the way into a community. It would be more organic and acceptable if the houses were in the familiar vernacular style whose features were functional components rather than fashionable indiosyncracies. The settlement would—to put two of his phrases together—provide 'a full life in an honest place'.

But to see the seminal influence of Unwin on what has come to be known as council housing, it is necessary to look back at housing legislation and the advisory reports that were connected with that legislation. Fundamental was the Public Health Act of 1875. The Act for Consolidating and Amending the Acts relating to Public Health in England (as it was called in full) gave local authorities powers to control the conditions of their district, even if the powers were permissive rather than mandatory.

The sanitary provisions were wide ranging and effective. Each new house was to have a proper privy, even if there was some disagreement on what that was. Authorities were exhorted to clean the streets and to provide an adequate water supply. New cellar dwellings were prohibited, and those already in existence had to comply with new stipulations.

But the most definitive provision, in terms of housing design, was Section 157 of the Act, which empowered local authorities to make by-laws governing the layout of streets and the construction of new buildings. Minimum widths of roads were established: roads were to be at least 24 feet at the front and 15 feet at the back. Minimum cubic contents of rooms were also specified. Unfortunately, since building costs tended to be less if the room was almost a cube, ceilings were often too high and floor areas too small.

In terms of space around the buildings, the Act stipulated that every house should have an open space in front and aimed to prevent building on back land and so avoid the unhealthy and crowded narrow courts with houses too close together. Space was as essential, said the Act, at the back as at the front.

The model By-laws were received with mixed feelings. The general principle was good, for action against insanitary conditions and back-to-back houses was long overdue. But what came to be known as 'by-law housing' tended to be dull and uniform—dutifully following the regulations, but unvaried and unimaginative. It commonly consisted of monotonous terraces of four, six or more houses in long, parallel, treeless streets. The houses had passages leading to walled back yards with a privy and sometimes a coal house. The doors opened directly on to the street. They were usually through terrace houses with a 'tunnel back' instead of the old 'back-to-back', built on a grid pattern in long straight lines which followed the minimum dimensions.

In appearance, by-law housing was the antithesis of all that Unwin championed. He accepted that 'a certain minimum standard of air-space, light and ventilation had been secured', but deplored the unpleasant appearance of the buildings, which seemed to go hand in hand with these otherwise welcome reforms:

The remarkable fact remains that there are growing up around all our big towns vast districts, under these very by-laws, which for dreariness and sheer ugliness it is difficult to match anywhere, and compared with which, many of the old unhealthy slums are, from the point of view of picturesqueness and beauty, infinitely more attractice. . . . We have in a certain niggardly way done what needed doing, but much that we have done has lacked the insight of imagination. (Unwin, 1909)

By-law regulations had other defects as well as ugliness. For one thing, they were geographically inconsistent, some authorities having no by-laws and others not enforcing those they had. But the by-law housing was superior to anything that had gone before. The houses were at least healthy, adequately exposed to air and moderately exposed to light. They were better insulated from cold, damp and noise, and better ventilated than earlier buildings. Staircases were less precipitately steep, timber flooring was beginning to replace stone flags, and there was greater provision of sinks, coppers and cooking ranges. Monotonous they undoubtedly were. What altered the situation was a movement brought about by two events during and immediately after the First World War.

In 1917 the Local Government Board, with a view to post-war planning, set up a committee to consider questions of building construction of dwellings for the working classes. It was chaired by Sir John Tudor Walters, MP. Raymond Unwin was one of its members. The Tudor Walters Report, published in 1918, was intended to 'profoundly influence the general standard of housing in this country'. Its proposals were revolutionary, initiating a major innovation in social policy, and ultimately affecting the character of working-class life; they were to remain a model throughout the inter-war years and indirectly much longer. Running to just under 100 pages, the Tudor Walters Report was the first comprehensive treatise on the political, technical and practical issues involved in the design of the small house. In the housing debates of 1918–19, its authority was virtually unquestionable.

For the Report dealt with the house itself—its standard layout and principles of design. It suggested that the standard house should be a two-storey dwelling with not less than three bedrooms. It considered the cost and availability of materials, as well as constructive ways of economising. It argued that good economy demanded an improvement in standards. In an implicit criticism of by-law building it showed that savings were made through high- not low-quality work. It was poor economy to build houses to anything but the highest standards; otherwise, before the loan period had expired, the house would be unlettable.

Not surprisingly, since Unwin was a member of the committee, the Tudor Walters report advocated the principle of not more than twelve houses to the acre (eight in the country). It stipulated that the maximum length of a terrace should be eight houses and that there should be a variety of types—an obvious rejection of by-law uniformity.

The Report proposed a wider-fronted house, in contrast to the narrow by-law frontages, with a 'through' living room to allow maximum air and sunlight—'medical opinion is unanimous in allowing plenty of sunshine to penetrate into the rooms'—and favoured simplicity of design—'simple straight-forward plans will usually prove most economical . . . ornament is usually out of place and necessarily costly both in execution and upkeep'.

The Committee emphasised that a third living room was a reasonable and proper expectation and that a house with a parlour was 'undoubtedly the type desired by the majority of the artisan class'. In the event about 40 per cent of post-war local authority houses contained parlours.

The body responsible for implementing the Report's recommendations was the Local Government Board. In 1919 the Board issued a housing manual in which the conditions of government grants were set out. It adopted the main features of the Tudor Walters Report, but extended the space recommendations. Every house was to have an internal WC positioned off the back lobby, as well as a bath in either a bathroom or the scullery. Like the Tudor Walters Report, the manual insisted that new housing should 'mark an advance on the building and development which has ordinarily been regarded as sufficient in the past'.

The manual's emphasis on physical beauty in layout again shows the influence of Unwin:

By so planning the lines of the roads and disposing the spaces and the buildings as to develop the beauty of vista, arrangement and proportion, attractiveness may be added to the dwellings at little or no extra cost. Good exterior design in harmony with the surroundings and adapted to the site should be secured. . . . By the choice of suitable local materials, and the adoption of simple lines and good proportion and groupings of buildings with well-considered variation in design and in the treatment of prominent parts, good appearance may be secured within the limits required by due economy. (Local Government Board, 1919)

The Tudor Walters report was quickly followed by the Housing and Town Planning Act of 1919, usually known as the Addison Act after its author Dr Christopher Addison, President of the Local Government Board and later the first Minister of Health. The Act set a precedent for the professional design of mass housing, when Addison commissioned a number of architects to submit plans for the guidance of authorities. Above all, because of the subsidies, it established council housing as we know it.

The majority of the cottage plans were the work of an architect, S B Russell, who attached importance to a clear layout of streets, sunny living rooms, as many bedrooms as possible, a cool place for the larder, easy access to the coal store and an avoidance of rear projections.

The plans were not mandatory and acted only as guidelines. Local authorities were free to design as they wished, provided they adhered to the space and other requirements. Most authorities produced their own plans within their own architects' or engineers' departments; central government was instrumental in setting standards and making suggestions.

The different interpretations of the Act produced a healthy diversity of housing throughout the country. In London the County Council developed two main house types. The most attractive were the 'Cottage Estates', influenced by the work of Unwin and his contemporaries. Excellent examples survive in Roehampton and the Docklands. But Becontree, described as 'the largest municipal housing estate in the world', though not a garden suburb, became the prototype of all housing estates.

The other main LCC type was that consisting of blocks of flats or 'Flatted Estates'. These consisted of five-storey blocks in a modified neo-Georgian style with sash windows; later versions had standard steel casements and plain brick surfaces. Each flat had its own bath and WC, a scullery (which was soon to become a kitchen), a larder and a coal store. A dust-chute was provided for each floor.

The average floor area of a flat was larger than before the war, and the restriction of blocks to a height of five storeys meant that the LCC flats avoided many of the problems that the high-rise boom was later to encounter. The flats had through ventilation and balcony access. Kitchens were well fitted and equipped.

There was one further development during the 1930s that was to affect the general housing scene in a dramatic way. The Government's attention became concentrated upon slum clearance. In the light of a calculation that there were about one million unfit houses in England and Wales, the Cabinet diverted its consideration to the huge numbers of families still occupying old, decaying slum property.

Of all the slum clearance schemes, the most famous and internationally recognised was in Leeds. Quarry Hill, at the east end of the Headrow, had been designated as the Quarry Hill Unhealthy Area at the beginning of the century. In 1934 the area was wholly cleared, and between that year and 1940 a new housing scheme was erected. The flats were designed in such a way as to enshrine the sanitary principle and prevent re-infestation. There was no timber except in the doors, and metal-framed windows were surrounded with concrete; skirting boards and other traditionally wooden structures were also made from concrete. But at the same time Quarry Hill made many desirable social and domestic innovations. It had quality fittings and its many amenities included a shopping centre, playgrounds, crèches and a laundry. It had a new system of waste disposal, a radio relay system, lifts to the eight-storey blocks, tennis courts and a community hall (see Figures 8.4 and 8.5).

On a site of 26 acres it had 938 flats housing over 3,000 people. The brief laid down that not more than one fifth of the site should be built upon. The rest was open space for gardens, fresh air, playing and relaxation. In the event, only about 18 per cent was built on. Quarry Hill was a showpiece of its kind and very popular with its tenants. Yet in 1978, only forty years after its completion, Quarry Hill was demolished. There were faults in the cladding and foundations;

Figure 8.4   A general view of Quarry Hill *c.* 1940

Figure 8.5   The communal laundry at Quarry Hill *c.* 1940

the houses were subject to damp and corrosion; the social buildings were incomplete; the landscape had degenerated.

The flatted estates and the estates erected for slum clearance had a lasting effect on the design of housing after the Second World War. For the problem now was even more obviously a demand for numbers. And the scene was transformed by the public housing drive.

In 1946, the majority of local authority dwellings were houses. By 1953, 77 per cent of public dwelling approvals were for houses, 20 per cent low-rise flats, and 3 per cent high-rise flats. The situation changed markedly in the next few years. The proportion of houses in building approvals continued to decline, while high-rise projects increased in height, numbers and importance. By 1960 and 1966 they formed respectively 15 per cent and 26 per cent of construction programmes.

The question that has to be asked about the housing of the 1950s, 1960s and 1970s is: why did the authorities decide to build high buildings in the first place?

The answer is that it was primarily a response to the need for numbers and speed. But there were also other, more idealistic reasons. High-rise housing was associated for many designers with progress and the expression of a new technological age. It seemed the inevitable expression of the modern movement in architecture. In a series of plans, exhibitions and books in the 1920s, Le Corbusier had argued for the adoption of high-rise housing as the essential building form of the modern city. 'We must create,' he declared, 'the mass production spirit.' (Le Corbusier, 1927) His imaginative designs for the city of the future included massive slabs of housing in wide, landscaped, open spaces.

Probably more profound was the influence of Walter Gropius, founder of the Bauhaus and author of one of the definitive texts on modern architecture, *The New Architecture and the Bauhaus* (1936). Gropius had studied how to obtain the best possible living conditions while maintaining the urban character of the city. His solution was to build high slab-like apartment blocks of about ten storeys. In two diagrams he showed (a) that at a fixed angle between the blocks of 30 degrees, the number of bed spaces (and therefore the number of inhabitants) could be increased by about 40 per cent, and (b) that if the bed spaces were kept to their original number, the angle of light between the blocks could be lowered from 30 degrees to 17.5 degrees. In short, the higher the blocks the greater the space and the better the sunlight. There could be cross-ventilation and a great deal of natural light. The idea of the 'verdant city' was, he said, a practical possibility.

In fact the number of high-rise blocks in this country was never the majority. Of all local authority housing only 6.5 per cent is in high-rise blocks. It just looks as if there is more; the image of the modern city is often one of masses of high blocks. Furthermore, the high-rise blocks were only put up for a period of about twenty years—from roughly the early 1950s to the early 1970s. By the middle of the 1970s local authorities were not building any more.

But why were they desirable in the early 1950s? It was not because of demand from the prospective tenants, although the top flats quickly became very popular when they were first opened. Nor were they the outcome of sociological study. In the early 1950s sociological research into housing had hardly started. I remember taking part in interviews to find a sociologist to join the housing research team in Edinburgh University in the mid-1950s. Most candidates had no suggestions to offer. The most experienced man suggested that we should put up some housing and he would return in twenty years to say what we had done wrong.

The housing of the 1950s and 1960s was not the product of theoretical studies; it was essentially a pragmatic solution to definable problems. To the professional trying to find a way through them, two of those problems were fundamental; the shortage of land, especially where planning policies were limiting the growth of the city outwards; and the overwhelming demand for accommodation. In one city, for example, the new city architect in the mid-1960s noted that, while his department was building less than 2,000 houses a year, the application list for houses was 60,000. Any possible answer must include high buildings on limited sites and almost certainly prefabricated 'system building' for speed.

As a guide to housing policy, the most basic text used by the architects of many authorities was the *County of London Plan* (1943) by Forshaw and Abercrombie. The authors included a number of detailed studies that suggested that at a density of some 135 people per acre it would be possible not only to provide 'improved living conditions for the differing income groups', but vastly superior facilities and adequate open space for health and recreation. In a mixed development of different housing types, some blocks would go high, others could stay nearer the ground. It was a practical, carefully considered solution; and it opened up some exciting possibilities.

As far as the dwellings themselves were concerned, the most influential document was a report on the design of dwellings produced by the Ministry of Health Central Housing Advisory Committee in 1944, chaired by the Earl of Dudley (Ministry of Health, 1944). The Dudley Report drew attention to two main defects in pre-war council housing. They were the lack of variety in housing types and insufficient living space.

Three types of house plan emerged from the study, each of which was to influence council housing for many years to come. The first was a living room combined with a kitchen, with a small scullery nearby. The second was a large living room combined with a dining room, and a working kitchen. The third was for an ordinary living room and a combined dining kitchen; that, of course, involved a separate utility room for washing etc. It was expected that heating would be by gas or electricity rather than by solid fuel. The question of whether there should be a separate parlour, which had been discussed continuously in the inter-war period, still remained a matter for speculation, but in due course the separate parlour disappeared. There would be higher standards of servicing and equipment—houses should contain refrigeration, and for families of five or more there should be two WCs; this practice was started in 1945 but abandoned in 1951.

The Dudley Report represented a considerable advance on the Tudor Walters Report which had influenced housing after 1918. The density of housing, confirmed in the subsequent *Housing Manual*, would vary between 30 and 120 people per acre. In terms of layout, what came to be accepted as a result of the Reports and the continued studies thereafter, was 'mixed development'.

The authority that exploited mixed development in the most remarkable manner was the London County Council (LCC)—the first authority, incidentally, to employ a sociologist to advise on housing. And the most complete and expressive scheme, which architects came from many parts of the world to study and admire, was at Roehampton, on the edge of Richmond Park.

Nearby was one of the best early LCC cottage estates, completed in 1927. Now, with a mature landscape, Roehampton offered an unusual opportunity —it was almost a garden city setting. Every tree possible was saved. The designers drew up a detailed plan of the site, including each individual tree, to ensure the minimum possible damage. The views to and from the blocks were carefully considered.

But above all, Roehampton was the prime example of mixed development. In pursuit of that ideal, the LCC evolved a concept of housing unlike anything on the continent. Instead of huge blocks of repetitive rows of low-density housing, a mixed development would have a combination of diverse dwellings suited to the requirements of diverse people. It would include single-storey cottages for the elderly, two- or three-storey terraced houses for families and a proportion of flats, in higher blocks, mainly for childless and elderly couples. At a density of about 120 people to the acre this would still allow ample room for landscape, for play and exercise. Mixed development, therefore, would produce some of the best of both low- and high-density housing.

Roehampton was built in two phases. The first phase, with its point blocks and low housing, was distinctly Scandinavian in character. The architects had studied Scandinavian housing at first hand and were convinced that it was appropriate. Groups of eleven-storey point blocks were sited among the trees, five-storey slab blocks were surrounded by a stretch of meadow, there were terraced houses and four-storey maisonettes on the narrower parts of the plot.

The second, later and bigger development was designed by the new wave of keen young architects in the Department, devotees of Le Corbusier and of his Unité d'Habitation at Marseille. This took the form of slab blocks with balcony access, later very unpopular, and rough concrete, later more unpopular still.

But the other housing types were still there—the point blocks, the four-storey maisonettes, the two-storey terraced houses and the single-storey houses for old people. The total environment was incomparable. Its major fault, very visible today, is the lack of space for car parking; at the time it was not anticipated that car ownership would increase to the level it has today.

As an estate Roehampton has not diminished in popularity. There have been, of course, variations in the popularity of different types of block. The tower blocks remain popular, as do the two-storey houses. The least popular are the four-storey maisonettes and the slab blocks. But the findings of Roehampton did not in the end influence the general pattern of housing in the country. In other parts of London, densities were increased to 200 people per acre and more. In many parts of the country the most successful and popular dwelling types, for the time being at least, were the tower blocks. In 1988 there were 429 tower blocks in Birmingham alone. Great Britain could boast 4,600 such blocks.

High-rise housing was popular not only with the architects, but with local councillors and their officials—especially the borough engineer. The argument of the borough engineer was that the cost of drainage and bringing in services could be reduced by concentrating the whole project. Fewer roads were needed. Furthermore, the high buildings were not usually of traditional construction, but were constructed through the adoption of proprietory *system building*. The major advantage was speed—both in the acquisition of land for a tower block and in the construction process using a prefabricated system. Contracting organisations vied with each other in producing systems. The long-term results of these are with us still.

Above all, high-rise housing was advocated and supported by central government. Local authorities were urged, through circulars, to build high. It was clear that building high must cost more per square foot than building a traditional two-storey house. Central government, therefore, supplied grants for building high. Everyone, it seemed, would be happy. The houses went up quickly, the politicians could congratulate themselves, the builders made fabulous profits. A few authorities might refuse to build high-rise housing—the chairman of York's housing committee, for example, refused to have anything to do with it—but generally the subsidies, the encouragement and the speed provided local authorities with the illusion of great achievement.

So what went wrong? How and why did attitudes change? First there was the problem of children. Surveys in the late 1950s indicated that while many single people and childless couples liked living in flats, the majority of families with children disliked them.

There were further revelations. The growing disillusionment of architects with the inherent weaknesses and substandard quality of high-rise housing went hand in hand with doubts as to whether there were any significant savings in either land or building costs. National data on building costs showed that in 1960 all forms of high-rise housing were more than twice as expensive per square foot as ordinary three-bedroomed houses. Even the alleged cheapness of high densities was a myth, as Unwin had perceived years before. Land was more costly in the inner cities, where the majority of tower blocks were built. And, despite the high price of flats, their quality was often poor.

By 1970, ministry policy had come round to a firmly anti-high-rise position. Cost controls were enforced which effectively eliminated high-rise and high-density public housing developments. The planning assumptions that had produced and dominated high-rise were questioned. The Department of the Environment limited new housing to a density range of 70–100 rooms per acre, with housing for families normally in the lower part of the range. Neo-vernacular building using traditional materials was soon to dominate the local authority output of houses and low-rise flats.

The main question that remains about high-rise and mass housing, after more than thirty years of development and disaster, is whether it is possible to transform or reorganise unsuccessful mass housing so as to make it a positive force in social architecture?

In any housing situation the crucial factors are design, management and maintenance. So, given a poor design, is it possible to redeem the housing through better management and maintenance? An increasing number of experiments suggest that the answer is positive. The key to it, in every case, has been giving the people in a housing scheme authority over their own area—to help them to participate in the formation of a community responsible for the management and maintenance of their dwellings.

An important recent development has been the conversion of some high-rise blocks into homes for the elderly. In Birmingham, where two-thirds of the housing demand in the city is for single-person accommodation, both for the young and the elderly, the council accepts that the targeting of selected blocks for specific social groups, reminiscent of the ethos behind mixed development, is fruitful.

So fifty-four blocks have been transformed since 1979 into sheltered housing for the elderly, with wardens in residence. Following the success of these blocks, more are now in the pipeline. The conversion involves gutting a ground-floor flat to create a community area, installing an intercom service throughout, and employing a permanent warden for each block. The evidence shows that the elderly who were already living in high-rise flats almost unanimously welcome the transformation of tower blocks; those who moved there from traditional houses are less enthusiastic. Most people prefer a house, and tend to look upon flats as a temporary mode of dwelling.

Looking back at the story of mass housing, it has to be said that high-rise housing was not merely the product of architectural egotism or of an artistic and technological dream. It was thought to be an answer to very pressing housing needs. The problem was that the reality did not fulfil the dream. The numbers game subsumed everything else.

Kenneth Campbell, head of LCC and GLC housing between 1959 and 1974, attributed the failure of high-rise housing to three basic faults: first, the inadequate state of the lifts, which were constructed too cheaply; secondly, young couples who moved into tower blocks could not easily be moved out again as soon as they had children; thirdly, the size of the Director of Housing's organisation meant that management and maintenance were slow working, often with unfortunate consequences. If lifts and security worked and could be guaranteed, the story would be very different.

In fact, high-rise has never been universally unpopular. Many childless couples positively like them. Wealthy people, in particular, often enjoy living in high buildings, especially if they have another house in the country. It is in the public sector that high-rise is most resented. The chief problems of the tower blocks—alienation, vandalism and crime—are the results of mass, rather than high-rise building.

Yet high-rise housing did make some useful contributions. Ultimately it highlighted the necessity of having a sociological basis for housing, and for consulting people about what they required and what needed to be done. When local authorities and private developers have the power to destroy whole communities and create new ones, with far-reaching human consequences, a concern not only for bricks and mortar but for people must be the key to any solution of the housing question.

For any housing, and especially social housing, a fundamental question is: what should the standards be? If the Tudor Walters Report of 1918 and the

Dudley Report of 1944 had both been revolutionary and enormously influential in the development of housing types and housing sizes, the Parker Morris Report (Central Housing Advisory Committee, 1961) was arguably more progressive: it advocated standards for all new houses both public and private. It aimed to keep pace with rising expectations and better post-war conditions. Increased prosperity meant that one in three households now owned a car. Two out of three owned a television set. As the Report said:

These changes in the way people want to live, the things which they own and use, and in their general level of prosperity . . . make it timely to re-examine the kinds of homes that we ought to be building.

The Report laid special emphasis on space and on heating. It maintained that the family house should be bigger, that in a house for five or more people there should be two day rooms and two WCs. It recommended a larger kitchen to accommodate the growing range of kitchenware, and a generous amount of storage space. Better heating was a central stipulation. The most common form of heating was still the open fire with a back boiler, which could heat only one or two radiators. Parker Morris suggested that houses should be equipped to heat the kitchen and circulation areas to a minimum of 55 degrees F, and living areas to a minimum of 65 degrees F. There should be a system whereby the tenant could regulate the temperature level—and therefore the expense.

In short the Report advocated larger, better planned and better constructed houses than had hitherto been provided. It believed that the higher standard of living ought to be reflected in a higher standard of housing:

An increasing proportion of people are coming to expect their homes to do more than fulfil the basic requirements. . . . There is therefore an increasingly prevalent atmosphere in which improvements in housing standards will be welcomed and indeed demanded, and in which stress will be laid upon quality rather than mere adequacy. (Parker Morris, 1961)

In the years following that publication, a number of major reports and events have changed the public attitude towards housing. In 1985 Alice Coleman published *Utopia on Trial*, the most sweeping condemnation of local authority ever produced. Subtitled *Vision and Reality in Planned Housing*, it was an indictment not only of the local authorities, but also of central government. It analysed, on the basis of comprehensive surveys, items such as vandalism, graffiti, litter, excrement and the number of children in care. All the results suggested that the local authorities had failed disastrously in terms of management as well as of design.

Coleman's starting point was to study the dilemma in relation to the people living on the estate. Her research showed that design had a noticeable impact on behaviour. She fastened on the Department of the Environment the ultimate responsibility for what she called 'socially disadvantaging designs'. The housing types that came in for most criticism were the five- or six-storey blocks with balcony access, virtually an open invitation to criminals. She suggested that breaking down the long balcony walkways into shorter spaces, which could be more easily supervised by tenants, would help to provide the 'defensible space' made popular by the American writer Oscar Newman. Bad housing, in short, could be attributable not only to bad design but also to bad management.

Her report received enthusiastic support from the Audit Commission in its own report, *Managing the Crisis in Council Housing* (1986). The main theme of the study is that the housing crisis is chiefly attributable to bad design and management. Its solutions are generally managerial ones. If the two areas of activity which have handicapped mass housing since it was erected—good management and good maintenance—could be assured, there would still be hope for the housing situation.

The major movement that seems to be having a positive effect upon the social scene is what has come to be known as 'community architecture'. Studies of mass housing confirmed that good management and proper maintenance were essential to the happiness and health of tenants. But, above all, tenants commented that they wished to have a larger share in the management of their homes. The key to the rediscovery of the great housing tradition and the creation of a satisfactory environment may therefore lie in the involvement of communities.

A number of pioneering projects in England have demonstrated, through community architecture, that the housing scene can be dramatically improved. The renovation of Lea View House, in Hackney, was the first project in which local authority tenants on London were wholly involved in the rehabilitation of their homes. Before refurbishment, Lea View was a typical problem estate, difficult to let, beset by crime and racial tension, continually vandalised. Ninety per cent of its tenants wanted to leave.

After renovation, crime and vandalism virtually disappeared. Health and spirits improved. There was a renewed sense of community. In contrast, the Wigan Estate, renovated by the same authority but without tenant involvement, reverted to a slum. John Thompson, the architect for Lea View, commented on the difference between the Wigan and Lea View Estates: 'It is a vivid example of how social behaviour responds to design . . . Lea View is housing for people . . . Wigan is unit housing, committee housing . . . uncaring in both its execution and its management.' (verbatim) If design has an effect on behaviour, the involvement of tenants in the management of their estates is important.

What, at the very least, is clear is that the era of the great architectural concept is at an end. The grand projects—whether at the periphery of great cities (as at Easterhouse in Glasgow) or in the outer reaches of London (as at Maiden Lane or Alexandra Road)—are over. But there is not much evidence that either the clients in the form of governmental agencies or the executants in the form of architects or planners will take much notice. And although there are numerous sociological studies, there are not many that bring sociological penetration to the perception of the designers—a kind of social comment and prescription that does not turn its back on the design and shrug its shoulders at the three-dimensional results but sees such studies as integral to each other, so that a social theorist might be able to play a creative part in the early stages of design and at the very beginning bring a social vision to inspire an architectural concept.

My experience of visiting and studying many housing schemes confirms for me that design cannot in itself result in a happy community and guarantee social success. But its failure can — and manifestly does — make social integration and fulfilment difficult and sometimes impossible. Good design is not a sufficient condition for social success, but it is a necessary one. And it is neglected at disastrous social cost.

References

Ackroyd *On improved dwellings for the working classes*, London, Shaw, 1861, pp. 4–5.

Audit Commission for Local Authorities in England and Wales (1986) *Managing the crisis in Council housing*, London, HMSO.

Burnett, J A (1986) *A Social History of Housing (1815–1985)*, London, Methuen.

Central Housing Advisory Committee (1961) *Homes for today and tomorrow*, Report of a sub-committee of the Central Housing Advisory Committee, London, HMSO (The Parker Morris Report).

Coleman, A M (1985) *Utopia on Trial: Vision and Reality in Planned Housing*, London, H Shipman.

Forshaw, J H and Abercrombie, P (1943) *County of London Plan*, LCC.

Howard, E (1985) *Garden Cities of Tomorrow*, London, Attic Books.

Le Corbusier (1927) *Towards a new architecture*, London, Etchells, p. 227.

Local Government Board (1919) *Manual on the preparation of State aided housing scheme*, London.

Ministry of Health (1944) *Design of Dwellings*: Report of the Design of Dwellings Sub-Committee of the Ministry of Health Central Advisory Committee, London, HMSO.

Parker Morris (1961) *Homes for today and tomorrow*, London, Ministry of Housing and Local Government.

Roberts, R (1973) *The Classic Slum: Salford Life in the First Quarter of the Century*, Harmondsworth, Penguin.

Rowntree, B S (1980) *Poverty: a Study of Town Life*, London, Garland.

Tudor Walters Report (1918) *Report of the committee appointed to consider questions of building construction in connection with the provision of dwellings for the working classes*, Cd 9191.

Unwin, R (1909) *Town Planning in Practice: an introduction to the Art of Designing Cities and Suburbs*, London.

Unwin, R (1918) *Nothing Gained by Overcrowding*, Garden Cities and Town Planning Association, London.

Unwin, R (1937) Journal of the Royal Institute of British Architects, April, p. 562.

Further reading

Creese, W L (1966) *The Search for Environment: the Garden City before and after*, Yale University Press.

Creese, W L (1967) *The Legacy of Raymond Unwin: a Human Pattern for Planning*, MIT.

Donnison, DV (1967) *The Government of Housing*, Harmondsworth, Penguin.

Knevitt, C and Wates, N (1987) *Community architecture*, Harmondsworth, Penguin.

Pawley, M (1971) *Architecture versus Housing* Studio Vista

Swenarton, M (1981) *Homes fit for Heroes: the Politics of Architecture of Early State*

Housing in Britain, London, Heinemann Educational.

Tarn, J N (1973) *Five per cent Philanthropy: an Account of Housing in Urban Areas between 1840 and 1914*, Cambridge, Cambridge University Press.

Willmott, P (1988) *Social Polarisation and Social Housing*, London, Policy Studies Institute.

9 Housing management: an historical perspective

Peter Kemp and Peter Williams

Introduction

The nature and effectiveness of housing management by social housing landlords has attracted increasing attention in recent years. This concern is relatively new for, while never entirely neglected, housing management was previously always a poor relation to the construction of new dwellings (Power, 1987). In a way, this was hardly surprising, for the impetus behind the development of council housing, as Kemp shows in Chapter 4, was always the need to tackle the shortage of housing or clear the slums. Hence it was how many new houses were built, rather than how well they were subsequently managed, which was the primary concern of politicians.

Yet housing management is big business and has been so for quite some time. By 1938, to take what is admittedly an extreme example, the London County Council owned and managed over 86,000 dwellings, occupied by more than 382,000 people—not far short of the population of Bristol at the time—with an annual rent roll (in 1938 prices) of £3.2 million (Gibbon and Bell, 1939). Today, local authorities in England and Wales alone manage some 4.5 million dwellings and spend approximately £3 billion a year on housing management and maintenance out of a total housing revenue account expenditure of over £6 billion (CIPFA, 1989). According to the Audit Commission (1986) over 55,000 people are employed in housing work by local councils. Yet many people have never heard, and still less thought much about, housing management as a career. In many ways it is a hidden profession, though one which has had a considerable impact on the lives of people who live in rented housing.

In this chapter we draw on a relatively sparse but growing literature to sketch out the development of housing management, focusing mainly on the council sector. In doing so, we attempt to show that there have been considerable continuities over time in this important activity and that many current issues, while they attract more attention now than they have done in the past, reflect what are recurring influences and debates. The key themes which we have identified and which we address in this chapter are: the initial influence of private sector management practice and the ambiguous nature of 'social' as opposed to private housing management; the changing role of council housing and the impact this has had on the style and practice of housing management; the influence of gender and of the struggle for professionalism on conceptions of how housing management should be organised and orientated; and the apparent gap between central advice on, and local implementation of, 'best practice' in the management of council housing. We begin by looking at the origins of housing management, which lie in nineteenth-century private sector practice.

The origins of housing management

Local authority housing management largely began with the Housing and Town Planning, etc., Act 1919 (the 'Addison Act') which introduced Exchequer subsidies for council house-building. Prior to the First World War, approximately nine out of ten dwellings were rented, almost all of them from private landlords. Although a few local authorities (most notably Liverpool, Manchester, the London County Council and Glasgow) had built some rental housing, by 1914 the national total was only an estimated 24,000 (Merrett, 1979). However, in the twenty years after the First World War, local authorities built, and had subsequently to manage, over one million houses. For the overwhelming majority of the 1,802 local housing authorities in England and Wales in 1919, housing management was a completely new task. Yet central government, in the shape of the Ministry of Health, was more concerned with the production of housing in the immediate post-war period, and management of the new houses was a secondary issue. Although the management ideas of Octavia Hill were not unknown, they were not widely applied and, in effect, virtually all that many of the new municipal housing managers had to draw on for their new task was private sector experience. And indeed, it was in the privately rented, profit-orientated housing market that Octavia Hill worked.

The aim of this section, therefore, is to outline briefly the nature of private housing management as it existed in England and Wales prior to the First World War. With hindsight it is perhaps all too easy to be critical of the way local authorities adapted to their new responsibility (e.g. Power, 1987). But the new municipal housing managers did not have the benefit of hindsight and, instead, had to draw on contemporary knowledge, perceptions and experience — all of which were informed by, or were based on, the way housing to let was managed in the private sector.

There is an essential ambiguity about the *modus operandi* of housing management in social housing which does not exist in the private sector. Local authorities and housing associations are usually perceived as motivated, at least in part, by 'social' considerations, although these are rarely defined in any rigorous or adequate way. Indeed, definitions of 'housing management' in the literature (e.g. Smith, 1977) usually amount to little more than an outline of the various *activities* (allocation of tenancies, collection of rent, carrying out of repairs, etc.) which comprise management, all of which are of course also carried out in the private sector. The *raison d'être* of housing management in the private sector, by contrast, is clear: to make a profit on capital invested. Property management, whether carried out by the landlord or an agent, is simply a means to this end. As we shall see, the commercial imperative informed and structured housing management practices prior to the First World War, even if the response to that imperative on the part of different managers varied. However, in considering housing management in the pre-1914 private rental sector, it is necessary to understand the wider housing and societal context within which it took place.

The management of privately rented housing in the nineteenth century

The development of capitalist housing provision, which accompanied the rapid urban growth of the late eighteenth and early nineteenth centuries (Ball, 1981) seems to have brought with it a distinctive, more impersonal and commercial, management of working-class housing to let. According to Dyos and Reeder (1973, p. 380):

Whereas in the old pre-urban days, when the rent receiver was often visible as employer or social better within a tolerable frame, and when the rent-night gathering might sometimes almost be said to have been celebrated 'as if the thing, money, had not brought it here', the relations between landlord and tenant in the [capitalist] city were characteristically impersonal, conducted through agents called rent collectors, and the rent itself seldom bore any demonstrable connection with the human container itself.

A related aspect of this transformation concerned tenancy arrangements. Previously, rented dwellings seem generally to have been let on yearly leases, with the rent being paid on the four quarter days or half yearly (Englander, 1983). Many tenants enjoyed tenure rights that covered the span of their lives and that recognised the succession rights of widows and their children. Tenants could be evicted only after a lengthy legal process (Nevitt, 1970). All this changed with the shift of population from the countryside to the rapidly growing towns and the development of a much more mobile force of wage labour (Kemp, 1987). Many of the new, urban working class found themselves reduced to mere weekly tenants with limited rights of occupation. The displacement of a moral economy by a political economy in rental housing was itself given legal expression in the Small Tenements Recovery Act 1838, which made it much easier to evict tenants who were unwilling to leave (Englander, 1983; Nevitt, 1970). Under this Act, landlords of working-class dwellings (those with an annual rent of up to £20) in England and Wales had only to apply to a JP to secure a warrant for possession after 21 days. No grounds for eviction had to be provided; it had simply to be proved that a notice to quit had been given. As Nevitt (1970, p. 131) has remarked,

The 'will' of the landlord no longer had to be 'reasonable' and it would not be an exaggeration to say that as far as the law was concerned the mass of the population occupied their dwellings from 1838 to 1915 at the whim of their landlord.

Nevertheless, landlords' exercise of their strong legal position was tempered by their need to keep sitting tenants in order to secure a flow of rental income.

Contemporary English property managers claimed that so long as an occupier was a 'good' tenant (itself a subject on which landlord and tenant might disagree) and paid the rent regularly, she or he was unlikely to be evicted (Kemp, 1987). Moreover, the management of rented housing was affected by the long cycles of boom and slump that characterised the urban housing market prior to 1914. As Daunton (1983) has pointed out, landlords could be more choosy and tenants less so when houses were scarce, but when the level of vacant properties increased beyond a certain level the balance of advantage shifted in favour of the tenants.

Whether carried out personally by the landlord or by an agent, the management tasks to be performed were essentially the same as those subsequently taken on by the new municipal landlords after the First World War. In carrying out these tasks, commercial considerations were paramount, though this is not to say that individual acts of genuine philanthropy did not occur. The overriding factor, however, was that rental housing for the landlord was an investment, a source of income, the amount of which was to be maximised and the costs kept to a minimum. In general, the decision as to whom to allocate a tenancy, whether or not to allow (a limited amount of) arrears to accrue, whether to carry out 'non-essential' repairs or to decorate a dwelling, all were informed by the commercial imperative (see, for example, Griffin, 1893–4; Howarth and Wilson, 1907).

This commercial imperative was translated into different property management practices by different landlords and agents. Thus some landlords were very strict, issuing a notice to quit immediately a tenant fell into arrears or was in some other respect found to be unsatisfactory. Others were more flexible in their approach, conforming more closely to the 'model' practice advocated by contemporary property managements experts (e.g., Griffin, 1893–4). Central to this model practice was an informal grading of tenants, involving careful character assessments by the landlord or managing agent.

Thus normally 'satisfactory' tenants who paid the rent with regularity but who fell on hard times were sometimes given a certain amount of leeway (a discreet lowering of the rent, for example) not accorded to 'unsatisfactory' tenants (Englander, 1983). Likewise, 'good' tenants were more likely to be able to persuade the landlord to redecorate the dwelling than were 'unsatisfactory' tenants (Kemp, 1987); this was necessary in order to prevent the best tenants from leaving to take up a tenancy elsewhere in a better-decorated dwelling. As Englander (1983) has remarked, the reliable rent-paying artisan had a certain amount of 'purchase' among landlords looking for tenants: 'Tenants of the best class are not to be picked up everyday; and having such, it is well to keep them', wrote one contemporary expert on the subject (Urlin, 1902, p. 48). With tenants below the labour artisan class, the managers of house property had largely to work within the constraints of the local labour market — especially seasonal and cyclical trade fluctuations — in making decisions. Thus managers had often to allow rent arrears to accrue during trade depressions or at certain times of the year in order to ensure that they had a tenant at all, in the hope and expectation that the arrears would be paid off when trade and employment had recovered (Kemp, 1987). The Outer London Enquiry team reported, for example, that 'One agent, dealing with better-class property in the poorer districts, told us that he found it necessary to allow every one of his tenants at one time or another to fall into arrears' (Howarth and Wilson, 1907, p. 177).

So as Englander (1983, p. 11) has remarked, in many instances a 'bond of debt united landlord and tenant'. With the poorest class of tenants, such as casual workers, however, the bond of debt sometimes deteriorated into a war of debt, with both landlord and tenant disregarding the law as well as each other's rights and obligations. At its extreme, property let to 'non-respectable' tenants became almost unmanageable, with the landlord virtually abandoning responsibility for the property (see Howarth and Wilson, 1907; Englander, 1983). It was tenanted property of this type that was originally the focus of attention of the housing reformer and manager of slum property, Octavia Hill. In order to properly understand Hill's contribution to the history of housing management, it is important to locate it within the private sector context that we have just sketched out.

Octavia Hill

Much has been written about the management methods of this formidable Victorian (e.g. Wohl, 1977; Brion and Tinker, 1980; Malpass, 1984), and there is not sufficient space here to provide a detailed outline and evaluation of her work. We would like to stress a number of points, however, about her system of management in relation to that of her contemporaries. First, we should note that Hill was as much, if not more, concerned with her tenants' moral condition as with their housing condition (see Hill, 1875). Housing was, in a sense, a medium through which she could seek to improve the moral welfare of the poor. Indeed, it was her view that moral improvement was the key to housing improvement since it was that, rather than the wider structural forces in society, that accounted for the existence of housing problems now that legislation existed to prevent the building of slum property.

Second, it was a basic premise of her management philosophy that it was necessary to deal with the tenant and the dwelling together; that the physical improvement of a dwelling had to go hand in hand with—indeed, was contingent upon—the education and moral improvement of the tenant (Hill, 1875). While her contemporaries in property management, as noted earlier, did make distinctions between types of tenant when deciding whether to redecorate a dwelling or allow a limited amount of arrears to accrue, their purpose for such action was different. Hill sought to offer rewards for good behaviour; her contemporaries 'rewarded' tenants whom they wished to keep because it was in their long-term interests to do so. Hill operated with a moral imperative, her contemporaries with a commercial one.

Third, Hill's moral imperative entailed the strict enforcement of punctual rent payment. Arrears of rent were simply not tolerated (Malpass, 1984). In this she was less flexible than many mainstream property managers of this period (Daunton, 1983) who adjusted their methods to the realities of working-class financial insecurity. Hence while Hill operated with a moral imperative, it was one that involved a belief in the 'discipline' of the market. It was not a return to the 'moral economy' referred to above in relation to the pre-urban housing markets.

A fourth and related point is that it is not clear whether her 'success' in housing management was the result of 'improving' her tenants or of simply the weeding out of 'undesirables'. Since Hill saw it as her moral duty to evict forthwith those of her tenants who fell into arrears, and given that fluctuations of employment and income level were endemic, the latter rather than the former would seem to account for her success in keeping bad debts to a minimum. Beatrice Webb, a volunteer rent collector in Katherine Buildings in London's East End, expressed the dilemma well in a diary entry of 1885:

Tenants, rough lot—the aborigines of the East End. Pressure to exclude these and take in only the respectable—follow Peabody's example. Interview with superintendent of Peabody's. 'We had a rough lot to begin with, had to weed them of the old inhabitants—now only take in men with regular employment.'

The practical problem of management: are the tenants to be picked, all doubtful or inconvenient persons excluded or are the former inhabitants to be housed so long as they are decently respectable? (Webb, 1982, p. 134)

Yet Hill (1875, pp. 50–1) claimed that her tenants were 'of the very poor' and yet that none had continued 'in what is called "distress" except such as have been unwilling to exert themselves'. This seems to suggest that she may have been somewhat out of touch with the realities of life for the late Victorian urban poor and that her approach to management could not have worked on a wide scale if the poorest of the poor were ever to be properly housed. This conclusion is in contrast to that of Power (1987), whose glowing account of Hill's work does not, in our view, adequately grasp the social and economic context within which house property was managed prior to 1914.

Fifth, it is often claimed that Octavia Hill was the founder of 'housing management' (Malpass, 1984; Clapham, 1987; Power, 1987). Certainly, if that term is intended to mean management for purposes other than just concern for the income-generating potential of property, the claim may well be justified. Although she relied upon the voluntary work of (middle-class) women rent collectors, towards the end of her life she saw the value of paid, trained, professional workers (Brion and Tinker, 1980). And in helping to increase the employment opportunities open to women (albeit within a sphere seen as women's work) she was a positive force in developing housing management. Yet while Hill may well have been the founder of public sector housing management, it is somewhat ironic that she was deeply opposed to subsidised or municipal housing.

'Property management' as a separate activity did exist on a wide scale before the First World War and was not confined to Octavia Hill and her followers. (What distinguished Hill was her stress on management as more than just rent collecting, her emphasis on moral improvements, her use of female volunteers and her authoritarian outlook.) In order to minimise the 'troubles and anxieties' involved in the management of working-class house property, many landlords chose not to carry out this task personally but instead employed an agent to do it. The contracting out of management tasks ranged from rent collection to all aspects of management (Kemp, 1982; Daunton, 1983).

Property management was carried out by a range of different types of exchange professionals, including house agents, auctioneers and surveyors. Although some firms specialised in property management, for many it was simply one source of income to supplement their main activity (such as surveying or conveyancing). Their fees were usually based on a percentage of the rental income, the precise amount varying according to how frequently the rent was collected (Kemp, 1986). Followers of the Octavia Hill approach were in direct competition with these more mainstream property managers. As a report on property management published in 1921 pointed out:

Women managers (mostly paid on percentage) have hitherto undertaken the work at a sacrifice. Introducing as they did a new system of management, their work was intensified, but their percentage remained the same as that of the former agents. (Jeffrey and Neville, 1921, p. 93)

The emergence of public housing management

Since 1919 housing management practice has been strongly influenced by local authorities and the ways in which their role has changed over time. Although private sector housing management continued as an important activity in most areas until the 1970s it was increasingly viewed in the light of local authority practice and was often the subject of considerable criticism. Aside from the charitable trusts, which are now seen as part of the housing association movement, the image of the private landlord from the 1950s, at least, has been poor. Indeed it was to allay fears of 'Rachmanism' by landlords of hived-off council estates that the Government introduced the so-called 'social landlords' charter' in 1988. Moreover, it is also evident that as local authority housing management grew in stature, as well as in physical scale, it rapidly took on a lead role with respect to the development of good management practice. In a special reprinted issue of *The Times* published in 1938 devoted to building societies, the unknown author of a short article on the management of houses commented (p. 38):

Private enterprise . . . has without doubt a good deal to learn from those organisations, both municipal and voluntary, which have been thinking hard and acting boldly in an attempt to adapt housing management to modern conditions.

But in 1914, housing management was not substantially established within local government. The London County Council, with over 10,000 dwellings, was very much an exception in having set up a housing department under a director of housing in 1912 (Power 1987). The management of council housing was at this time seen as the management of property and as such there appears to have been little to distinguish public from private landlords in these early days. Indeed, some local authorities actually employed private sector house agents. For example, immediately after the war, Manchester made use of private sector agents to manage part of its stock (MoH, 1920). In the 1930s, Chester-le-Street UDC (Urban District Council) hired a firm of private estate agents to handle all rent collection, on a commission of 3 per cent (Ryder, 1984).

After the First World War, the newly established Ministry of Health gave plenty of advice and encouragement to councils about house design, non-traditional methods of construction, and other aspects to do with facilitating the speedy production of 'homes fit for heroes' to live in. But it gave very little guidance to councils on the subsequent management of the newly built stock. One exception to this was the single issue of its fortnightly magazine *Housing* that it devoted to what it called 'the problem of management'. Even there it declined to offer councils any detailed advice on how they should manage their new asset, preferring to leave each council to devise its own management scheme in the light of local circumstances.

This local autonomy in housing management has largely continued up to the present. While governments have been keen to provide authorities with advice about good practice, they have none the less generally left it to each local authority to decide whether or not to take that advice. This has led to a noticeable gap between what is often regarded by central government as good practice and what is actually carried out at the local level. And there has often been considerable variation between different authorities in their policies and practices in the management of council housing. This is in marked contrast to the relationship between the Department of Social Security and local DSS offices, where there is much tighter control by the centre over what is done in practice at the local level.

One piece of advice the Ministry of Health did give in 1920 was to advise against what it regarded as the 'unsatisfactory' system of entrusting manage-ment to commissioning agents who 'usually do little more than send a junior clerk to pay a fleeting call on the tenants once a week for the purpose of collecting the rents' (MoH, 1920, p. 2). Apart from this the Ministry did not feel it necessary to suggest in what sense council management should be different from that provided by the private sector. If there was to be anything 'social' about management by local authorities it was left unstated. Instead, the Ministry provided what amounted to a content definition of the new task facing local authorities, one that was no different from good practice in the private sector: 'Whatever system is adopted,' said the Ministry, 'arrangements will have to be made for carrying out the following objects:-

(1) The careful selection of tenants;
(2) The elimination of unsatisfactory tenants;
(3) Constant supervision of the property and its occupants by officials directly employed and paid by the owners;
(4) Systematic and punctual collection of rents.'
     (MoH, 1920, p. 2)

Housing management and the role of council housing

The way in which housing management has been carried out in practice since 1919 has to a greater or lesser extent been influenced by the changing role of local authority housing. Initially, as part of the homes fit for heroes campaign, preference was given to rehousing ex-servicemen and their families (Daunton, 1984; Ryder, 1984). In the 1920s, as Bowley (1945) has remarked, council housing was oriented towards the better-off working-class households rather than the poor. One important reason for this was that, because of very high (if after 1920, falling) building costs and interest rates, the rents of these new homes were very high, notwithstanding the subsidies that were provided. The poor were in this way largely excluded from council housing for most of the 1920s, while the intense housing shortage meant that better-off workers were often keen to accept the 'privilege' of a council tenancy of a house built to much higher standards than those constructed before the war. Even so, some councils had difficulty letting their most expensive houses and some had to resort to advertisements (Dickens and Gilbert, 1981; Ryder, 1984; Power, 1987). Dresser (1984) notes that Addison Act tenants in Bristol were originally selected on the basis of their ability to pay the rent.

In part because they were housing the 'respectable', better-off working-class households, who were not seen as a management problem, housing management was given relatively little attention in the 1920s. Moreover, the political imperative behind the provision of Exchequer subsidies was to reduce the housing shortage, so effort was concentrated on the production of new houses.

As the 1920s progressed and the housing shortage abated, it seems that local councils gradually moved down-market and began to let accommodation to other groups in the community (see Daunton, 1984). After 1930, council house-building was directed towards rehousing slum clearance tenants who were of course much poorer, generally speaking, than the households to whom they had previously allocated tenancies (Byrne, 1974). This meant that councils were increasingly forced to confront the problems of reconciling prudent estate management with local social policy (Ryder, 1984). In its annual report for 1929–30, for example, the Ministry of Health suggested that local authorities could not:

be governed by the same considerations as other property owners. The latter naturally select the most eligible, ie., the most respectable and prosperous, tenants available and may even take into account the absence of children who may knock the house about. Local authorities on the other hand have to provide for those tenants, amongst others, who are least eligible in the eyes of the private owner . . . (Ministry of Health, 1930, pp. 81–2.)

This new emphasis on housing 'unsatisfactory families', such as those rehoused through slum clearance schemes, led to a concern about how management services should be provided to meet this new situation. Thus in 1935 the Ministry of Health set up the Central Housing Advisory Committee (CHAC) which, in turn, set up a sub-committee to investigate the management of municipal housing estates. The sub-committee noted in its 1938 report that the municipal landlord:

may have found that the tenants of his first houses, built under earlier Acts, had generally accommodated themselves to their new environment with a minimum of supervision, but he does not find that a policy of interested detachment can be maintained in his dealings with tenants rehoused from slums. (CHAC, 1939, p. 8)

The Committee noted that the slum clearance rehousing emphasis of the 1930 Housing Act 'introduced an entirely fresh principle in housing administration', that the very poorest were to be rehoused. To CHAC this seemed to imply that 'closer supervision' of this new class of council tenants was necessary, and it proposed what was a more interventionist and paternalist style of management, one that had overtones of Octavia Hill:

What kind of advice and assistance do tenants need? We have already stated that contact with new tenants in their homes prior to removal is essential. During this period arrangements will be made for cleansing furniture and clothing and for giving information on matters connected with the change . . . Later, during the course of day-to-day administration, help can be given in a variety of ways and hardship often alleviated. (CHAC, 1939, pp. 24–5)

Thus the authorities' role as housing providers, and the types of tenants whom they rehoused, had an important influence on the philosophy, content and style of housing management practice between the wars. The more property-oriented, hands-off approach of the 1920s was replaced in the 1930s by a more intensive style, geared to people as well as to dwellings, as councils began to rehouse slum dwellers. This more intensive approach was explicitly seen by many to involve a need for social control of the rehoused tenants and an attempt at 'social engineering'. In *The Slum: its Story and Solution*, Barnes (1934) claimed that 'many of the people our [slum clearance rehousing] programme is intended to provide for need some training before they live decently in our decent houses'. As well as the Octavia Hill approach, a few councils experimented with isolating 'slum minded tenants' in special blocks under close supervision until they proved themselves capable, as Barnes put it, of 'living decently' and so deserving of a normal council tenancy. This was the so called Dutch system (also referred to as the Paisley system). An alternative, strongly promoted by Manchester on its own estates, was the training of estate managers so that 'they became not only the rent collectors of 600 houses a week, but also the guides and friends of 600 families' (*The Times*, 1938, p. 77).

After the Second World War the more intensive management styles were themselves subjected to criticism. Until the mid-1950s, as Kemp shows in Chapter 4, both Labour and Conservative Governments gave municipal house-building a wider orientation than it had in the 1930s, to provide general needs housing. The removal in 1949 of the requirement to house the 'working classes' was a symbolic reflection of this wider remit. One consequence of this changed conception of the role of municipal housing was that, as in the 1920s, it was often not the poorest families who were housed. The interventionist, paternalist management style that emerged in the 1930s was felt to be much less appropriate in the 1950s. For example, one borough treasurer asked 'Does the council tenant get too much management?' (Allerton, 1950). His answer was that there was 'a distinct danger of quite respectable normal people being unduly harassed by visits and inquisitions'. He argued that:

The first essential of good management seems to be the realisation that tenants of council houses are not a special race of people. The majority of them are prepared with but little supervision, to observe all reasonable requirements. That being the case, they are entitled to be largely left alone. (Allerton, 1950, pp. 77–8)

So the 'interfering' paternalism of the 1930s was being challenged with the establishment of council housing as a more widely available option within the housing market. In 1952 the Metropolitan Boroughs Association report on *Housing Management* suggested that only a small minority of tenants were what it called 'friction cases' and the general approach was one of efficient and businesslike property management. This view received official sanction in the 1959 CHAC report, *Councils and their Houses* (CHAC, 1959). The Committee took the view that much had changed since their earlier reports were published and that a fresh look at management was needed. It was noted that in 1938 the Committee had been concerned with 'municipal housing essentially as a social service' and with 'tenants of very limited means'. By 1959, however, the public sector was much larger and a social security system had been established. The Committee went on to point out that

tenants today are much more representative of the community as a whole and are, for the most part independent, reliable citizens who no longer require the support and guidance which was often thought to be necessary in the past. *Local authorities must recognise that this is a major social change which is likely to become more marked in the years ahead: and that this recognition must be given positive effect in their management practice. Though the basic functions of management remain the same, methods must be continuously adjusted to keep ahead of changing conditions.* It is this which constitutes the present challenge to all those engaged in housing management. (CHAC, 1959, p. 2; emphasis in original)

In passing it is also worth noting the committee's concern to ensure that elected members played a full part in housing provision and management—a far cry from today's debate about political 'interference' from councillors in the housing service.

Gender and professionalism in housing management: the struggle for ascendancy

The question of what style of management was appropriate to council housing was not only affected by the role it played in housing provision. It was also affected by the emerging professionalisation of housing management in the public sector. Between the wars the debate about, and move towards, the professionalisation of management had an important gender dimension that, arguably, was the main practical legacy of Octavia Hill's work. For not only did Hill stress the importance of housing managers keeping close personal contact and involvement with tenants, in essence acting as welfare officers or social workers charged with 'improving' the tenants (Clapham, 1987), she also argued forcibly for women being used as housing managers. Although she died in 1912 her legacy was a small but growing number of women property managers working in the private sector, who in 1916 formed an association (the name of which changed several times) which sought to codify and formalise the kind of training and management style that Hill had argued for (Brion and Tinker, 1980; Power, 1987).

It was common for advocates of the Octavia Hill approach to link it with a stress on the need to employ women in housing management. For example, a committee appointed in October 1920 by the women's section of the Garden Cities and Town Planning Association to consider the question of housing management argued in its report (reproduced in Jeffrey and Neville, 1921) that whether the housing manager was a man or a woman was less important than that the Hill system be adopted. Nevertheless, the Report added, 'it should not be overlooked':

(1)   That the housekeeper is always a woman;
(2)   That the woman usually pays the rent;
(3)   That housekeeping and repairs are closely connected;
(4)   That, therefore, a woman will usually be better equipped than a man to deal with the problems arising out of the management of working-class property. (ibid., pp. 87–8)

In seeking to create a sphere in which it was 'legitimate' for middle-class women to be engaged in the labour market, the committee was obliged to fall back on notions that did not conflict with the dominant patriarchal assumptions of a woman's proper place being in (or to do with) the home. Like the Association of Women House Property Managers, the committee sought to construct a conception of housing management in which 'the personal, human factor' was an integral part of the activity rather than being seen, as critics claimed, as 'unbusinesslike' (ibid., p. 86).

One important consequence of employing Octavia Hill-type generic housing workers capable of dealing with a variety of management functions (including rent collection, arranging for repairs to be carried out, and social work), was that each worker could only supervise a limited number of tenancies, perhaps 300 in all (CHAC, 1939). The so-called Octavia Hill 'system', therefore, was very expensive in staff resources. Not surprisingly, and quite apart from any other reasons, not many local authorities introduced this system into the management of their housing stock. The first local authority appointment of a woman housing manager took place as late as 1927, though by 1936 there were 75 women employed in such positions (CHAC, 1939). The encroachment of women into the world of public sector housing management was a very slow process even though Hill's ideas had been acknowledged for some while.

An alternative perspective on housing management to the generic approach advocated by the Women's Society came to be associated with the (male-dominated) Institute of Housing, founded in 1931 (Brion and Tinker, 1980; Power, 1987). In contrast to the Society of Women House Property Managers, the Institute of Housing promulgated a more extensive style of management. This stressed the importance of rent collection and property maintenance, while giving the social work function (which was seen as being best carried out by women visitors) a very minor role. The male-dominated Institute of Housing saw the task very much in property management terms, a conception not that different from private sector practice, and hoped to push the Women's Society into a peripheral and subordinate position. There were several reasons for this, not least the fact that many of the early housing managers seem to have had technical qualifications and were more concerned with issues to do with the physical stock rather than with the social fabric of the estates. Typically, they were men seeking a career in local government and were locked into the competitive and hierarchical structure of local authorities. Questions like the relative status of departments, the size of their budgets and their organisational structure may perhaps have assumed a greater importance than the welfare of individual tenants.

It was not only that the Women's Society saw the welfare aspect as vital to management while the Institute saw it as peripheral. A further significant difference was that whereas the Society advocated a generic approach the Institute was happy to see the fragmentation of the various management tasks. The latter perspective largely reflected the way in which local authorities often dealt with their newly acquired role as landlords. Although some councils did set up housing departments, others simply parcelled out the various tasks to existing departments, for example, rent collection to the Treasurer's Department, lettings to the Town Clerk's Department, and repairs to the Surveyor's or Engineer's Department (CHAC, 1939). Many of the Institute's members came from these other local government professions, hence their interest in a fragmented approach to housing management (Laffin, 1986).

Thus in the inter-war years the question of how to organise housing management was debated at length. The debate was addressed in the investigation into the management of municipal housing estates carried out by a sub-committee of the Ministry of Health's Central Housing Advisory Committee (CHAC, 1939), referred to earlier. Perhaps not surprisingly, they reached the conclusion 'that there can be no hard and fast rule, and we are unable to recommend for general adoption in its entirety any of the [two] systems which have been described to us' (CHAC, 1939, p. 28). Similarly, the LCC reviewed its management approach in 1939 and came to the conclusion that the Octavia Hill system offered no advantage over its current scheme, which fell somewhere between the two ('AHS', 1939). In the same year, Greenwood-Wilson (a member of the CHAC enquiry) elaborated an approach which had more in common with the Institute's view and probably most local authority practice, than with that advocated by the Society:

My criticism of the Octavia Hill system is that it attempts too much, or shall I say that for the municipal landlord it undertakes more than is necessary? The private landlord or the voluntary housing association may be almost obliged to combine in the one officer rent collection, maintenance, and social education. But I suggest that the municipal landlord does not need such an officer. He has his municipal treasurer or accountant for rent collection, his surveyor, architect, or building inspector for repairs and maintenance, his sanitary inspector for disinfestation and general cleanliness, and his health visitor for social education. There is no reason why the activities of any of these persons should not be coordinated successfully . . . (Greenwood-Wilson, 1939)

The Second World War interceded in this debate and in the early post-war years the great pressure to build new dwellings tended to overshadow questions of management, though there is little doubt that the more extensive approach to management which was advocated by the 1959 CHAC report became increasingly dominant. Moreover, by then the professionalisation debate had moved on. In its evidence to the 1959 CHAC investigation, the Institute of Housing indicated that there was now a general feeling that the issue was no longer simply one of what type of management should prevail. The Institute argued that two key principles had to be established. The first was the establishment of unified housing departments and the second was the creation of management systems whereby the 'tenant looks to one person . . . to deal with all matters affecting his municipal tenancy' (Anon., 1958).

This seems to have marked a significant shift of view by the Institute, in part taking it closer to the approach advocated by the Society of Women Estate Managers. Although the intensive, welfare-oriented style associated with the Octavia Hill 'system' was not taken on board (hardly surprising given the general needs orientation of council housing), the Institute now recommended the generic, rather than the fragmented, approach to carrying out the management functions. Significantly, in 1955 the two professional associations had set up a joint committee of the two bodies (and in 1965 they finally merged). Cullingworth suggests that this rapprochement between the two 'traditions' was a reflection of the rise in the general standard of living, the development of the social services as well as the extension of council housing already mentioned and an acceptance that the housing department 'should in no way duplicate these other services' (1966, p. 84). Significantly, in the light of community care, Cullingworth notes that welfare work is not easily distinguished from general management and it is precisely this issue which continues to run through debates about the division of labour between the various departments.

The establishment of the two 'key' principles of generic workers within a unified housing department which the Institute sought were closely bound together. They were necessary features for the establishment of housing management as a profession in its own right, separate from the related professions in local government. For the fragmented approach that was then so common implied that the various management tasks could continue to be performed as an adjunct to the work of other local government departments and, therefore, other professions. The argument for generic housing managers could be used, then, to justify the establishment of separate housing departments, which was itself a vital step towards the professionalisation of this activity. Instead of being an association of people from other professions who happened to work in housing, the Institute was becoming more akin to a collection of housing workers seeking recognition as a valid and separate profession in its own right.

Unification and centralisation

By the Second World War, although housing management had become firmly established as something that local government did, it was still largely a fragmented activity. According to Cullingworth (1966, p. 73) only about a fifth of local authorities had appointed a housing manager by 1939 and 'many of these worked in the department of another chief officer'. The fragmentation of housing management within local government was noted by the 1938 CHAC report, but the Committee found no evidence that existing arrangements were ineffective. The Scottish Housing Advisory Committee took a different line in its 1946 report on housing management. It noted that the overwhelming majority of Scottish local housing authorities operated the functional system, but went on to argue that the generic approach should be more widely adopted

(SHAC, 1946). The 1952 report of the Metropolitan Boroughs (Organisation and Methods) Committee (MBA, 1952) stressed the need for authorities to review the situation and decide what was best for them—a position mirrored in the 1959 CHAC report, *Councils and their Houses*.

The 1959 CHAC report argued that there were four main types of organisation of housing management within local government at that time. Of 57 councils and new towns responding to their questionnaire, 27 had a housing manager in charge of a separate department, 11 had a housing manager in charge of a section of a department under another chief officer, 8 had a housing manager but no separate department or section, and 11 had no housing manager at all (CHAC, 1959).

However, in his address to the 1959 Institute of Housing conference, the Minister of Housing and Local Government argued that:

A system whereby responsibility for day to day management is spread over perhaps as many as four officers—for instance, the clerk, the treasurer, the surveyor and a housing manager with very limited functions may have been suited to a small number of houses. But it does not suit housing management on the large scale as we know it today.

A turning point seemed to have been reached, because all subsequent reports on the organisation of the housing service have stressed the need to create unified housing departments.

In 1965 the Ministry of Housing and Local Government requested information on housing management from all local authorities in England in an attempt to see to what extent change had taken place since the 1959 CHAC report. The 1,135 replies which it received suggested that 'there had been some further move towards the development of the profession of housing management' but that 'while many qualified Housing Managers had extensive responsibilities, the organisation of housing management still varied greatly between local authorities' (MHLG, 1967, p. 73). The Ministry found that, since 1959, 118 authorities had appointed housing managers for the first time or had set up a separate housing department. Nevertheless, little more than half (632) of those responding to the survey employed a housing manager, of whom only two-thirds were in charge of their own department.

The progress towards unified housing departments gained further momentum and support from both the Seebohm report on *Local Authority and Allied Personal Social Services* (Seebohm, 1968) and from the Cullingworth report *Council Housing: Purposes, Procedures and Priorities* (Cullingworth, 1969). Both reports argued that the effective implementation of housing policy made the establishment of unified housing departments imperative. They also argued, however, that local authorities should be concerned not just with council housing management but should look to identifying, and facilitating the meeting of, housing need in the housing market as a whole. Cullingworth argued strongly for the establishment of the 'comprehensive housing service' embracing all aspects of both public and private sector management.

Consolidation of the various housing management functions into unified housing departments was also given a considerable boost by the local government reorganisations of 1965 in Greater London and of 1974 in the rest of England and Wales. This reorganisation was influenced by a desire to

increase efficiency and effectiveness in the delivery of services in local government and was linked with the introduction of corporate planning as well as
other management and budgetary techniques imported from the USA (see
Cockburn, 1977, for a critique). This was an era in which it was widely
believed that significant economies of scale could be achieved through the
creation of larger and more comprehensive units of service delivery.

Although each authority was left to decide how to deal with its housing
functions, most set up a housing committee as recommended by the Bains
Report (1972) though the question of departmental responsibility was left
unresolved. The reorganisations of 1965 in London and 1974 elsewhere in
England and Wales (1975 in Scotland) created the opportunity for housing
managers to achieve a consolidation of the various housing management
functions. A report by the Metropolitan Boroughs Association's Organisation
and Methods Committee (MBA, 1962, p. 62) argued, for example, that the
number of dwellings owned by a local authority was an important determinant
of the most suitable way of organising housing management:

Applying this test to housing in the metropolitan area it is clear that the new authorities
to be set up under the London Government Act 1963 will be more than justified in
combining many if not all their housing management functions in the hands of one
senior officer whose concern is exclusively housing.

As Cullingworth (1966) has pointed out, however, housing departments could
only be established if some functions were taken away from an existing
department or departments. So as well as considerations of what is the most
efficient organisation of the housing management functions, vested interests
were at stake; and the struggle between different professions in local government was inevitably an important influence on the rate at which housing
departments were established. Reorganisation was important because it created
the opportunity of starting afresh, of looking towards the most efficient
structure and of cutting through vested interests. As an Institute of Housing
Managers' report (1972, p. 1) pointed out, the 1974 reform of local government brought 'the opportunity of a century for the creation of the right
organisation for the housing service'. For the Institute, the aim to be achieved
by reorganisation was the creation of 'all-purpose departments under a
qualified housing director'. This, it claimed, would not only end confusion in
the minds of the public, but would also 'ensure that the housing service is fully
co-ordinated within the authority and not weakened by fragmentation' (ibid.,
p. 7).

The reorganisation of local government that took place greatly reduced the
number of local housing authorities (down from more than 1,333 in England
and Wales to only 308) and significantly increased their size. As Gittins (1974,
p. 5) pointed out;

From 1200 authorities owning fewer than 5000 dwellings the position will have
changed to 60 authorities owning fewer than that number; from 166 authorities
owning over 5000 dwellings it will have changed to 253 owning over that number.
Before reorganisation there were 540 authorities owning less than 1000 dwellings; after
reorganisation there will be none owning less than 1500.

The consolidation of housing functions that took place at this time also involved an increase in scale as local authorities were grouped together into larger units. Moreover, the mass housing boom (Dunleavy, 1981) of 1945–75 involved not only an increase in the total number of council houses but also an increase in the size of new schemes. This meant that housing estates almost certainly increased in size and this further helped to increase the scale of municipal landlordism.

Throughout the 1960s and 1970s local authorities moved further and further away from close, personalised contact with their tenants, partly in attempting to achieve economies of scale. Apart from their increased size as landlords, conslidation of housing functions often meant centralisation as well. Concern with systems, economy and efficiency led to the withdrawal of resident caretakers and the adoption of 'flying squads', as well as the gradual abandonment or withdrawal from door-to-door rent collection (Power, 1987) and the closure of estate offices. High-rise housing, in any case an impersonal built form, was an important element in this process as it was clearly harder to retain contact with households in a twenty-storey tower block than it was with tenants in a row of houses. Thus social and physical distance crept into the municipal landlord/tenant relationship, making housing management more extensive, more remote and increasingly depersonalised.

Emerging problems and trends

In the 1970s and 1980s the inadequacies of this large-scale, bureaucratic approach to housing management became very evident. In many difficult to let estates housing management had begun to break down with voids, arrears and uncompleted repairs increasing daily (DoE 1981). As the rate of new build continued to decline so the new emphasis on better management of existing stock became an overwhelming priority for many authorities. The size of many council housing departments and the scale of their stock, the lack of suitably trained staff, the erosion of capital and revenue budgets, the design and construction faults of much of the system-built housing, problems of dwellings that are both difficult to let and to live in, and the emergence of rundown estates combined with high unemployment and other social problems, have placed great stresses and strains on housing management, particularly in the inner city and on the suburban periphery. The Audit Commission (1986) has even talked about a 'crisis' in housing management. These problems are very real but have been diagnosed differently by the Government, the opposition and housing experts.

One reaction has been to reduce the scale of housing management. For example, many local authorities have decentralised in order to improve service delivery and get closer to the tenant. Some authorities, such as Glasgow and Islington, are going further and encouraging tenant management cooperatives (Clapham et al., 1987). The Department of the Environment has also become more directly involved in housing management than it has in the past. It set up the Priority Estates Project in 1979 which is an experiment in intensive, tenant-focused estate management (DoE, 1984). Anne Power, who leads the programme, in advocating localised participatory management, is acutely conscious of the historic connections stretching back to Octavia Hill (see Power, 1987). The DoE has also funded for the first time a major programme of housing management training and development, involving a variety of organisations, including universities and polytechnics. So the state is itself now engaged in promoting the professionalisation of housing mangement. This is no different from what has occurred in other spheres of work—it has just come a lot later.

An alternative reaction to the perceived crisis in council housing management has been to emphasise consumer sovereignty through the market-place by means of privatisation. This is at least one part of the remit of Estate Action (formerly the Urban Housing Renewal Unit) in the Department of the Environment. While the reaction of the left has been to re-emphasise community, on the right it has been to call in the market (Donnison, 1986). As discussed elsewhere in this book (Chapter 4), the Government has made it clear that it wishes to hive off as much local authority housing as possible, either to housing associations using private finance or to private landlords. In justifying this policy, great emphasis has been placed on inefficient, 'bureaucratic' local authority housing management (Kemp, 1989).

Initial impressions suggest that the 1988 Housing Act has done a great deal to stimulate local authorities' housing management function and that, in combination with the 1989 Local Government and Housing Act, it may produce important gains in efficiency and effectiveness. One aim of the legislation has been to introduce a businesslike ethic into both housing associations and local authority housing, thus raising important questions of how this can be balanced against their core function of housing those in need. This move towards a more market-orientated system of ownership, financing and management reflects the Government's deep-seated mistrust of local councils and a strongly held belief in the virtues of the market and of business methods. It constitutes part of its expressed desire to wean people off what it sees as a 'culture of dependency' on the state and to cultivate instead an 'enterprise culture'.

Yet the available evidence suggests relatively little desire among most council tenants to have their homes transferred to alternative landlords, and least of all to the private sector. Nor is there much evidence of a widespread 'crisis' in housing management (MacLennan et al., 1989), though this is not to deny that problems do exist. It is important to remember, as David Donnison has noted in relation to 'privatisation', that the word 'crisis' is highly symbolic, often 'intended by advocates and opponents . . . to dramatise a conflict and mobilise support for their own side' (Donnison, 1984, p. 45).

Nevertheless, the momentum towards the demunicipalisation of rented housing is increasing and it seems likely that the next decade will see considerable fragmentation in the ownership of social housing and changes in the nature and scale of housing management. This move towards a pluralist and more market-orientated system will inevitably have implications for the way in which housing management is carried out. The introduction of competition, the increasing reliance on private finance and the growing importance of private and quasi-private landlords seems likely to produce a new commercialism in housing management. This will involve renewed emphasis on maintaining the value of the property, a new concern for the rent-paying ability of tenants and stricter control over rent arrears and reducing void intervals between lettings. Yet, at the same time, the stimulus of competition between social housing landlords may possibly erode some of the worst elements of paternalism that have characterised local authority housing management and produce a more urgent concern for tenant satisfaction.

It is clear that housing management in Britain has reached a crucial stage in its development and significant changes are likely over the next decade. While a full return to the ethics of the market that characterised housing management in the private sector before 1914 is unlikely, neither is the bureaucratic organisational framework that has dominated public sector housing management to date going to remain fundamentally unchanged. If housing management has had a contested history up to the present, the struggle for its future nature and orientation is now under way.

Acknowledgements

Thanks are due to Tony Collinson and Peter Malpass for their comments on our interpretation of the history of housing management.

References

'AHS' (1939) 'London County Council representation on housing management', *Housing*, June, pp. 167–8.

Allerton, R (1950) 'Housing management', *Housing*, Jan./March, pp. 77–8.

Anon. (1958) 'The management of municipal estates', *Housing*, March, pp. 104–10.

Audit Commission (1986) *Managing the Crisis in Council Housing* London, HMSO.

Bains Committee (1972) *The new local authorities: management and structures* HMSO, London.

Ball, M (1981) 'The development of capitalism in housing provision' *International Journal of Urban and Regional Research*, 5, pp. 147–77.

Barnes, M (1934) *The Slum: Its Story and Solution*

Bowley, M (1945) *Housing and the State 1919–1944* London, Allen and Unwin.

Brion, M and Tinker, A (1980) *Women in Housing* London, Housing Centre Trust.

Byrne, D S (1974) *Problem families: a housing lumpen-proletariat*, University of Durham Department of Sociology and Social Administration working paper 5, Durham.

CHAC (Central Housing Advisory Committee) (1939) *Management of Municipal Housing Estates*, London, HMSO.

CHAC (1959) *Councils and their Houses* London, HMSO.

CIPFA (1989) *Housing Revenue Account Statistics. 1987–88. Actuals* London, Chartered Institute of Public Finance and Accountancy.

Clapham, D (1987) 'Trends in housing management', in D Clapham and J English (eds) *Public Housing: Current Trends and Future Developments* London, Croom Helm, pp. 107–25.

Clapham, D, Kemp, P A and Kintrea, K (1987) 'Co-operative ownership of former council housing', *Policy and Politics* 15(4), pp. 207–20.

Cockburn, C (1977) *The Local State* London, Pluto Press.

Cullingworth, J B (1966) *Housing and Local Government* London, Allen and Unwin.

Cullingworth, J B (1969) *Council Housing: Purposes, Procedures and Priorities* London, HMSO.

Daunton, M J (1983) *House and Home in the Victorian City* London, Arnold.

Daunton, M J (ed) (1984) *Councillors and Tenants: Local Authority Housing in English Cities. 1919–1939* Leicester, Leicester University Press.

DoE (Department of the Environment) (1981) *An investigation into difficult to let housing*, 3 Vols, HMSO, London.

DoE (Department of the Environment (1984) *Local Housing Management* London, Department of the Environment.

Department of the Environment (1987) *Housing: The Government's Proposals* London, HMSO.

Dickens, P and Gilbert, P (1981) 'Inter-war housing policy: a study of Brighton, *Southern History* 3, pp. 201–31.

Donnison, D (1984) 'The progressive potential of privatisation', in J Le Grand and R Robinson (eds) *Privatisation and the Welfare State* London, Allen and Unwin, pp. 45–57.

Donnison, D (1986) 'The community-based approach', paper presented at the City Renewal Through Partnership conference, Glasgow, 6–10 July.

Dresser, M (1984) 'Housing policy in Bristol 1919–30' in M J Daunton (ed) *Councillors and Tenants* Leicester University Press, Leicester, pp. 155–216.

Dunleavy, P (1981) *The Politics of Mass Housing in Britain* Oxford, Clarendon Press.

Dyos, H J and Reeder, D A (eds) (1973) 'Slums and suburbs', in H J Dyos and M Wolff, *The Victorian City* London, Routledge and Kegan Paul, pp. 359–86.

Englander, D (1983) *Landlord and Tenant in Urban Britain 1838–1918*, Oxford, Clarendon Press.

Gibbon, I G and Bell, R W (1939) *History of the London County Council 1889–1939*, London, Macmillan.

Gittins, A C (1974) *Local Authorities and Housing* Chichester and London, Barry Rose, for the Local Government Review.

Greenwood Wilson, J (1939) 'Problems of estate management', *Housing*, October, pp. 7–11.

Griffin, H (1893–4) 'Weekly property as an investment', *Transactions of the Surveyors' Institute* 26, pp. 331–76.

Hill, O (1875) *Homes of the London Poor* London, Macmillan.

Howarth, E G and Wilson M (1907) *West Ham: A Study in Social and Industrial Problems* London, J. M. Dent.

Institute of Housing Managers (1972) *The Comprehensive Housing Service — Organisation and Functions* London, Institute of Housing Managers.

Jeffrey, M and Neville, E (eds) (1921) *Housing Property and its Management* London, Allen and Unwin.

Kemp, P A (1982) *Housing Property as Capital: Private Rental Housing in the Late Victorian City* (Urban & Regional Studies Working Paper 28), Brighton, University of Sussex.

Kemp, P A (1986) *The House Market in Late Victorian Britain* (Centre for Housing Research Discussion Paper 11), Glasgow, University of Glasgow.

Kemp, P A (1987) 'Some aspects of housing consumption in late nineteenth century England and Wales', *Housing Studies* 2, pp. 3–16.

Kemp, P A (1989) 'The demunicipalisation of rented housing', in M Brenton and C Ungerson (eds) *Social Policy Review 1988–9* London, Longman, pp. 46–66.

Laffin, M (1985) *Professionalism and Policy*, Aldershot, Avebury.

MacLennan, D, Clapham, D, Goodlad, R, Kemp, P A, Malcolm, J, Satsangi, M,

Whitefield, L (1989) *The Nature and Effectiveness of Housing Management in England* London, HMSO.

Malpass, P (1984) 'Octavia Hill, 1838–1912', in R Barker (ed) *Founders of the Welfare State*, Routledge, London, pp. 31–6.

MBA (1952) *Housing Management* London, Metropolitan Boroughs Association.

MBA (1962) *General Review of Housing Management* London, Metropolitan Boroughs Association.

Merrett, S (1979) *State Housing in Britain* London, Routledge and Kegan Paul.

Ministry of Health (1920) *Housing* London, HMSO.

Ministry of Health (1930) *Eleventh Annual Report of the Ministry of Health, 1929–30* London, HMSO.

MHLG (1967) *Report of the ministry of housing and local government for 1965 and 1966*, London, HMSO.

Nevitt, A A (1970) 'The nature of rent-controlling legislation in the UK', *Environment and Planning A* 2, pp. 127–36.

Power, A (1987) *Property Before People: The Management of Twentieth-Century Council Housing* London, Allen and Unwin.

Ryder, R (1984) 'Council house building in County Durham, 1900–1939', in M J Daunton (ed) *Councillors and Tenants: Local Authority Housing in English Cities, 1919–1939* Leicester, Leicester University Press, pp. 39–100.

SHAC (Scottish Housing Advisory Committee) (1946) *Housing Management in Scotland* Edinburgh, HMSO.

Seebohm Committee (1968) *Report of the Committee on local authority and allied personal social services*, London, HMSO.

Smith, M (1977) *Guide to Housing* London, Housing Centre Trust.

The Times (1938) 'British Homes; The Building Society Movement', reprinted from *The Times* 31 May 1938, London.

Urlin, R D (1902) *A Handbook of Investment in Houses and Lands* London, Wilson.

Webb, B (1982) *The Diary of Beatrice Webb, Volume One, 1973–1892* London, Virago.

Wohl, A S (1977) *The Eternal Slum* London, Arnold.

10 Housing associations: 1890–1990

Richard Best

This chapter traces the development of housing associations over the last century and seeks to answer two conflicting questions:

— *Why have housing associations achieved so little over the last century?* They own barely 3 per cent of the nation's stock. Their counterparts in many European countries provide ten times this proportion;

— *Why are housing associations expected to achieve so much?* While the private landlord and the public landlord are both in dramatic decline, housing associations have become the principal developers of social housing. It is housing associations that are expected to provide the accommodation for those needing 'care in the community', to renovate Victorian streets in inner-city areas, to build for shared ownership sale to young families in rural areas, and much else besides. And the present government hopes they will take over the ownership of much of the existing property held by local authorities.

Definition

In this chapter 'housing association' is taken to mean any not-for-profit housing provider which is controlled by a voluntary committee and is constitutionally independent of government. The title, therefore, embraces charitable housing trusts (including almshouse trusts) and 'public utility' housing societies (including housing cooperatives). From the Housing Act of 1936, the generic term has been 'a housing association' (Section 30).

1890–1920: Housing associations as the pioneers

Long before the municipalities ever thought of providing accommodation, charitable housing associations were at work. The oldest member of the National Federation of Housing Associations was founded in 1235: this is the St Lawrence housing association formed (by Edith Bissett) to house 'two female lepers', which started a tradition of accommodation for people usually rejected by society which can be traced right through to the 1980s and the creation of 'special needs' associations, not least for those people with AIDS/HIV+.

A hundred years ago many of the pioneering estates of the Peabody Trust were twenty years old and Octavia Hill had created a model for 'housing management'. Between 1890 and the First World War, several philanthropists endowed new housing associations including the Guinness Trust founded in 1890, Samuel Lewis Housing Trust and the Sutton Dwellings Trust in the 1900s—and the great Quaker pioneers Cadbury and Rowntree started building the villages of Bournville in Birmingham and New Earswick on the edge of York.

After such a lengthy and successful build-up, why was it that local authorities, not housing associations, thereafter became the principal providers of low-cost homes?

Perhaps the first reason is that the housing associations themselves did not see their role in terms of mass provision.

Throughout the nineteenth century, when most homes were supplied by private landlords, the associations saw themselves as pioneers demonstrating how responsible landlords, and discerning investors, could meet the needs of those on modest incomes. So when the Society for Improving the Condition of the Labouring Classes was founded in 1830 it saw its role as demonstrating that good-quality homes could be achieved by private enterprise. As the Earl of Carlisle said at the time:

Let it be proved that the act of doing good . . . would pay its way and ensure its fair profit, and it would follow that the benevolence, instead of being an ethereal influence in the breasts of a few—fitful and confined in its operations—would become a settled, sober habit of the many. (Jones, 1985, p. 7)

With Queen Victoria as Patron, Prince Albert as a central participant, and with strong support from Lord Shaftesbury, this organisation wanted to prove a point.

The Metropolitan Association for Improving the Dwellings of the Industrial Classes, established in 1841, had specifically intended to show that a 5 per cent return was possible from good housing for the 'labouring man'. These organisations and several others which copied their example were intent on producing schemes, such as Prince Albert's cottages built for the Great Exhibition of 1851, which could be replicated in their design, management and financing by the private sector on a wide scale.

However, even away from the high costs of central London where most of these developments took place, the standards which were acceptable to reformers placed the accommodation well beyond the means of those most in need. Either the accommodation did not produce sufficient return to attract profit-making landlords to follow the pattern, or the rents that achieved acceptable returns were too much for poorer households.

An illustration of this is the Alexander Cottages development on the Prince of Wales's Sandringham estate, built in the 1880s at £195 each. Working on the assumption that the average labourer should not be expected to devote more than one-seventh of his earnings to rent, this produced a return of only

1.5 per cent on capital—too low for ordinary landlords to accept (Burnett, 1986, p. 136). Similarly, the Medical Officer of Health for Exeter reported in 1885 that the Industrial Dwellings House Company, which had been founded with philanthropic motives, had never paid dividends of more than 2 or 2.25 per cent and its shares were at a 50 per cent discount (Holmans, 1987, p. 31). It is clear that without public subsidy, these not-for-profit organisations could not produce affordable rents.

In the years that followed, although incomes rose in real terms, so did the cost of land and of capital; when combined with expectations of rising standards, the cost of unsubsidised housing has doggedly remained beyond the reach of those with low incomes. So the Royal Commission on Housing in Scotland concluded in 1917 that: 'private builders had for a long time prior to the war failed to provide in anything like adequate numbers the houses necessary for the working class population . . . the fundamental [reason was] that an economic rent could not be got' (para. 1964). They concluded that since this section of the community could not improve their earnings, no private owner would ever let to them. 'Who is to house them?' says the Commission. 'It can only be the local authority' (para. 2022).

The early housing charities and non-profit bodies may have demonstrated what needed to be done. But they could not show that their models worked for the profit-making landlord.

Seebohm Rowntree's 1901 study in York showed that although rent took an average of just under 15 per cent of income, the poorest housholds in York spent the largest proportion—about 29 per cent compared with only 9 per cent for the wealthiest working-class families. Rowntree estimated that only the most well-off working people could afford to house themselves adequately. His father, Joseph Rowntree, acquired land and established a charity in 1904 to create a new community. His village was to house a range of people, not all of whom would be on low incomes. Joseph Rowntree was much influenced by his fellow Quaker, Ebenezer Howard, who had published *Tomorrow: Peaceful Path to Reform* in 1898, advocating the creation of garden cities. Through the inspiration of his architect/planner, Raymond Unwin (a Fabian), the homes were carefully planned and attractively designed; they were set in a 'green' environment but with easy access to local employment. The village incorporated a model school (with many original design features), shops and other amenities. The whole was to be a 'self-governing community' with an elected Village Council.

As with its planning and architectural features, Joseph Rowntree hoped that the financial arrangements could be replicated by others elsewhere. He envisaged a return on investment in the properties of around 3–4 per cent. Like the other pioneers of the time, the Rowntrees were not seeking to replace the private sector but to reform it.

1914–19: The critical moment

In 1914 the Liberal Land Inquiry Committee for England asked who should build the homes of the future. Lloyd George was more familiar with developments like the Cardiff Workers Co-operative Garden Village Society than with municipal housing. The Committee placed its emphasis on voluntary and cooperative enterprise, exemplified by the 'public utility societies':

These bodies might be less resourceful than an individual speculator, and offer less financial security than a municipality backed by the rates, but they did promise enough of both in order 'to constitute a most happily-blended instrument for a meeting so great a national need as for housing of the workers'. (Daunton, 1987, p. 50)

The Liberal version saw the state as enabling citizens to stand on their own feet, without dependency on the public sector to house them. But the impact of the First World War was to change this perception. The scale of the problem mounted and as the war progressed, government involvement moved on from its original public health role to intervention in controlling private rents from 1915.

Seebohm Rowntree was close to the centre of policy making during the First World War. As part of Lloyd George's Reconstruction Committee in 1917, he devoted himself to a study of post-war housing needs. He estimated that housing shortages would mean a requirement for 300,000 new houses in England and Wales during the first 12 months after the war (not 120,000 as the Local Government Board had estimated). In preparing for this enormous house-building programme, he felt that state intervention was essential. But he turned his back on grants going exclusively or mainly to voluntary bodies:

He accepted the case for large-scale building either by the State or the local authorities, and favoured the latter on the grounds that it would be more desirable for local authorities to own and to let the new houses than for the State to do so. (Briggs, 1961, p. 138)

Nevertheless he felt that capital grants to local authorities should be seen as a temporary measure. He hoped that, five years after the end of the war, assistance to local authorities could be confined to loans: 'Like most members of the Reconstruction Committee, he was a Liberal and not a Socialist, and he stated explicitly that normal economic patterns should be disturbed as little as possible' (ibid., pp. 138–9).

1919–39: Local authorities take over

Anxious about the possible consequences of the return of troops facing acute housing shortages—and in need of productive employment—and with the Bolshevik revolution afoot elsewhere in Europe, Lloyd George's Government was prepared to act.

Threatened with industrial dislocation and social unrest, both Cabinet and Parliament accepted the housing programme of 1919 as the necessary price of social stability, the unavoidable premium of the 'insurance against revolution'. (Swenarton, 1981, p. 111)

Local authorities by definition existed throughout the country: unlike housing associations they were a resource available in this emergency in all areas. Almost all had some building knowledge; and all were non-profit and unlikely to abuse public funds entrusted to them.

The Housing Act of 1919 (the 'Addison Act') followed and the municipal authorities got into their stride. While the promises of Lloyd George were only partly fulfilled, some 'Homes for Heroes' were built, slum clearance and estate building on an extensive scale did begin; and these became the accepted tasks for the local authority.

Once the momentum of the post-war effort was lost, government might have turned to other providers. But the local authority road had now been taken. And Neville Chamberlain, as the minister responsible for housing for most of the 1920s, was a true believer in local government, having seen its success as a councillor—and as Lord Mayor—in Birmingham.

Nevertheless, some new trends were started by the housing associations of the 1920s and early 1930s: by raising loan stock at low rates of interest the St Pancras Housing Association in Camden tackled inner-city areas of appalling slums. Similar associations, often inspired directly by Father Basil Jellicoe, the key figure behind St Pancras, followed suit. Many of the housing associations of the 1920s and 1930s followed a pattern set earlier by Octavia Hill. She had used the money and influence of her middle-class circle to buy houses to let at modest rents. She maintained a personal relationship with the properties and the residents which, while giving them the benefit of her determination and commitment, made it unlikely that her work would expand on a major scale. Her influence was in establishing a firm but caring approach to housing management, based on training for women housing managers, (most of whom worked for large-scale private landlords, such as the Ecclesiastical Commissioners); but in terms of quantity her housing achievements were modest. So too was the work of those who followed: the Kensington Housing Trust in 1922; the St Marylebone Housing Association in 1926, set up by Mrs Cicely Davies and six friends who contributed loan stock and raised charitable money; Liverpool Improved Houses, founded in 1928 by Dorothy Keeling and the local MP, Eleanor Rathbone; these, closely following the housing management practices of Octavia Hill, acquired and rehabilitated Victorian properties in the inner-city areas.

At the same time, several of the older housing trusts continued to expand using the same subsidies as local authorities. By the late 1930s, for example, the Sutton Dwellings Trust had produced 6,000 homes up and down the country.

When the National Federation of Housing Societies was formed in 1935 there were estimated to be 224 potential members, and 170 joined up. It was not envisaged that these organisations would represent an alternative in numerical terms to local authorities as the chief source of social housing. But, as in its earlier forms, the sector could change attitudes and influence policy and practice. The relevant Minister, Sir Kingsley Wood, said in 1936:

What I have already seen gives me confidence that the work of housing societies will be of vital importance. . . . I believe the value of this contribution will not be limited by the number of houses they build. I have in mind the importance of their work in the field of education and propaganda on housing in general (Jones, 1985, p. 19)

The housing association movement was certainly an energetic lobby. And it introduced many in the middle classes to the problems of homelessness and bad housing.

In these inter-war years one quite different model for social housing was successfully tested. In 1935 the government set up the North Eastern Housing Association to build in the depressed areas of Durham and Tyneside where industrial decline and unemployment were acute. This supplemented the local authorities—whose own resources were meagre because of the low rateable values—and the association went on to build 20,000 homes. The organisation became a constitutionally 'normal' housing association—North Housing Association—in 1980. By then it demonstrated quite clearly that, in the good times and the bad times, an agency independent of local government could be a safe recipient of very substantial public funds.

In those inter-war years, it is estimated that housing associations built about 24,000 homes; these were added to the 50,000 homes created before the First World War (Holmans, 1987, p. 206). Meanwhile, from 1919 to 1939, 1.112 million houses were constructed by local authorities out of a total of 3.998 million. Associations had come through this period having done some important new work but with only a modest quantum of extra homes to show for their efforts.

Perhaps as a consolation prize, housing associations at the time could draw satisfaction from their influence overseas. Ebenezer Howard was the first Chairman of the International Federation of Housing and Planning formed at the end of the First World War and based in Holland. Model dwellings along the lines of those created in Britain appeared in many European cities and there the concept of social housing became expressed principally in provision by housing associations. In Scandinavia, inspired by both the housing cooperatives in the UK and the Garden City movement, housing associations made considerable strides in the 1920s.

As so frequently happens in political or social philosophy, the propagated ideas flourish more readily outside the country of their genesis. Housing co-operatives and related forms of association for building, owning or managing housing, have developed far more strongly and extensively in Denmark, Norway and Sweden (and in several other countries of Western Europe) than in Britain. (Greve, 1971, p. 83)

Was it that the lesser impact of the First World War had not propelled the Scandinavian countries into more drastic state intervention? Was it that the political scene there was less divided? Or was it, particularly in the aftermath of war in Germany itself, that citizens had to help themselves because the state could not do so?

In the mid-1930s Seebohm Rowntree had a chance to think again about the provision of 'social housing' free from the overtones of crisis which had influenced policies on post-war reconstruction. The National Housing Committee of which Rowntree was a prominent member reported in 1934:

Though the local authorities must play an essential part in putting through the housing programme we have suggested, an alternative method of procedure is both useful and desirable. We have therefore proposed that, where the local authorities desire it or where circumstances indicate that it is necessary, public utility societies should be organised and encouraged and financed by a statutory central body.

The report indicates that these bodies can take different forms

ranging from the completely voluntary and independent Society to one which may be
promoted and supported by a local authority as a convenient agency to carry out on its
behalf any section of housing work, including the management of houses already
owned by it. As the scale of local housing activities increases, this form of organisation
may prove of great value in taking the work out of the sphere of local politics,
maintaining continuity of progress and saving the members of the Council from
embarrassing concern in the details of tenancy relations with large numbers of their
constituents. (Amulree et al., 1934, pp. 34–5)

But these far-sighted proposals—in effect for the creation of a Housing
Corporation and an expansion of the housing association movement—were
overtaken by the dictates of another world war.

1940–70: Housing associations 'filling the gaps'

In September 1945, the Federation did not receive a rapturous reception from
the new government. Its vice-president told a council meeting that they 'had
always been sure of a welcome at the Ministry of Health, but now there was a
note of hesitation' (Jones, 1985, p. 21). Aneurin Bevan, in charge of housing,
said:

I am prepared to approve arrangements made by a local authority with a housing
association under the Housing Act 1936, where I am satisfied that the houses which the
association propose will be of the kind most needed, and will effectively supplement the
local authority's own programme. But I am not prepared to encourage local authorities
to farm out their housing responsibilities.

Not all Labour politicians felt the same way. The Labour MP for Norwood,
Ronald Chamberlain, had been Secretary to the Federation from 1936 to 1940
and he argued passionately for a new role for housing associations, not least in
the new towns. But in the heady days of Harold Macmillan's term as Housing
Minister in the 1950s—when over 225,000 council houses appeared in a
single year—housing associations operated on the outer edge. The role for
associations was now in 'filling the gaps' left behind after the public sector had
done its work.

The largest of these gaps took the form of specialist housing for particular
categories of need, principally elderly people. Under the National Assistance
Act 1948, local authorities were given a duty to make provision of care for the
elderly; and associations such as Servite Houses, and Church Army Housing
with its 'Churchill Homes', began building schemes specifically for elderly
people. The Abbeyfield Society, providing shared accommodation usually in
existing properties, came into being; and, in order to hold together the 1,700
local almshouse charities (mostly for elderly people) the National Association
of Almshouses was created in 1950.

In the 1950s, one new approach was the 'self-build' housing association. In
1952 Harold Macmillan wrote to the Federation: 'I am especially pleased that
your Federation is helping self-build groups, and I want to encourage people
who are enterprising enough to build their own homes' (Jones, 1985, p. 32).
Perhaps there is one clue here to the relative unimportance of housing
associations in the UK: the building society movement, which began with

people clubbing together to build the homes they needed, led to owner occupation, not homes for rent. Similarly the self-build housing associations dissolved when the properties were transferred into individual home ownership. When the building societies stopped building and became permanent bodies, their mutual role was to raise and invest the finance in home ownership. This contrasted with the self-help movement in continental Europe. There those who worked together more often provided their homes in rented housing. Was the difference just that the British preferred to be owner-occupiers? Or was it that in this country we have preferred to live in separate houses which can be easily managed by their occupiers, rather than in blocks of flats which require communal management and lead more readily to a rented tenure?

By the mid-1950s, under Duncan Sandys as the Housing Minister, the Housing Act 1957 provided the legislative framework for loans and subsidies to be passed to housing associations.

One gap that local authorities could not fill was for 'key workers' needed to meet the demands of new, expanding industries. Westfield Housing Association in Cumbria was set up for steel workers; British Airways Staff Housing Society—which copied the pre-war Great Western Railway Housing Association with a self-governing ingredient—appeared near Heathrow, with a similar association to follow outside Gatwick. The break-up of these associations occurred much later, in the 1980s when the tenants obtained the statutory 'right to buy'.

Another gap to be filled in the post-war period was of newcomers to the UK (not least in helping some of the 20,000 Hungarians who sought refuge in 1957). Most significantly, there was the arrival of immigrant workers from the Commonwealth countries. Local authorities had local needs to meet and frequently required lengthy residency qualifications. The new black community was left to take its chances in the slum properties of Notting Hill, Nottingham, and elsewhere. A number of new associations were created at this time specifically to help: Birmingham Friendship Housing Association (which included refugees from Egypt following the Suez Crisis in its early days), Nottingham Coloured People's Housing Society, and what is now the Metropolitan Housing Trust. The Federation's Secretary, Meg Merrylees wrote in *The Times Weekly Review* in December 1958:

we can and must all do something, and the burden that falls upon our particular shoulders is that of helping to ease the housing situation. The answer, 'but our hands are full with our own housing problems' is not acceptable. The housing of the immigrants is our problem, because anti-racialism is a germ that festering inward, ultimately kills the social system that harbours it.

In meeting 'minority needs', a number of associations concentrated on the needs of people with physical disabilities. The Federation itself founded the St Giles Housing Society by way of demonstration: larger houses were converted into flats with the ground floors being adapted for disabled people. Purpose-built homes followed. Long-standing charities like the John Groom's Association for the Disabled (founded in 1866) gained new impetus.

In 1960 the Federation had 638 members and had provided 45,000 homes since the war (Jones, 1985, p. 41).

During the 1960s, sheltered housing became a major part of housing association work. Most successful was the Hanover Housing Association created in 1963. Using the loans and grants that came through local authorities, the Association demonstrated that a large-scale operation was possible: by combining the values and committee control of the volunteer with the acumen and skills of professional management, a substantial impact could be made. It produced 2,000 homes in the 1960s. The contrast with the majority of associations was clear:

for the most part these housing associations are locally based and are organised and managed on an entirely voluntary basis. These characteristics tend to create a built-in limitation to the size of the building programme which can be undertaken by any association. (Stack, 1967, p. 2)

It was the commitment by a charity (the National Corporation for the Care of Old People) to finance the development and promotional overheads in advance of any schemes being built which placed Hanover in this position.

A quite different strand was cost rent housing, intended for those who could be expected to pay an unsubsidised rent. Under the Housing Act 1961, the National Federation sponsored the formation of new associations through an initiative by Sir Keith Joseph. With extra staff seconded from the Housing Ministry, the Federation passed on loans (at the then going rate of 6.75 per cent) mostly to new associations set up for the purpose. But this soon went the way of all other attempts to produce affordable homes without subsidy. The Department of the Environment's central Housing Advisory Committee said in 1971 (in the report of Sir Carl Cohen's Housing Associations sub-committee):

Cost renting has come to a dead halt. The high promise of 1964–66 has resulted in less than 1,600 houses. . . . Without either a subsidy, which destroys the whole point of cost-renting, or a substantial fall in interest rates, which cannot confidently be predicted, there seems no prospect of a change in this situation. (Para 3.42)

The answer lay in 'co-ownership' schemes with subsidy provided through tax relief. The Housing Act 1964 brought the Housing Corporation into being and £100 million was allocated to it for loans, alongside building society mortgages, for co-ownership.

Over the next decade, 1,000 societies were formed producing nearly 40,000 co-ownership homes in England, Wales and Scotland. But in filling the gap between traditional renting—subsidised in the public sector and controlled in the private sector—and full owner occupation, co-ownership was also a short-lived exercise. Production petered out as the cost of capital, and the price of land, rose in the early 1970s to the point where resulting charges were unattractively high: for similar outgoings, with the same level of tax relief, potential occupiers could be buying their own homes and benefiting from the whole of the increase in their value. And when the opportunity came along to acquire their homes on the basis of the outstanding mortgage commitment, co-owners in the 1980s moved swiftly to become ordinary owner-occupiers. Today the 'co-ownership' is virtually non-existent.

The other major interest of the 1960s, for the voluntary housing sector, was the growth of the 'inner-city' housing association, the charities rescuing families and properties from unacceptable landlords of the Rachman variety.

Even if these associations could not muster sufficient resources to modernise the properties to high standards, they could give the occupiers security.

In 1966, five national organisations came together to form SHELTER, the National Campaign for the Homeless. Chaired by the Reverend Bruce Kenrick of the Notting Hill Housing Trust (formed in 1963), SHELTER was created to channel charitable finance into housing associations: these bodies received 85 per cent of the new charity's net gift income. Under dynamic leadership and greatly helped by the drama documentary *Cathy Come Home*, SHELTER raised over £1 million in just 2 years (1967–8). These funds had an immediate and disproportionate impact on housing association activity. The SHELTER grants—as with the charitable grants to Hanover, and also to the Anchor Housing Association (then Help the Aged Housing Association) in the world of sheltered housing—financed the staffing costs which made possible an ambitious development programme.

Public funds specifically for property improvement were given a boost with the Housing Subsidies Act of 1967: this contained provision (Section 12) for grant-aid not just for modernisation but to offset the costs of acquiring property. The clause that achieved this was inserted in the Bill by Anthony Greenwood following representations directly from John Coward of Notting Hill and Father Eamon Casey of the Catholic Housing Aid Society. The Labour Government saw this as the major gap for associations to fill. The municipal authorities, now used to large-scale demolition and estate building, seemed an unwieldy instrument for the labour-intensive task of taking over tenanted properties and sorting out the needs of the (often elderly) occupiers. It is interesting to note that subsidies for property acquisition were not made available in this Act to the local authorities. Indeed, except for a burst of 'municipalisation' in the mid-1970s (mostly in inner London) purchase and rehabilitation has never been a significant part of local authority work. But over the twenty years following the 1967 Act, about half of all housing association investment was devoted to this activity.

So while it was left to local authorities to undertake the mainstream provision of social housing for those households—who were mostly families—needing new low-cost rented homes, housing associations picked up on the more small-scale and seemingly less important tasks.

1970–80: Dramatic growth

When municipal housing came to the fore, it was London that had showed the way at the turn of the century. In 1970 the Greater London Council again started what was to become a major trend. The GLC set aside £125 million over five years for housing association work, principally for the purchase and modernisation of older property. Housing associations were now to be trusted with some real money. When the Housing Finance Act of 1972 introduced 'fair rents' for associations—fixed by the local rent officer—the GLC pledged support from the rates to meet the difference between the rents received and the rents needed to recover costs. This meant security at last. Nor was the trend confined to the GLC: it was not only the Conservative boroughs, like

Westminster and Kensington and Chelsea, but Labour authorities such as Haringey and Newham who followed suit; in Birmingham, Nottingham and especially in Liverpool (under the Liberal administration), local authorities formed strong partnerships with housing associations.

Why this apparent change of heart? And how deep did this support run? By taking on specialist tasks over the preceding twenty-five years, housing associations had carved out some important niches in housing provision. Gradually these activities moved from the wings to a central position. Demographic, social and economic changes had emphasised the value of the particular operations pursued by associations:

— The ageing population and the fragmentation of larger households into smaller units had highlighted the importance of projects for elderly people and young people; these were needs which associations had specialised in meeting.
— The value of preserving communities, and conserving properties, was increasingly emphasised as a better alternative for many areas than wholesale clearance and replacement with council estates. System-building techniques and industrialised methods had turned public sympathy away from the tower blocks, immense estates on the periphery of towns, the concrete walkways and the sometimes brutal design; the painstaking and piecemeal renovation practised by housing associations gained popularity accordingly.
— In terms of housing management, the scale on which local authorities now operated inevitably brought with it large and sometimes distant bureaucracy. A 'small is beautiful' philosophy combined with an interest in community involvement and 'power to the people', which seemed more achievable through the more intimate structures of a localised housing association.

So by 1970 the specialisms of housing associations had increasingly become central to housing provision. Their reputation was untarnished by the failed architecture and planning of ugly estates. No doubt if housing associations had been the chosen option for social housing on the grand scale, then they would have become tainted by the same problems of defective developments. Perhaps it is more by good luck than sensitive judgement that associations escaped unscathed from the era of unsuccessful mass construction.

The depth of the support for housing associations was to be tested during the 1970s. Associations were vulnerable to criticism not just on the basis of their lack of direct accountability within the democratic process, but on the grounds that some of those benefiting from their work were professionals— architects, solicitors, estate agents—who sat on committees of management and awarded contracts to themselves. These organisations were mostly the non-charitable enterprises which had been created to produce cost rent housing and, later, to sponsor co-ownership societies. While some of these professional people undoubtedly acted altruistically, others did not. The London Housing Associations Committee, formed in 1970, took the first steps to weed out this element from the 'voluntary' sector. The issue remained an irritant, despite representations from the Federation to central government right through the 1970s, and despite the creation of a code of conduct for Federation members in 1977, until government outlawed the practice in the Housing Act of 1980.

In other respects, housing associations claimed cross-party support for their work. Labour local authorities were sometimes antagonistic to a collection of organisations which—despite nomination arrangements that dated back to the 1920s and secured homes for those on council waiting lists—were independent of local government.

The real test came when the Conservative Government under Edward Heath fell in 1974 to Harold Wilson's Labour Administration. The previous Secretary of State for the Environment, Geoffrey Rippon, had just introduced the Housing and Planning Bill, which was intended to concentrate public resources on specified housing action areas and was to provide a new charter for housing associations. In 1973, the Housing Minister Paul Channon had told the Federation's annual conference:

the time for piecemeal proposals is past: we shall bring forward measures to take our worst areas of stress by the scruff of the neck and improve them. We shall be particularly concerned to preserve a stock of good, well-maintained, rented accommodation which our poorer families can afford. And this is where we shall ask you—the housing associations—to take on a spearhead role. (Jones, 1985, p. 58)

The Housing Corporation had already widened its scope in 1972, moving onward from co-ownership projects to supporting schemes let at fair rents. Lord Goodman, known to be acceptable across political frontiers, was appointed in 1973 to chair the Housing Corporation, alongside its new Chief Executive, Dick Madge from the DoE.

In an unusual political move, Anthony Crosland as Secretary of State for the Environment picked up the Conservative Party's Housing Bill and pressed it through the new Parliament. Not only did the resulting Housing Act 1974 provide associations with a generous system of capital grants and revenue deficit grants, it was backed by government investment on an unprecedented scale.

Along with the legislation and the money, came the new 'policing' role for the Housing Corporation as the body which registered, monitored and could ultimately control each housing association in receipt of public funds. An important linkage had been created between the state and the voluntary sector.

In 1970, housing associations—with 700 years of history behind them—owned about 170,000 homes (Cohen Committee evidence, 1971). In the next twenty years their stock was to rise to over 600,000 homes (including 50,000 in hostels and shared housing). The peak years for development were in the late 1970s when the impact of the 1974 Act worked its way through the system and over 40,000 homes were being produced each year. Even the impact of the 1976 'IMF Budget' which led to substantial public expenditure cuts in all spheres, failed to halt this progress. The many strands of the housing association movement all joined in to achieve this growth: the old Victorian and Edwardian trusts; the inner-city associations, from the 1920s to those supported by SHELTER in the late 1960s; the specialist providers for elderly people and for a range of other groups.

Why had housing associations fared so well under Labour, the party identified with municipal housing?

Practical government ministers and civil servants had seen that housing associations could deliver the goods in fields where councils had not proved so agile. Politically, many 'grass-roots activists' — not least linked to SHELTER's campaign — were both energetic Labour Party and housing association supporters. Anthony Crosland, with his Fabian background, held a broad, pluralistic view of subsidised housing which allowed for diversity, variety and indeed flexibility.

Another component in Labour Party thinking throughout the period 1974–9 was exemplified by the Housing Minister, Reg Freeson. He came from the Co-operative Party as did a number of key people such as Harold Campbell, earlier Deputy Chairman of the Housing Corporation and in 1975 the Chairman of the Housing Associations Registration Council which guided the Corporation's policy on registering and supervising housing associations; David Page who, as Chair of the Housing Committee at Haringey promoted a housing association programme in the borough of over 500 homes per annum in the early 1970s; and Richard Balfe who maintained support to associations when the GLC became Labour controlled and he was elected Chair of the Housing Committee. Although housing cooperatives themselves remained a relatively insignificant proportion of the total housing association programme, their supporters in the Labour Party were not wedded to municipal enterprise. They proved invaluable supporters of the whole housing association movement; for them, state control was never as good as control by the consumers and producers.

1980–90: Radical change

In the 'Thatcher years' that followed, the fortunes of the housing association movement fell and rose. First, housing associations were a casualty of the public expenditure constraints of the early 1980s, particularly in respect of their funding through local authorities: this source of financing had led to approvals for over 16,000 homes in 1975–6 but the numbers now dwindled as councils came under financial pressure, to just 2,500 in 1981–2. Finance through local authorities dropped from a peak of over £400 million in 1977–8 to £100 million in 1983–4 (at 1983 prices) (NFHA, 1983, p. 7).

The position could have been worse. Provoked by a moratorium on their funding by the Housing Corporation in September 1980, the National Federation launched a major campaign: in November 1980, 'Housing Associations Week' was declared and nineteen Church of England bishops, led by the Archbishop of Canterbury, boarded up properties which could not now be modernised. Committee members were mobilised in all parts of the country. The Federation was rewarded with a statement from the Secretary of State for the Environment, Michael Heseltine, of an increase in the Housing Corporation's programme for 1981–2. Funding has never fallen so low again.

Associations then faced a threat from the government's emphasis on home ownership. On the one hand, this affected associations through government hopes that they too should sell properties at discounts to existing tenants under the 'right to buy'; this became a requirement on non-charitable housing associations in 1980. And on the other hand, it emerged in the enthusiasm of the Housing Minister, John Stanley, for associations to move into a more extensive programme of 'shared ownership' (part-owning, part-renting) and 'improvement for sale', but at the expense of its rental programme.

Associations resisted these changes. For the first, by mounting a strenuous campaign in the House of Lords, exemption for charities was secured from the compulsion to sell properties at discounts, in the Housing and Building Control Bill of 1983. For the second, in asserting the need for a rented housing programme for the less affluent, associations received increased public support following the street riots in Toxteth, Brixton and elsewhere in the summer of 1981. Following further campaigning, 1982 saw 'funding through the Housing Corporation returning to the level of its best year' (NFHA Annual Report). And the following year saw an injection of an extra £150 million. After the general election of that year, however, the sums were trimmed again. But the economic recovery of the late 1980s was reflected in a gradual increase in the programme of housing associations.

Attention now switched to the financial framework in which these organisations were operating. The trouble with the generous subsidy system which had fuelled the growth of associations for a decade, so it was argued, was that it lacked incentives to produce the most cost-effective solutions; tenants were unaffected by the level of expenditure incurred by associations in producing their homes since rents were fixed by the rent officer (and the grant arrangements balanced the books). To place associations in a more competitive environment, to encourage more entrepreneurial skills, and indeed to produce more homes for the same amount of public money, new arrangements were introduced by the Housing Act 1988. This legislation abolished the fair rent system for future lettings, leaving associations to set rents on a basis that would cover their costs after receipt of grant on a predetermined basis. To stretch the public finance further, the new system encouraged associations to borrow from private sources, rather than through the Housing Corporation or through a local authority. But grant levels set in the spring of 1988 were formulated on the basis of private sector loans available at the then building society rate of 9.5 per cent; as interest rates rose to 15.5 per cent without revision to the level of grants, rents rose to absorb around 30 per cent—and sometimes even more—of the net income of some new tenants.

The Housing Act 1988 marked some other important changes affecting housing associations. This legislation meant an end to 'right to buy' for all new lettings and re-lettings by the non-charitable associations and, therefore, confirmed the softening of the Government's virtual obsession with promoting owner occupation.

The Act also introduced mechanisms designed to encourage local authority tenants to transfer their homes from the public sector into the ownership and management of other landlords. Opportunities for 'tenants' choice' were coupled with mechanisms for housing action trusts which concentrated resources on specific areas (predominantly comprising council housing). After such a prolonged period of local authorities holding the majority of all rented homes in the UK, these measures—reinforced by financial pressures in the Local Government and Housing Act of 1989—were intended dramatically to shift the balance. But, at the beginning of the 1990s, there is little evidence that council tenants want to change the status quo in the ownership of their homes (although they are willing to vote for this, in some cases, where the council itself voluntarily proposes a transfer). At the same time, the existing housing associations have shown very little inclination to take on the ownership of council housing.

Government plans for the 1990s indicate a rise in public expenditure through the Housing Corporation from £815 million in 1989–90 to over £2 billion in 1993–4. Major cash flow problems resulting from the switch to the new system, and the cloud of 'unaffordable' rents, generated by high interest rates on mortgage loans, hang over this programme. But clearly the housing association movement is now centre stage for the development of social housing in the UK. Its programme is scheduled to be at least four times that of local authorities by the early 1990s (over 40,000 homes p.a., compared with less than 10,000). If the stick of heavy rent increases on the one side, and the chance of better services on the other, lead to large numbers of council tenants voting for a change in the ownership of their homes, then the shape and size of this movement could change even more dramatically.

In Conclusion

Over the last century, housing associations have received the good wishes of all governments. But mostly they have not received the funds necessary to operate on an extensive scale. Charitable gifts or philanthropic loans cannot substitute for government investment. Without large-scale public funding their role has inevitably been modest. And reliance on volunteers has confined most associations to a small size (albeit a size which both the committees and the tenants of many associations regard as beneficial).

When urgent action was needed, nationwide, at the end of the First World War, housing associations did not have either legal powers or the national coverage necessary for the task: local authorities covered every area and provided a safe channel for government funds. Nurtured by sympathetic ministers during the 1920s, council estates became the norm for social housing provision. Although the National Housing Committee of 1934 advocated a more pluralistic approach—with a central role for non-profit societies—the crash programme necessitated by another world war set this aside again.

For fifty years, housing associations have been the second best option, whichever political party has been in power. The Conservatives have favoured the private sector, believing that market forces will deliver best what the consumer wants. Labour governments have favoured direct provision by the public sector where democratic control should ensure that the needs of the majority are met.

Conservatives can point to the private sector's success in the field of home ownership: but this emphasis has diminished opportunities (and resources) for rented housing. And private renting for low-income households, as this chapter shows, has never been profitable. If government opts for the provision of subsidies to a scatter of profit-making landlords to meet these needs, difficulties seem inevitable—of policing the public funding, of ensuring value for money, of maintaining public confidence. So housing associations have been accepted by Conservatives as the half-way option.

The Labour Party can justifiably point to the successes of council housing. But it has not been blind to the deficiencies of a policy which leads to 100 per cent of rented housing being provided by a single landlord in each locality; inertia, inflexibility and insensitivity to consumers can appear if one provider holds a virtual monopoly on an area's low-cost housing. So housing associations can be used to meet priority needs and, in doing so, create some variety and give tenants the power that comes from choice.

Viewed the other way around, the Conservative Party—particularly with its recent desire to roll back the frontiers of local government provision—has seen public expenditure for associations as a lesser evil than public spending through the councils. Meanwhile Labour, with its deep-seated dislike of profit-making landlords, has found housing associations the only acceptable co-providers of homes to rent, alongside their traditional option of the local authority.

This 'second best' attitude to associations in the UK may indicate why they have not received the level of governmental finance needed to run a larger social housing programme.

But this chapter has pointed out that, historically, the housing association movement itself also saw the role of associations as secondary. As well as relieving a social evil on a relatively small scale, associations have recognised their value as a lobby in influencing public and government opinion, and in demonstrating how either the private sector (from 1830 onwards) or the public sector (from the turn of the century) might successfully meet mass needs.

In digging deeper, one wonders whether the curious divisions in British society may not also have contributed to the limited role of associations. In Scandinavia and in much of Northern Europe, the participation of producers and consumers has helped greatly in securing the rise of this sector. Here, trade unions have not involved themselves in the ownership or management of housing associations (and have channelled their support to the public sector); home-seekers helping themselves—backed by the building societies which, originally, they founded—have become individual owner-occupiers. If representatives of the building trades, and the occupiers themselves, had been a more central part of the housing association movement, surely the continental model would be more prevalent here. Has there been a suspicion in the past that, with their philanthropic origins, associations were run by middle-class 'do-gooders' helping their inferiors? However well-meaning they have been, perhaps there has been a cultural gap between these voluntary agencies and both producers and consumers.

Today's voluntary sector is increasingly bringing together the charitable theme—the 'haves' reaching out to the 'have nots'—and the self-help theme—groups setting out to do for themselves what the Welfare State failed to do.

Today's philosophy is the 'hand up, not the hand out'. In so far as housing associations not only offer opportunities for work to the construction industry, but also offer a sensitive response to consumers (shared owners as well as tenants), powerful pressures could accelerate the progress of this movement.

In blending the historic threads of philanthropy and self-help, of volunteering by the well housed and involvement by the tenant customer, the associations of the 1990s also create alliances across old divides: people from the business community can understand and support less affluent neighbourhoods; tenants can be empowered by learning new organisational skills. As in the past, housing associations can have a wider value in helping create a fairer and more successful nation — but perhaps tomorrow on a bigger scale.

References

Amulree, Lord Balfour, et al. (A National Housing Committee) (1934) *A National Housing Policy* P. S. King and Son.
Briggs, A (1961) *Seebohm Rowntree* London, Longmans.
Burnett, J (1986) *The Social History of Housing, 1815–1985* London, Methuen.
Cohen Committee (1971) *Housing Associations* London, HMSO.
Daunton, N J (1987) *A Property Owning Democracy?* London, Faber and Faber.
Greve, J (1971) *Voluntary Housing in Scandinavia* Birmingham, CURS.
Holmans, A E (1987) *Housing Policy in Britain* London, Croom Helm.
Jones, P (1985) *NFHA Jubilee Album* National Federation of Housing Associations.
NFHA (1983) *Housing Associations: Their Contribution and Potential* National Federation of Housing Associations.
Stack, U (1967) *The Development of a Housing Association* Birmingham, CURS.
Swenarton, N (1981) *Homes fit for Heroes* London, Heinemann.

Further reading

Tarn, J N (1973) *Five Per Cent Philanthropy* Cambridge, Cambridge University Press.
Wilmott, P and Murie, A (1988) *Polarisation and Social Housing* Policy Studies Institute.

11 Local political attitudes and council housing

Jane Darke

Introduction

Writing in 1990 it is tempting to draw parallels between the history of council housing and that of the Labour Party. Both had their origins in the late nineteenth century, both grew rather fitfully, with setbacks in the 1930s, both had a few years of glory in the period immediately following the Second World War. In national terms this was followed by a decline but with continued vigorous activity in some areas, then both institutions enjoyed a revival in the mid-1960s, of which the outcomes proved a disappointment to many of their supporters. In the 1980s, the defenders of council housing and of the Labour Party have been split amongst themselves and constantly attacked from outside; both institutions have seemed beyond recovery at times but both have emerged into the 1990s with unexpectedly high levels of support.

In fact the dawn of council housing predated that of the Labour Party. Labour has championed and defended council housing rather more vigorously than have other parties but the two main parties have both changed their position over time, only partly in response to the changing content of the housing problem. Each party is likely to set different priorities as policy makers in *local* government as compared to central government. Any account of political attitudes must therefore consider the particular situation at different levels of government, in different places and at different times. Local attitudes and achievements cannot be examined in isolation from the parties' policies nationally.

The issues that have divided the parties can be summarised as *quantity*, *quality* and *pricing*. The Conservatives have usually set lower targets than Labour in quantitative and qualitative terms, and have expected occupiers to contribute a higher proportion of costs. Labour has tended in principle to advocate high output to high standards and at low cost to users, but economic realities have forced at least one of these goals to be compromised at any one time. If Labour's policy has appeared inconsistent, this may be due to different decisions on how to compromise.

These party differences arise from fundamentally different beliefs on the *role* of council housing. The Conservatives have wished to minimise direct state involvement in housing provision, so have seen council housing as limited to a short period of exceptional shortage (1919 and 1923 Acts and the early 1950s), limited to particular target groups (1933, 1935 and 1956 Acts), limited to those who could not afford the full cost of adequate housing (the mid-1950s and early 1970s) or as a provision no longer required at all except perhaps for economically marginal households (the 1980s). Labour by contrast has generally seen council housing as a mainstream part of housing supply, catering for a broad section of the working class or even potentially for almost the whole population (1945–50). We shall examine how these philosophies have manifested themselves over the century since the 1890 Act.

Early examples

The extension of the franchise in 1884, the formation of the Social Democratic Federation and the Fabian Society in the 1880s and the Independent Labour Party in 1893 and the reform of local government in 1888, all contributed to permit some sections of the working class to have a direct influence on housing and other policies. Gauldie (1974, p. 294) has pointed out that the 1890 Housing of the Working Classes Act gave few powers to local authorities that they did not already possess, and certainly did not *require* a local authority to build housing. The use made of the 1890 Act can thus be seen as a sort of barometer of local political conditions, relying as it did on political pressure. It appears that those authorities that made use of it were indeed those with a well organised labour movement. Gauldie cites London, Sheffield, Bradford, Liverpool and Manchester as areas of particular housing activity (ibid., pp. 298–301). Merrett (1979, p. 26) estimates that 24,000 dwellings had been provided by 1914, almost half of these by the London County Council and some of the London boroughs. In quantitative terms this was tiny: less than a half of one per cent of the national housing stock. Yet the form of building had exemplary significance disproportionate to the numbers involved.

The pattern between 1890 and 1914 appears to be of limited use of rehousing powers before 1900, with the form of building generally high-density tenement flats on the sites of the cleared slums. Although the facilities provided were far superior to the norm for working-class housing at the time, the appearance of the new blocks was criticised. Even the lovingly designed Boundary Street estate in Shoreditch, built from 1893 to 1900 by the LCC under 'Progressive' (that is, mainly Liberal) control, (Beattie, 1980, pp. 18–54) was referred to as 'crude yellow brick . . . barrack dwellings' by Arthur Morrison in *Child of the Jago*, which described the semi-criminal existence in the rookeries that had been torn down to make way for the estate (1971, p. 160.) In Sheffield the flats built on the site of the Crofts Insanitary Area, with their curved facade and internal garden, were considered an improvement on slum clearance replacement schemes in Manchester but were in turn overtaken by a policy of cottage building (Gaskell, 1974, pp. 103–13).

The 1900 Housing of the Working Classes Act gave local authorities the power to build on suburban sites, which the LCC already possessed but had not used until 1898 (Young and Garside, 1982, p. 113). In the early twentieth century, advocacy of cottage estates, under the influence of the Garden City movement, was strongly identified with the Liberal and embryonic Labour parties, whilst Conservatives favoured non-intervention or grudgingly allowed limited building of tenement flats when prodded to do so by the Local Government Board (Gaskell, 1974, p. 114). Gaskell maintains that these policy preferences were not related to policies articulated by the parties at national level, but were consistent with the Conservatives' wish to minimise municipal expenditure, the Liberals' belief in self-help and Labour's 'romantic attachment not only to the Garden City idea but also to a utopian socialist ideal of a pre-industrial society' (1976, p. 194).

The ideals of utopian socialists such as William Morris, who inspired audiences all over Britain in his public speeches in the 1880s and early 1890s, and Edward Carpenter, who was living the simple life and lecturing to working people in Sheffield in the same period, must have influenced schemes such as Sheffield's cottage estate on High Wincobank, started in 1903 and continuing up to and after the First World War. This scheme was the subject of intense controversy, leading to changes in political control of the council from Liberal to Conservative in 1908 and back to Liberal in 1910 (Gaskell, 1976, pp. 193–4). The small Labour Party supported the Liberals in favouring cottages but were concerned that rents of over 6 shillings a week could not be afforded by families from the slums, whom Labour saw as the intended beneficiaries of cottage building. The Conservatives too criticised rents of 7 shillings but their solution, vetoed by the Local Government Board, was to lease the remaining land to private builders who would presumably build for private renting more cheaply and to lower standards. Many of the cottages built by the Corporation had three bedrooms and an upstairs bathroom: a very high standard for working-class housing at the time, and many were in fact occupied by non-manual workers.

We thus see an early emergence of the debate on quantity, quality and costs. There has been a continuing tension in Labour's thinking between the desire to build to exemplary standards and the desire to target policies at the poorer sections of the working class. In practice the former aim has tended to predominate, with the result that council house-building has generally tended to benefit artisans, the more financially secure and better organised section of the working class. The less skilled or economically marginal population has had to rely on the slow process of filtering, or at times on slum clearance policies which admitted them to the ranks of council tenants but in a specially targeted poor-quality part of the stock.

By the First World War Labour was still little more than a pressure group but Fabian socialist ideas were becoming a significant influence on official thinking. Beatrice Webb was a strong believer in the role of local government and Raymond Unwin was the principal author of the important Tudor Walters committee report. There was socialist and feminist representation in the Women's Housing Sub-Committee, which set out to ascertain the views of working-class women on the standard of housing to be built after the war (Swenarton, 1981; McFarlane, 1984; Ravetz, 1989). During the war working-class organisation on Clydeside, in which women played a leading role, forced the government to impose rent control.

Political attitudes between the wars

After the war there was multi-party consensus that the state must build to high standards and must provide subsidies. However, the Conservatives and Liberals envisaged the intervention as being short lived, to overcome the temporary scarcity and to placate a potentially insurgent working class (Swenarton, 1981, *passim*). The decision to axe the housing programme in 1921, after unrest had died down, appears to have been almost equally uncontroversial within the Coalition Government although Addison resigned, having already been relieved of responsibility for the housing programme (ibid., Ch. 6). Nor does this cut appear to have given rise to political outrage or popular agitation. The trade union movement and the Labour Party were at the time preoccupied with internal issues (Pelling, 1978, pp. 48–50). However, the following year Labour overtook the Liberals in parliamentary seats and in January 1924 came the first Labour Government, a minority administration with Liberal support.

The different views on the role of council housing are seen particularly clearly in the comparison between the Housing Acts of 1923 (Chamberlain) and 1924 (Wheatley). The Chamberlain Act offered rather low subsidies for a limited period and allowed councils to build only if they could demonstrate that private enterprise was failing to meet the needs in their locality. Chamberlain saw and welcomed the growth in home ownership, which he thought promoted social stability. Wheatley saw council housing not as a short-term response to a crisis but as potentially the main source of housing for the working class. His own background as a militant Clydeside trade unionist active in the agitation leading to the 1915 Rent Act helped him to secure agreement with the building unions to expand their workforce in exchange for the guarantee of a fifteen-year programme with generous subsidies.

In the immediate post-war period most local authorities, whatever their political complexion, recognised the need to build housing. Nationally, the space standards of the Addison Act houses were higher than at any other point in the inter-war period (Merrett, 1979, Appendix 3) and estate layout was often imaginative, with curved tree-lined streets and picturesque vistas as recommended by Unwin in the Tudor Walters Report. The Local Government Board manual of 1919 had called for houses that would 'serve as a model or standard for building by private enterprise in the future'. However, not all those on the left were in sympathy with this approach. The Liverpool School under Professor Reilly criticised the backward-looking quaintness of Garden City planning and called for a more functional approach:

The standard cottage will depend for any attraction that it may possess, not upon the toolmarks of the workman, nor upon its peculiarity or idiosyncracy . . . but upon more general characteristics such as suitability to purpose and excellence of design. It will not be the home of an individual, of an anarchist; but the home of a member of a certain class, of a communist. (Adshead, 1916, quoted in Swenarton, 1981 pp. 63–4)

Adshead was also an early advocate of standardisation in housing as a means of rationalising the production process (Finnimore, 1989, p. 14). In practice, estates built under the Chamberlain and Wheatley Acts tended to be plainer and more functional than those built under the Addison Act (Jennings, 1971, pp. 126–7) but this is probably attributable to the fact that the local authorities, not the government, had to bear the cost of any extravagance, rather than to any ideological preference for simplicity.

By the mid-1920s there was greater variance both in political control (with Labour in charge in some town halls) and in readiness to build. The choice of some authorities to continue to use the Chamberlain Act, with no obligation to make a rate fund contribution but implying higher rents, is an indicator of local political priorities (Bowley, 1945, pp. 109–17; Dresser, 1984, p. 164). The evidence for Labour local administrations showing greater enthusiasm for building is strong but anecdotal rather than comprehensive (Bowley, 1945, passim; Jennings, 1971, passim; Ryder, 1984, pp. 50–1).

Some of the debates and accusations around housing management issues in the inter-war period are strikingly similar to those of today. The District Auditor in County Durham accused the Labour councils of Brandon in 1928 and Hetton in 1936 of laxity in their efforts to recover rent arrears (Ryder, 1984, pp. 88–9). There were discussions in Bristol on the relative advantages of a masculine, businesslike style of housing management and the more personal approach of the Octavia Hill school (Dresser, 1984, pp. 203–4). Labour councils sought to avoid the restrictive practices and cartels often operated by private builders by setting up direct labour organisations (DLOs) (Ryder, 1984, pp. 65–8). The 'moderates' took the view that DLOs led to low work rates at the council's expense.

On standards the picture was more complex: the relationship with political control was not always in the expected direction. Ryder (1984, p. 72) tells of a Conservative MP in 1935 criticising cramped housing built by Labour-controlled Chester-le-Street RDC (Rural District Council) and claiming that the council had deliberately built unsatisfactory housing in order to discredit the National Government. In Bristol, the Conservative chair of housing in 1923 designed the 'Bristol chalet', which had reduced space standards and a lower standard of construction and finishes than traditional housing. This gave rise to an outcry against 'kennels' and 'hen roosts', leading to the resignation of the chair (Dresser, 1984, p. 188). Dresser goes on to show how standards of space, amenity and layout declined over the 1920s, and how uncertain was the response of the left to right-wing attacks on the monotony and ugliness of council estates: 'aesthetic considerations could increasingly come to be seen by champions of a collectivist housing policy as an impractical luxury, or even an insidious diversion' (pp. 189–94).

A similar desire to keep housing within the reach of lower-income families was behind the policy decision taken in 1934 by the newly Labour-controlled LCC to concentrate on building inner-city flats rather than suburban houses (Young and Garside, 1982, pp. 179–81). In Sheffield the Labour council resisted government pressure to build small flats to high densities rather than houses, although the proportion of two-bedroomed houses increased in the 1930s. In Leeds, on the other hand, a Labour council elected in 1933, influenced by workers' flats in Vienna, embarked on the showpiece scheme of Quarry Hill Flats, planned to include nurseries, laundries and other collective facilities (Ravetz, 1974b; Finnigan, 1984, pp. 139–42). This scheme, still not completed at the start of the Second World War, was illustrated in virtually every pamphlet or newsreel of the 1940s on post-war reconstruction but failed to live up to the hopes of its idealistic creators. It was demolished in the 1970s.

There was controversy, particularly in Leeds, on whether rent levels should be related to ability to pay, with the consequent need to apply the hated means test (Finnigan, 1984, pp. 116–22). Labour was divided at national level on the issue of rebates, which were introduced by a Labour government on a permissive basis in 1930 and encouraged by the National Government in 1933 (Malpass and Murie, 1987, p. 64). A rent structure which targeted subsidies to poorer tenants and economised on subsidies to the financially secure was to the obvious advantage of the Exchequer, but such schemes were resisted by the majority of tenants, who stood to pay higher rents to support neighbours whose lower standards could be seen as sullying the reputation of their estates. Labour councillors could be placed in a difficult position as the respectable working class was a major source of their support. Tenants organised rent strikes to oppose differential rent schemes against a Labour council in Leeds and a Liberal-Unionist one in Birmingham (Merrett, 1979, p. 58).

Summing up the inter-war period, Labour's record on housing quality and pricing was rather variable, and only on the issue of quantity does the party appear to have maintained consistently high objectives, although Labour councils did not always achieve high output in practice. The Conservatives, as we have seen, sought to restrict state intervention to exceptional periods or target groups.

Post-war achievements

In the Attlee Government of the post-war period, Bevan as Minister of Health placed his priorities firmly on the side of quality. His era is remembered not simply for the most generous space standards ever achieved in council housing (Merrett, 1979, Appendix 3) but also for other aspects of quality: the houses were mostly two-storey and semi-detached, with good standards of privacy internally, in spacious layouts and sometimes planned to harmonise with the local vernacular without pretending to be anything other than council houses. It is instructive to compare the 1949 *Housing Manual*, which illustrates this, with its successors of 1952, 1953 and 1958, in which the only sparks of creative thought are devoted to ever more ingenious ways to save costs (Ministry of Health, 1949; Ministry of Housing and Local Government, 1952, 1953, 1958). Bevan intended council estates to be mixed communities serving a wide range of social classes.

In the immediate post-war period subsidies were also high: Bevan won a battle with the Treasury but even so rents rose to levels unaffordable by poorer families (Malpass, 1990, pp. 75–80). The commitment to high standards and high subsidies had the inevitable consequence of low numerical output. However, the need for state housing was recognised on all sides. In many villages the only evidence of state intervention is a handful of Addison Act cottages and a close of Bevan houses, now often purchased under the 'right to buy'. The 1949 manual illustrates superbly designed schemes in Dorset,

Devon, rural Berkshire, Suffolk and other areas not known since that era for their commitment to state housing.

Macmillan as Minister of Housing from 1951 achieved increased output but expected this to be followed by rent increases ('the houses must go up before the rents', quoted by Malpass, 1990, p. 89). Space standards were sharply reduced, following the trend started in 1950 under Labour. The real value of subsidy in relation to construction costs fell between the mid-1950s and the early 1960s from around one-third to about a quarter (Merrett, 1979, pp. 179–80).

In the mid-1950s the shift from universalism is evident in the persistent concern that subsidised council houses were being occupied by those who could afford to go private (Malpass, 1990, pp. 86–101); a concern not voiced over higher-income users of state education or the National Health Service. The housing problem was seen as an urban issue, shown particularly in the switch from general needs to slum clearance at this time. The larger urban authorities, mostly Labour controlled, became reasonably efficient machines for large-scale slum clearance and rebuilding, even if this efficiency was not always apparent to the objects of their zeal (see Ungerson, 1971, for an account of the devastating personal consequences to those in slum clearance). There was no consultation with those affected and very little attempt to keep them fully informed.

Pricing

It would be interesting to be able to present comparative data on changing rent levels over time, according to type of authority and political control, and in relation to the income levels of tenants and of manual workers in general. Unfortunately such data have not been assembled, so the evidence on political influences on rent setting is piecemeal. At national level, Merrett (1979, p. 184) estimates that for forty years from 1936, rents remained close to 7–8 per cent of male manual gross earnings. During the 1980s rents have risen rather faster than earnings: the average rent of £20.64 in April 1989 was 9.5 per cent of the average male manual wage. Furthermore, the 'average tenant' is no longer a male breadwinner on an average manual wage: that individual is likely to be a home owner. Over half of council tenants are not in the labour market. Cuts in government subsidies to local housing authorities have resulted in a doubling of the real costs of rebates or housing benefit (Hills and Mullings, 1990, table 5A.1).

There are some continuities between those county boroughs charging low or high rents in 1936, 1954 and 1964. Six of the ten highest-rent county boroughs for 1954 and five for 1964 were already high-rent authorities in 1936, and a similar comparison holds good for low-rent boroughs (Bowley, 1945, p. 115; Malpass, 1990, p. 96). All ten county boroughs with lowest rents in 1964 were Labour controlled or had Labour as the largest single party. Rent setting by Labour authorities has tended to follow the simple principle of 'keep 'em low'. Decisions appear to rest on a calculation of relative electoral advantage and obligations towards tenants as against ratepayers as a whole.

Judging by the level of organised protest from tenants, rent rebates have been a more controversial issue than rent levels. Protests against rebate schemes in the 1930s were noted earlier; this issue was also the cause of the most famous acts of defiance in post-war housing history: the St Pancras rent strike of 1960 (Merrett, 1979, pp. 180–2) and Clay Cross in 1972–4, where a left Labour council refused to implement rent increases required by the 1972 Housing Finance Act (Malpass, 1989). In Sheffield in 1967 there was widespread protest and a rent strike against a system of rebates which included what would now be called non-dependant deductions: tenants were enraged at a 'lodger tax' on resident adult sons and daughters (Hampton, 1970, Ch. 10). By contrast, the very steep rent increases of 1980–3 nationally produced hardship but no organised campaign of defiance. This issue will be further discussed later.

High-rise and system building

With few exceptions, politicians in both main parties supported the greater use of high rise and of system building, both in Parliament and in local councils (Dunleavy, 1981, pp. 151–8 and Chs 7–9). High-rise building reached a peak in 1966, with 25.7 per cent of dwellings in tenders approved in that year being in schemes of five storeys or over (Cooney, 1974, p. 152). System building, not necessarily high rise, peaked the following year, with 42.6 per cent of dwellings in tenders approved (Finnimore, 1989, p. 262).

Both high-rise and system building were virtually confined to large urban areas with substantial housing programmes to complete in the face of shortages of building land and of workforce in the construction industry. The moral panics of the day were about families waiting years in foul slums or countryside disappearing under bricks and tarmac, rather than the unacceptable quality of life in high flats. Tower blocks were a measure of a council's virility, especially if they attracted design awards and admiring visiting experts. Civic rivalry played a part: Leeds' Quarry Hill was amply matched by Sheffield's Park Hill.

There are several bitter ironies about this era. First, local councillors, architects, planners and housing staff were well aware that the overwhelming preference was for houses with gardens rather than flats, but attributed this to people's backwardness (Dunleavy, 1981). Secondly, many of the high-rise schemes were not to particularly high densities: in most of these cases low rise would have been a perfectly feasible alternative (Dunleavy, 1981, pp. 264–7, 308). Furthermore, despite the alleged savings in cost and productivity of system building, this was not consistently cheaper, and high rise was certainly far more costly than low rise (Finnimore, 1989, Appendix 7). Construction times were quite likely to be slower due to long lead-in times (Dunleavy, 1981, pp. 220, 269–78). Finally, there was unprecedented scope for corrupt relationships involving councillors, council officials, contractors and private consultants (ibid., pp. 293–5). In the end it was not just high-rise and system building that were discredited but the image of council housing as a whole, perhaps irreversibly.

Once clearance had removed the worst housing, and in view of the rehousing alternatives on offer, owners and some private tenants in future clearance areas started to form action groups. Most of the councils whose proposals they were opposing were Labour. Although both parties initially supported the use of high-rise and system building, the Conservatives can take marginally greater credit for ending their use. The unpopularity of the Labour Government in the late 1960s, and the campaigns of the action groups, led to widespread gains by the Conservatives in local elections, even for example taking control of Sheffield in 1968–9. By this time official advice and a new subsidy system discouraged the use of very high blocks and this accorded with the Conservatives' wish to cut municipal spending. Many high-rise projects were given the *coup de grâce*. The policies of all parties nationally started to favour improvement rather than clearance.

In some districts the Tory gains cleared away the older generation of paternalistic Labour councillors and paved the way for the rise of the 'new urban left' in the late 1970s (Gyford, 1985, pp. 24–8; Lansley et al., 1989, Ch. 1). Elsewhere it was local government reorganisation in 1974 that brought in a new generation of Labour councillors. There was a greater readiness to work *with* people rather than doing things *for* them. By the late 1970s, the more perceptive of the professionals working for local government were uneasily conscious that the services they delivered were seen as part of their oppression by the clients, rather than as a welcome increment to their quality of life (London Edinburgh, 1979; Dickens and Goodwin, 1981).

Housing in the 1980s

The pattern of party attitudes in the 1980s has been complex and sometimes contradictory. Both parties at the start of the decade had some perception of the need to improve service standards and treat tenants as customers rather than the fortunate but passive beneficiaries of municipal initiative. This awareness was rarely translated into practice (Kay et al., 1986). The Conservative Government in the 1980 Act willingly adopted most provisions in the Tenants' Charter that had been drafted under the previous Labour Administration, and added the 'right to buy'. They also added new financial provisions that gave them a sophisticated lever for raising rents, in contrast to the crudely conceived 1972 Act which had had the same objectives (Malpass, 1990, pp. 114–26, 137–41).

Where the legal drafting was careless was in the new rules controlling local authority capital spending. The intention to limit this was frustrated by three factors: the fact that housing investment programme allocations to individual authorities could not take account of the authority's level of capital receipts, the fact that receipts could 'cascade', yielding additional resources for spending in successive years, and the use of the remaining portion of receipts for 'non-prescribed' expenditure such as capitalised repairs. These loopholes were firmly closed by the 1989 Local Government and Housing Act.

On the issues of quality, quantity and costs, the record of the 1980s is clear on the last two but not the first. During the 1970s architects were relearning how to design homely, likeable housing, occasionally even talking to users in the process. Unfortunately, just at this point the possibility of building *anything* started on its fifteen-year decline to a current level at around one tenth of the level of the mid-1970s. The Parker Morris standards, introduced in the 1960s, had been mixed in their benefits, setting a reasonable (though not generous) level of space internally but ignoring so many other aspects of dwelling quality. This had permittted the continued building of large, ugly, over-dense estates, and the process of gaining approval for schemes had become excessively bureaucratic. However, the abandonment both of the Parker Morris standards and of collection by the Department of the Environment (DoE) of statistics on size of new dwellings means that it is impossible to tell what is actually happening on standards. It is therefore not possible to detect political differences in practice, but any party hoping in future to reverse the low status of council housing would have to ensure that new building was of high quality, and that it remained so in the face of pressures for increased output.

The financial regime controlling capital spending from 1981 to 1990 altered possibilities for both Conservative and Labour authorities. Although some Conservative local politicians opposed the right to buy (Stoker, 1988, pp. 178–9), most areas in Tory control, including key London boroughs such as Westminster and Wandsworth, were enthusiastic to sell their housing stock. The highest sellers are mostly rural southern authorities outside London, virtually all non-Labour (Forrest and Murie, 1988, pp. 116–21). The receipts from the right to buy and the ability to make a profit on the housing revenue account yielded resources that could be used to keep rates to low levels and still leave enough surplus for such authorities to undertake capital projects. In many areas the stock has been modernised to high standards and tenants enjoy a good-quality repairs service (Audit Commission, 1986b; DoE, 1989, Ch. 6). Where new build was undertaken it was often targeted at the elderly, with sheltered schemes or bungalows fitting the traditional Conservative view that council housing was to meet exceptional needs.

None the less, towards the end of the 1980s rural areas were feeling the impact of house price inflation, with local prices higher and wages lower than the national average. Some district councils in rural areas became concerned at the inability of local people to afford housing. This remains a continuing tension: the authorities must be 'enablers not providers' but housing associations have been denied the resources to meet the need, and authorities' attempts to do partnership deals, exchanging land for nomination rights, have been frustrated by changing and incomprehensible rules set by the DoE.

Labour-controlled areas, specifically the metropolitan districts, other industrial cities and most of inner London, have benefited much less than the rural areas from capital receipts. Many Labour councils fought against the right to buy, including the use of deliberate obstructive tactics (Forrest and Murie, 1988, pp. 207–16; Stoker, 1988, pp. 178–81) but have been forced into welcoming the receipts generated. (In fact the financial arguments against council house sales do not stand up to analysis, and the social arguments are equivocal to say the least, but this is not the place to pursue this debate.) The decade has been a constant struggle to maintain capital programmes and service standards for those authorities embracing such objectives. None the less, Labour party control is still a significant predictor of higher levels of investment by an authority, even after allowing for differences in housing needs, as it was earlier in the post-war period when housing showed greater differences by party than most other services (Kleinman et al., 1989; Eastall, 1989; Sharpe and Newton, 1984).

The pressure for a better service

All too many authorities, Labour as well as Conservative, still have no notion of operating a high-quality housing service in a collaborative relationship with their tenants. It is worth briefly tracing the trend towards greater awareness of quality of service. The impetus for changes in housing service delivery has come from three sources: housing experts, the 'new urban left' and from tenants themselves (Moseley, 1984). The term 'experts' rather than 'professionals' is used, as the Institute of Housing was not in the vanguard of pressure for change (Laffin, 1986, Ch. 9). Rather the DoE in the late 1970s discovered the difficult-to-let problem and started to advise on housing management issues, in contrast to its earlier advice centred on development (Andrews, 1979; DoE, 1981; Laffin, 1986, Ch. 5). At the same time, a research team at City University was providing evidence of an undertrained, unqualified workforce delivering poor-quality services (Education and Training, 1977, 1978; Housing Research Group, 1981).

The history of the new urban left has been amply chronicled (Gyford, 1985; Seyd, 1987; Stoker, 1988, Ch. 9; Lansley et al., 1989). In housing terms, their main objectives have been firstly, decentralisation, following the lead taken by Walsall (Seabrook, 1984) and secondarily the introduction of an equal opportunities and especially an anti-racist perspective.

The intended outcome of decentralisation, which sometimes involved other services as well as housing, was as likely to be convenience of access as empowerment of local people. The short-lived Walsall experiment was widely admired and copied without the councils concerned necessarily articulating the anticipated benefits: decentralisation came to be seen as the progressive course of action to be taken. Resistance by white-collar unions was widely reported, often with exaggerated horror stories being given credence by the very councillors who were victimised by press fantasies about children being indoctrinated with gay rights and 'Baa Baa Green Sheep' (Sharron, 1985; Lansley et al., 1989).

In retrospect, the unions' fears for their members' jobs were not misplaced: left-wing councillors, impatient for change, wrongly diagnosed the obstacle as staff attitudes rather than the institutional constraints on staff attempting to allocate scarce resources according to rules set by councillors. A thorough reorganisation, with staff having to reapply for their own jobs and (invariably) an overall increase in staffing, could bring in large numbers of younger, better-qualified staff with a strong commitment to high service standards and equal opportunities. These new staff may sometimes have been viewed with suspicion by the old hands, but they soon discovered a common interest in securing adequate working conditions and recognition of the stressful nature of their work, from councillors more concerned to provide a model service than to act as model employers.

Although tenants, councillors and housing staff all shared an interest in improving services, this was not recognised and relations which should have been collaborative were often confrontational. Tenants and other clients were sometimes involved on one side or another of a dispute, but often suffered in silence from the lack of services. Poor services were as likely to be due to the chronic underfunding of local government throughout the 1980s as to industrial action or bad management, but there have at various times been inexcusable failures to deliver a housing benefits service, homelessness assessment or a repairs service. Inefficiencies in letting empty property or recovering arrears were also common (Audit Commission, 1986a; DoE, 1989), but have had less impact on tenants up to 1990. This will no longer be the case in future: high arrears and void levels will result in higher rents as their cost will fall on the Housing Revenue Account.

More widespread still, in authorities of all political colours, is extremely poor performance on tenant involvement. Despite the setting up of the Tenants Participation Advisory Service in 1988, it is rare for tenants even to be fully informed, let alone to have real opportunities to influence decisions (Kay et al., 1986; DoE, 1989, pp. 25–30). The belief that councillors know best and that tenants' only role is to pay the rent and be grateful is deeply ingrained. Council housing has received stronger support from council tenants than it deserves, in the campaigns against the 1988 Act and against voluntary transfers by individual authorities. Admittedly, actual examples of better ways of managing a housing service are hard to find, but 'the devil you know' (Duncan and Greaves, 1989) is hardly a positive choice.

Rents in the 1980s

The provisions in the 1980 Act allowing the Secretary of State to force rents up were only partly successful as more and more authorities went out of subsidy: by the late 1980s few authorities outside London received any government subsidy. Many authorities, of all political colours, have until 1990 maintained low rents as a result of a decision to keep the Housing Revenue Account in balance, or not to extract a high surplus. Only half of the ten authorities with lowest rents in 1988 (Malpass, 1990, p. 148) were in Labour control; the others were rural areas or cathedral cities.

The high rent group, all London boroughs, were all Conservative controlled except Hammersmith and Fulham which had only recently changed control. Elsewhere in London, particularly in boroughs controlled by the new urban left, rents were not increased for several years running during the mid-1980s, despite strong advice from some chief officers. For such authorities low rents became a political fetish, with perverse refusal to raise rents even though tenants would have welcomed additional spending on repairs; and the necessary rate fund contributions were subject to harsh penalties and, eventually, capping. The result was that when the true seriousness of the authorities' positions became apparent, shortly after the 1987 general election, tenants were abruptly confronted with very steep increases, a trend likely to continue under the new financial regime introduced in the 1989 Local Government and Housing Act. This Act allows the Secretary of State virtually to dictate local rents, and to exert strong upward pressure in areas with high capital values.

Local authorities' autonomy on rent setting until 1990, even though eroded in the 1980s, has meant that the Labour Party nationally did not need to decide a principled basis for rent setting. The position has now changed: if arguments against rent increases are to have any credibility Labour must arrive at a position on appropriate rent levels, and degree of local autonomy on this (see Labour Housing Group, 1989). Pooling of historic costs within any one authority would now produce such anomalous local variations as to be unworkable. The Conservative Government's intention to move towards rents related to capital values represents an attempt to introduce a principle into a chaotic situation. Labour needs an equally strong principle, but it will be difficult to arrive at a suitable system that would work both after fifteen years of low investment *and* after a few years of increased investment.

A future for council housing?

Council housing is still equated with high-rise flats by many of the public. To reverse its negative stereotype will require a proliferation of the positive thinking that has turned round many priority estates, with a commitment to creating a high-quality environment, excellently managed with tenants able to participate in decision making. The 1980s have been a time for learning, sometimes painfully, how to recover from past mistakes. There is an excellent level of awareness of the situation, understanding of what should be done and willingness to act, among housing staff, local politicians and tenants. The prospects for a second century could be exciting, if politicians at national level allow council housing a future.

It is not necessary to elaborate on the Conservative agenda for housing: this has become increasingly clear since 1979. If the Conservatives were to win a further election the future would appear to be one of continuing defensive action to hang on to parts of the service: the scope for innovation would continue to be limited. The Social and Liberal Democrats published a policy document in 1989, but it contains few firm proposals. The Labour Party, after a period of distinct coolness towards council housing, now takes the view that although housing associations and co-ops should be encouraged, only the public sector has the capability of meeting the current extent of housing need.

But Labour's policy still has gaps. The party has refused to set targets, either numerical or in terms of dealing with particular issues in so many years. Their intentions on standards of new build and modernisation are vague, although there is a welcome commitment to tenants' rights and to tenant involvement. The proposals on housing finance are still under discussion. Whether Labour could achieve both quantity and quality of provision at reasonable cost remains to be seen.

References and sources consulted

Adshead, S D (1916) 'The standard cottage', *Town Planning Review* 6 pp. 244–9.

Andrews, L C (1979) *Tenants and Town Hall* London, Department of the Environment HMSO.

Audit Commission (1986a) *Managing the Crisis in Council Housing* London, HMSO.

Audit Commission (1986b) *Improving Council House Maintenance* London, HMSO.

Beattie, S (1980) *A Revolution in London Housing: LCC Architects and their Work 1893–1914* London, Greater London Council and Architectural Press.

Bowley, M (1945) *Housing and the State 1919–1944* London, Allen and Unwin.

Clapham, D (1989) *Goodbye Council Housing?* London, Unwin (The Fabian Series).

Cooney, E W (1974) 'High flats in local authority housing in England and Wales since 1945', in A Sutcliffe (ed) *Multi-storey Living: the British Working-class Experience* London, Croom Helm.

Dickens, P and Goodwin, M (1981) *Consciousness, Corporatism and the Local State*, Working paper No. 26, Brighton, Urban and Regional Studies, University of Sussex.

DoE (Department of the Environment) (1981) *Priority Estates Project 1981: Improving Problem Council Estates* London, HMSO.

DoE (Department of the Environment) (1989) *The Nature and Effectiveness of Housing Management in England* London, HMSO.

Dresser, M (1984) 'Housing policy in Bristol, 1919–30', in M J Daunton (ed) *Councillors and Tenants: Local Authority Housing in English Cities, 1919–1939* Leicester, Leicester University Press.

Duncan, S and Greaves, K (1989) 'Better the devil you know?', *Housing* 25 (5), June, pp. 20–3.

Dunleavy, P (1981) *The Politics of Mass Housing in Britain 1945–1975* Oxford, Clarendon Press.

Eastall, R (1989) *Local Politics and Housing Investment: an Investigation of the Relationship between Political Control of Local Authorities and their Housing Expenditure*, Housing Working Paper 3, Department of Land Economy, University of Cambridge.

Education and Training for Housing Work Project (1977) *Housing Staff*, The City University, London.

Education and Training for Housing Work Project (1978) *Housing Training: Finding and Recommendations* London, Department of the Environment.

Finnigan, R (1984) 'Council housing in Leeds, 1919–39: social policy and urban change', in M J Daunton (ed) *Councillors and Tenants: Local Authority Housing in English Cities, 1919–1939* Leicester, Leicester University Press.

Finnimore, B (1989) *Houses from the Factory: System Building and the Welfare State 1942–74* London, Rivers Oram Press.

Forrest, R and Murie, A (1988) *Selling the Welfare State: the Privatisation of Public Housing* London, Routledge.

Gaskell, S M (1974) 'A landscape of small houses: the failure of the workers' flat in Lancashire and Yorkshire in the nineteenth century', in A Sutcliffe (ed) *Multi-storey Living: the British Working-class Experience* London, Croom Helm.

Gaskell, S M (1976) 'Sheffield City Council and the development of suburban areas prior to world war I', in S Pollard and C Holmes (eds) *Essays in the Economic and Social History of South Yorkshire* Barnsley, South Yorkshire County Council.

Gauldie, E (1974) *Cruel Habitations: a History of Working-class Housing 1780–1918* London, Allen and Unwin.

Gyford, J (1985) *The Politics of Local Socialism* London, Allen and Unwin.

Hampton, W (1970) *Democracy and Community: a Study of Politics in Sheffield* Oxford, Oxford University Press.

Hills, J and Mullings, B (1990) 'Housing', Chapter 5 in J Hills (ed) *The State of Welfare: the Welfare State in Britain since 1974* Oxford, Oxford University Press.

Housing Research Group (1981) *Could Local Authorities be Better Landlords?* London, The City University.

Jennings, J H (1971) 'Geographical implications of the municipal housing programme in England and Wales 1919–39', *Urban Studies* 8 (2), pp. 121–38.

Kay, A, Legg, C and Foot, J (1986) *The 1980 Tenants' Rights in Practice* London, Housing Research Group, The City University.

Kemp, P (1989) 'Why council housing?', *ROOF* March-April, pp. 42–4.

Kleinman, M P, Eastell, R and Roberts, E (1989) *Local Choices or Central Constraints? Modelling Capital Expenditure on Local Authority Housing* Discussion Paper No. 23, University of Cambridge, Department of Land Economy.

Labour Housing Group (1989) *Housing Finance: Interim Policy Statement*, Labour Housing Group, 8A St Thomas Crescent, Newcastle-upon-Tyne.

Laffin, M (1986) *Professionalism and Policy: the Role of the Professions in the Central–Local Government Relationship* Aldershot, Gower.

Lansley, S, Goss, S and Wolmar, C (1989) *Councils in Conflict: the Rise and Fall of the Municipal Left* Basingstoke, Macmillan Education.

Local Government Board (1919) *Manual on the Preparation of State-aided Housing Schemes* London, HMSO.

London Edinburgh Weekend Return Group (1979) *In and against the State* London, Conference of Socialist Economists.

Malpass, P (1989) 'The road from Clay Cross', *ROOF* January-February, pp. 38–40.

Malpass, P (1990) *Reshaping Housing Policy: Subsidies, Rents and Residualisation* London, Routledge.

Malpass, P and Murie, A (1987) *Housing Policy and Practice* 2nd edn, Basingstoke, Macmillan Education.

McFarlane, B (1984) 'Homes fit for heroines: housing in the twenties', in *Making Space: Women and the Man-made Environment*, Matrix, London, Pluto Press.

Merrett, S (1979) *State Housing in Britain* London, Routledge and Kegan Paul.

Ministry of Health (1949) *Design Manual 1949* London, HMSO.

Ministry of Housing and Local Government (1952) *Houses 1952* London, HMSO.

Ministry of Housing and Local Government (1953) *Houses 1953* London, HMSO.

Ministry of Housing and Local Government (1958) *Flats and Houses 1958: Design and Economy* London, HMSO.

Morrison, A (1971) (first published 1896) *A Child of the Jago* London, Panther.

Moseley, R (1984) 'Liberating the public sector', in Labour Housing Group, *Right to a Home* Nottingham, Spokesman.

Pelling, H (1978) *A Short History of the Labour Party* 6th edn, London, Macmillan.

Ravetz, A (1974a) 'From working class tenement to modern flat: local authorities and multi-storey housing between the wars', in ∴ Sutcliffe (ed) *Multi-storey Living: the British Working-class Experience* London, Croom Helm.

Ravetz, A (1974b) *Model Estate: Planned Housing at Quarry Hill, Leeds* London, Croom Helm.

Ravetz, A (1989) 'A view from the interior' in J Attfield and P Kirkham (eds) *A View from the Interior* London, The Women's Press.

Ryder, R (1984) 'Council house building in County Durham, 1900–39: the local implementation of national policy', in M J Daunton (ed) *Councillors and Tenants: Local Authority Housing in English Cities, 1919–1939* Leicester, Leicester University Press.

Seabrook, J (1984) *The Idea of Neighbourhood: What Local Politics Should Be About* London, Pluto Press.

Seyd, P (1987) *The Rise and Fall of the Labour Left* Basingstoke, Macmillan Education.

Sharpe, L J and Newton, K (1984) *Does Politics Matter?: the Determinants of Public Policy* Oxford, Clarendon Press.

Sharron, H (1985) 'Overcoming trade union resistance to local change', *Public Money* 4 (4), March, pp. 17–23.

Social and Liberal Democrats (1989) *Housing: a Time for Action* English White Paper No. 2, 4 Cowley Street, London.

Stoker, G (1988) *The Politics of Local Government* Basingstoke, Macmillan Education.

Sutcliffe, A (1974) 'A century of flats in Birmingham, 1875–1973', in A Sutcliffe (ed) *Multi-storey Living: the British Working-class Experience* London, Croom Helm.

Swenarton, M (1981) *Homes Fit for Heroes* London, Heinemann.

Tudor Walters, Sir J (chairman) (1918) *Report* of the Committee appointed by the President of the Local Government Board . . . etc. Cd 9191, Parliamentary Papers 1918, vii.

Ungerson, C (1971) *Moving Home*, Occasional papers on social administration No. 44, London, Bell and Sons.

Young, K and Garside, P L (1982) *Metropolitan London: Politics and Urban Change 1837–1981* London, Edward Arnold.

12 Retrospect and prospect
Stuart Lowe and David Hughes

In this chapter we attempt to draw together the key themes from the text and, informed by lessons from the past, discuss what the future direction and purpose of social housing might be. That some form of provision will continue is unquestionable. What is less certain is the form of the provision, and for whom it will cater? Readers of this book will by now recognise that these were the very same issues to tax the minds of the housing reformers of a hundred years ago.

Retrospect

The initial emphasis on the 'public health' aspect of housing, and on local authorities having powers over areas of substandard accommodation has a modern ring. This must be set alongside an historic resistance on the part of many authorities to build houses on any sort of scale. Indeed, some authorities are today disposed to transfer their stock of housing, in whole or in part, to other landlords, although as Peter Kemp points out, there are various motives for doing this in the uncertain world of local authority finance. Those authorities, however, are in a minority. Nevertheless in our beginning is our end for in Chapter 1 Stuart Lowe demonstrates that the controversy over using local rate funds to sustain council housing budgets and disposal of local authority stock can be shown to have had precursors in the 1890 Act itself; likewise early policy preference for social housing provision to be made by charitable bodies. Does the historic failure of those charitable bodies, as detailed by Richard Best in Chapter 10, to provide a sufficiency of social housing in the years down to 1914 point a moral for the future?

Why 'council' housing?

The prior question, however, is why the British local authorities emerged as the major providers of social housing, and this is discussed by Jane Morton, Peter Kemp and Richard Best. There is some unanimity of view among our authors that this decision was implicit in the pre-1914 situation. Part III of the 1890

Act was important in preparing the legislative framework, and it expressed a political will which, although anxious about the impact of intervention in the market and equivocal in its intentions, nevertheless is the origin of a nationally mandated local authority housing sector. Jane Morton and Richard Best highlight the point that the municipal alternative to the model dwelling companies and other potential providers was well established for a variety of practical reasons. There was to some extent a 'market failure' and the local authorities were seen as offering at the very least a stop-gap function. More positively Jane Morton emphasises that the relatively high standard of much of the housing that had been built in the years immediately before 1914 by the local authorities (even if it was at this stage beyond the reach financially of the poorest families), gave credibility to the municipal option because it compared very favourably with standards in the private sector. Second, the nationally structured system of local government provided what Jane Morton calls, 'a certainty of provision' compared to the uneven spread of the philanthropic housing bodies based mainly in the South, and there was a strengthening administrative base of officials ready and willing to deliver the new housing. That local authorities were the chosen recipients is further explained by Kemp in political terms: wartime rent strikes and profiteering by private landlords made the private rented sector less than acceptable for subsidisation. Voluntary bodies were acceptable in subsidy terms but were not considered able to cope with making the amount of housing provision needed, nor was it, as Best demonstrates, a role they wanted. Central government itself had not the necessary local knowledge to undertake local housing programmes.

It is useful in this context to consider what happened in other countries and why at this time most other European nations did not follow the British route. Recent work by Daunton highlights, as do Kemp and Lowe in this book, the important point that the administrative response is only part of the explanation of the British experience. Daunton points to the 'social and political relationships which arose in the housing market as . . . in the case of the rent strikes and the politicisation of landlord–tenant relations which took place in some cities' (Daunton, 1990, p. 23). In Berlin, Paris, Budapest (to a lesser extent) and Vienna the municipal solution was not a preferred option. In Berlin alone, for example, some 11,000 dwellings were built between 1890 and 1914 by non-profit, cooperative building societies using cheap loans provided by the central government. The important point here is that even these enterprises were opposed by the powerful property owners' interest groups who certainly would not have tolerated the outright adoption, through the national legislature, of a municipal building programme. The key element, according to Daunton, in Germany (and most other North and Central European nations), compared to Britain, was the very powerful political base of the small property owners. In Britain the Conservative Party represented rural as opposed to urban landowners, and the Liberals' political programme favoured heavy taxation of landowners, which in the towns was synonymous with the private landlord.

A second reason highlighted by Daunton for the choice of the municipal route to social housing in Britain concerns the acceptance of the legitimacy of the parliamentary system and the state itself by the British Labour movement. Thus the option of the working-class movement developing their own housing agencies—cooperatives and trade union housing were common on the European continent at this time—was never on the agenda in Britain, where the Labour movement looked to the state, and in particular the local state, as the agent of social housing provision, rather than their own industrial and political organisations. As Daunton suggests,

The German path was to develop autonomous trade union or political organisations in order to build and own houses which, although they might accept cheap loans from the state, nevertheless retained a large measure of independence in the selection of tenants and the management of the property. There was a sense that the state was biased, a class interest which was hostile to the unions and Social Democrats. (Daunton, 1990, p. 25)

Indeed it was the radical Glaswegian Labour politician, John Wheatley, Health Minister in the First Labour Government, who unequivocally established 'council' housing as the major alternative to the private landlord. Since his earliest days as a politician Wheatley had consistently campaigned for *municipal* housing as the solution to the needs of working-class families for good-quality housing. Although a radical reformer Wheatley, in his 1924 Housing Act, used the existing framework of subsidies established under the 1919 Act but increased the levels of subsidy very significantly, as well as permitting the rates to support development programmes. The fact that during the next eight years over 500,000 houses were built under this legislation is a tribute to Wheatley's practical knowledge of the building industry and his grasp of housing finance. He cultivated close connections with the builders, recognising that most council housing would be built by private companies. This very 'hands-on' political vision was typical of the response of the British Labour movement to the improvement of the housing conditions of the working class. It should also be added, in parenthesis, that the existing literature on the political ideas and career of John Wheatley are far from adequate. This gap needs filling because the key 1924 Housing Act was very much the product of his ideas and political skills; in this case, the role of the individual was seminal.

An important subsidiary point to emerge from the comparative dimension is the diversity of response to the provision of social housing that emerged in late nineteenth-century Europe. Only sometimes, as in Budapest, did local councils become heavily engaged in provision (Gyáni, 1990). As Daunton observes, 'There was no single way of housing the worker' (1990, p. 28). But it should also be noted that what was true in Europe was equally true *within* Britain itself. The tenements of Glasgow contrast sharply with the self-contained cottages which became the usual building style followed by local authorities in England and Wales. Progress was uneven and, as Jane Morton shows, the initial contrast between local government in London (which she sees as part of the problem) and the progress made by some city corporations even before the 1890 Act, was striking. Some twenty to thirty years earlier cities such as Liverpool and Glasgow had won discretionary powers to rehouse clearance families by private Acts of Parliament. As Morton suggests, 'National legislation had for years been modelled on their innovations.'

The relative unevenness of development is a point made by Roger Smith and Paul Whysall in their case study of Nottingham. They show how the city responded to opportunities set by the national legislation and subsidies, but also responded to their particular circumstances by building without subsidies in advance of legislation while, on other occasions, proceeding with great caution in adopting centrally directed opportunities. Local political attitudes to housing provision is also an issue brought into the 'weave' of this volume by Jane Darke. It has played a major part in the provision of housing by local authorities, thus introducing the notion that an important formative influence in social housing has been its landlords' perception of themselves and their political and social desires. Richard Best's chapter picks up this theme in relation to housing associations as an explanation for their failure to become prime providers of social housing: they did not see themselves as having the role. Local authorities also were everywhere in a position to take on the task of providing non-profit housing, while associations were much more geographically limited.

The trends and patterns established after the First World War were confirmed and enhanced by the Second World War. Political, and indeed obviously *party* political, forces drove the housing programme in the post-war years. A strong Minister, Aneurin Bevan, was able to channel these forces in the direction of local authority housing provision. Even when the Conservatives returned to power in 1951 they were not, as Kemp has demonstrated, easily able to direct the social provision of housing away from local authorities, despite their overall housing preference for owner occupation, and a 'reluctant collectivism'.

Kemp's chapter further demonstates the political *cum* administrative forces at work in relation to council housing by reference to the subsequent development of Conservative housing policy. Though overall content to restrict local authority building to slum clearance replacement, the Conservatives discovered by the early 1960s that the private rental sector was not reviving sufficiently to supply general housing needs. Their 1961 Housing White Paper had to acknowledge a continuing need for general local authority provision, though subsequently they were to take up the notion of voluntary or other non-profit housing as something of an alternative to council housing. Likewise the Labour Party, as Richard Best demonstrates, despite its historic attachment to council housing, was to espouse the cause of housing associations in the 1970s. In Best's words, 'since the Second World War housing associations have been the second-best option whichever political party was in power'. For many years the view of central government on associations was that they were there to 'fill the gaps' in other public sector provision, particularly with regard to the elderly. Housing associations for their part, because of the importance of role perception, became enmeshed in that recurring argument in social housing provision and management—quantity versus quality. This argument is part of an issue already alluded to: the question of what the function of social housing is. Authorities also, of course, were likewise engaged in this argument, but historically associations were very much concerned with matters of housing quality, management (in terms of both style and local structures), policy and practice, rather than numbers of units.

The social composition issue

A key theme in this book, and one which is high on the contemporary agenda, is the question of for whom social housing is intended. Two main points emerge here. First, that there were important changes in the social composition of the entrants to council housing between the 1920s and the 1930s, a fact which the judges were insensitive to in their legal definition of the 'working class'. As David Hughes points out in his chapter on tenants' rights, the courts came to define the phrase 'working class' where it appeared in legislation as meaning poorly paid people in unskilled/semi-skilled jobs. Those even poorer, for example those not in employment, tended historically not to enter social housing, at least not until subsidies were used almost exclusively for the demolition of slums and the rehousing of their occupants after the 1932 'Greenwood' Housing Act. However, in the 1920s there was to an extent a mismatch between the legal definition of 'working class' and the social reality because, as Bowley suggests, the social composition of the new council tenants was very much artisan in character. What she calls 'small clerks' were common entrants to council housing, and the best housing was sought after even by the lower professionals in some parts of the country (Bowley, 1945). Council housing was qualitatively superior to most houses built for sale in the private sector during the 1920s. But as private speculative house-building boomed in the 1930s the social composition of new council house tenants changed. Subsidies now favoured slum clearance and replacement housing and general needs provision was met almost entirely by the private developers. This interaction of the fortunes of the private sector building industry with the social role played by council housing is an important theme in our historical evaluation, and points a lesson about the relationship between the tenures and more generally between the public and private sectors in housing. We return to this latter point below.

The second key point on the theme of social composition to emerge, and one which is closely connected to the first point discussed, is that social housing provision in the 1980s and 1990s is socially residualised and contains the vast majority of the nation's most underprivileged and poor households. This is hardly a 'new' point but it is nevertheless essential that it be reiterated. It is clear from this book that this characteristic of council housing today is not only the product of Thatcherite social policy, but is contingent upon the ambiguities and controversies that have surrounded this housing tenure since its inception. This is not to say that there was any inevitability in what has happened. Social housing, however, has been vulnerable because the context in which it developed was set by the dominant interests of the private enterprise economy. This in turn has left it exposed to party political and ideological interests rather than those of housing policy *per se*.

Council housing has now taken the place of the privately rented sector in accommodating the poorest of our citizens and, in this regard, stands in marked contrast to the situation of sixty years ago. This change has occurred despite the achievement of the Minister of Health (who held the housing duties), Bevan, and the law in 1949 in making council housing technically available to all by removing the requirement that it was for members of the 'working class'. Peter Kemp's chapter draws attention to Bevan's vision of the possibilities of council housing, as does Jane Darke's. Stuart Lowe points out that Bevan and his predecessor in the 1920s, John Wheatley, were the only ministers with responsibility for housing to be truly committed to the ideal of municipal housing provision with an open access and appeal across the social class divide.

In practice council housing today, in many parts of the country, is a residual form of provision to be accessed only by marginalised groups of people, for example numbers of divorced or separated women, single parents and those otherwise homeless. 'Social' has become equated with 'welfare'. The creation of communities where all social classes can co-mingle is, in terms of strict law, feasible, but in practice those who can afford owner occupation opt for that tenure and it is society's residualised groups who increasingly make up the 'clientele' for social housing. A gathering trend in this pattern of events is for social services departments and housing departments to be merged. Housing management and social work are converging professions. A similar residual role has also generally been the lot of the voluntary housing sector in social housing, a matter considered by Richard Best in Chapter 10.

Currently housing 'policy' is directed to changing the role of local authorities to that of enablers of others to provide housing, as opposed to building new housing themselves. Social housing provision by local authorities has been concentrated only on special needs groups such as the elderly, and only housing associations have had a more general role, albeit very limited in terms of quantity, in general provision. Even in special needs provision, lack of adequate funding has produced slippages in particular forms of housing. This issue was highlighted by the July 1990 decision of the Government to postpone the introduction of the 'care in the community' programme, though it had been apparent for some time that the discharge of large numbers of people from psychiatric care and other long-stay institutions would bring about problems in relation to their housing. At the same time a different strand of the ideological armoury makes it clear that there is no legal obligation on local authorities to maintain a housing stock, even though such bodies have housing *obligations*, for example the homeless. A number of local authorities have already successfully divested themselves of their housing stock, and others, albeit small numbers, are seeking to do so. Quite where these contradictory strands of policy lead is uncertain although what is sure is that the *demand* for social housing will not be going away.

Rents and the subsidy question

An important skein in the weave of this history is the way in which the changing role and purpose of council housing began to be reflected in the *nature* and *form* of the subsidy system. Peter Malpass' chapter brings out the significance of the 'historic cost' approach to housing finance and particularly its influence on rent levels. Until the early 1970s the subsidy system was the main policy instrument by which central government was able to influence council house production. Peter Malpass very clearly shows how a reasonable balance between the various interests was struck through this system, but that the pressure of the social housing sector within a dominant private housing market was once again apparent in the gradual shift in the post-Second World War decades away from 'needs'-based rents to more market-orientated rents. Initially this was done by rent and subsidy pooling and soon this gave rise to, 'demands and exhortations to local authorities to adopt the rebating principle to protect poorer tenants from rising rents'. Malpass points to the significance of the 1972 Housing Finance Act as heralding a new era in housing finance, with the introduction of 'fair rent' and the loss of local authority powers to set rents innovating new sets of principles which, in effect, drew social housing much more closely into the logic of the market system. Trevor Buck's essay also brings out the seminal influence of the Housing Finance Act on the move away from 'bricks and mortar' subsidies, and towards individualised housing benefits for those unable to meet rising housing costs. The national rent rebate/ allowance scheme introduced by the 1972 Act brought local authorities into the business of making what were effectively social security payments, and this move was confirmed by the 1982 Social Security and Housing Benefits Act. The 1986 Social Security Act generally harmonised housing benefits with other income-support benefits. The consequence of this major shift in the pattern of giving assistance with housing costs, *away* from keeping down the cost of accommodation and *towards* helping occupiers to pay the increasing costs of their accommodation, is to associate housing costs assistance with welfare benefits.

Trevor Buck's essay also demonstrates how housing policy is subject, via the legal framework of housing benefits, to the requirements of overall social security policy. This is further reflected in the new arrangements for housing benefits subsidies to be subsumed into the new housing revenue account subsidy under the Local Government and Housing Act 1989. As Peter Malpass comments, 'rent rebates are combined with housing subsidy and [rebates] are properly regarded as a form of social security'. All this contributes powerfully to the residualisation of social housing and, certainly, of council housing, as provision for the 'worse-off' poor, a role which, as we have seen, it never had initially, and for which it was not intended.

Social housing and the private sector

An important theme which emerges strongly in some chapters and is implicit in nearly all is the nature of the relationship between the local authorities and, latterly, housing associations, as developers and managers, and the private sector which provided most of the loan finance, much of the land, and which has done most of the construction. As Peter Malpass shows, the impact of loan charges on rents has been a critical feature of council house finance. Non-market access to council housing is, however, a very distinctive feature of the tenure and Malpass shows how the historic cost accounting of local authorities' housing finance provided a crucial defence in rent setting against open market prices, at least until the early 1970s. Since then there seems to be something almost inexorable in the move from 'fair' rents to affordable rents to market rents and ultimately the transformation of council houses into owner occupation. It *was* not inevitable, but that *is* what happened.

The impact of private landlordism on the practice of housing management in social housing is another example of the interaction of the private and public sectors. Peter Kemp and Peter Williams in Chapter 9 show that there were many continuities in the practice and content of housing management which crossed the centuries and the private/public sector divide. Indeed only during the last two decades has there been anything distinctively 'social' about the management of council housing. Always the emphasis, especially in the formative years of the 1920s and 1930s, was on ensuring the protection of the property and the efficient collection of rent; in short, the same preoccupations and concerns which had for centuries been at the forefront of the minds of the private landlords.

Two important strands in our weave must be connected here with the earlier issue of the social composition of the estates. First, that so long as council housing was mainly occupied by 'the better class of poor' management problems were relatively limited and housing management itself was taken for granted. A second point is that the allocation process, in the context of the entry into council housing of less well-off households (for example, from slum clearance areas), has generated a social structure on the estates which reflects the 'deserving' and 'undeserving' labelling. Divisions between the tenant population, created by the allocation process, have created a series of knock-on effects for estate management, lettings policy and, latterly, the acceleration of the residualisation process via the 'right to buy' policy. Here large quantities of the best housing stock, occupied by the 'respectable', mainly skilled manual, working-class families have been sold, leaving a smaller, poorer-quality stock disproportionately occupied by low-income households, the elderly and young couples.

For almost all the one hundred years of social housing, management has been a neglected part of the debate and has been one of, if not the, most under-professionalised occupations of all the services provided by local government. The legacy of its private sector origins have only recently been fully understood. It must be high on the agenda for change and reform as the new century unfolds. Good, responsive and open management, in which tenant participation and consultation figure at every stage in the provision of housing, must be a core feature of social housing in the future even though, as David Hughes has shown, such principles are currently given scant legal recognition. Nor have either local authority members or officers regularly espoused such principles in the past, as Jane Darke argues.

Thus the private sector has woven threads deep into the very fabric of social housing, both at a policy level and in practice. The social sector has never been able fully to escape from the dominant environment of the private sector on both the supply and the demand sides of the housing system. Being aware of this and given sympathetic political circumstances, as the example of John Wheatley in the 1920s demonstrates, it is possible for large quantities of social housing to be built to a good standard and allocated without stigma. The question for the future of such provision is how best to utilise the private sector and where public subsidy can most effectively be engaged to harness the partnership of the public and private sectors. Even in the unfavourable circumstances of the 1980s there are many examples of successful liaisons between private finance, private construction and the production of social housing. The question-mark over this is just exactly the same historical issue which we found a hundred years ago—whether, within the mix of public and private finance, the affordability threshold is exceeded. The implication and conclusion are the same now as they were then: that the element of public subsidy needs to be higher for, as we argue below, all housing is to some extent subsidised and in that sense, if not indeed in a wider sense, is social.

Property rights and social housing

One important theme to emerge from several chapters, notably those by David Hughes and Trevor Buck, is the significance of the interaction of housing policy and property rights, particularly private versus communal rights in land. The critics of local authority, and more generally state-owned, assets argue that bureaucratic control and management provide low incentives to manage the properties well or efficiently because these managers do not have to live with the consequences of their actions. Moreover, as several contributors to this book have pointed out, public housing is subject to inconsistent and sometimes contradictory political pressures. Government intervention in housing is not simply an issue of economic efficiency, broadly speaking, to correct market failures, but has many dimensions related, for example, to the influence of interest groups, distributive justice or ideology. In the Anglo-American tradition the dominant notions of individual property rights have had an important bearing on housing policy and on the institutions affecting the housing market.

The change during the hundred years of housing under consideration here, from a housing system dominated by private landlordism to a system dominated by home ownership, is marked not only by the emergence of an institutional and financial apparatus to facilitate such a change, but has been underpinned by a continuity in law of the primary status of individual private property rights. Social housing has been unable to find features of its system of tenure to countervail those of owner occupation which, as Kemp points out, are resident control and capital accumulation. In the last decade this disparity between the two forms of housing provision has come more and more to the fore in public consciousness—greatly fostered, let it be added, by government policy which has concentrated on promoting yet further extension of home owner-ship, particularly in the form of the 'right to buy'. However, the disadvantages of social housing have been perceived by many, and certainly by government, as most marked in relation to council housing. This has led to a further strand of current central policy: the attempt to revive private renting, the transfer of housing associations into the private sector by, *inter alia*, changing the legal incidents of their tenancies, and new legal provisions allowing for both the voluntary and forced transfer of council housing stock to new landlords. The political justification for such changes has been stated, in an age of market ideology, very much in terms of consumer choice, management responsiveness, and meeting the demands of individuals. This policy reinforces an inbuilt tendency of law, as David Hughes argues in Chapter 7, to think of rights in relation to property in highly individual terms. Housing is then seen as an individual private good to be enjoyed on an individual basis, the subject of individual control and choice, paid for according to market bargains struck between willing providers and willing consumers.

Returning briefly to our comparative mode, it is worth pointing out in this context that the dominance of property rights in housing is not universal. Other societies, both in the erstwhile command economies and in capitalistic nations, regard property rights in housing as secondary to a citizen's *entitlement* to decent housing. The Swedish model is probably the best European example of a society which sees housing in this way, and where the state provides institutions and subsidies to support a high standard of social housing but also retains a private property market. As Kemeny shows, this collectivist view of housing rights stands in sharp contrast to the 'home-owning societies' (Kemeny, 1981). The association of home ownership and an emphasis in law and society in general on private property is close. Our point is simply that for, at the very least, the poor and those excluded from easy access to home ownership, there is nevertheless a social entitlement to good and decent housing, a right of citizenship which *supersedes* individual property rights.

Even amongst those who do not subscribe to a market-dominated philosophy of housing there is an acceptance that it is not the law of the Medes and Persians that local authorities must provide social housing, or that they should be the major providers of it. Yet, of course, the danger inherent in concentrating attention, as the government has done since 1979, on the shortcomings of *council* housing is that the wider, and more important questions, of what sort of *social* housing provision is needed, by whom, where and how provided, are simply not asked, or, if they are, are insufficiently investigated and debated.

All housing is 'social'

A further theme, illustrated variously by Peter Malpass' and Patrick Nuttgens' chapters, certainly from design and economic points of view, is that *all* housing is in a very real sense 'social'. As Malpass shows, intermediaries are necessary in the housing process between those who build and those who occupy, because the latter are rarely able to pay in one single sum all the price demanded for accommodation by the former. For owner-occupiers the inter-mediary is usually a building society providing mortgage finance to spread the cost of acquisition over a long period. For those who rent, the landlord is the intermediary. Both intermediaries fulfil a social function in that they are facilitating the meeting of a basic human need, that for shelter. The social role of housing finance in both owner-occupied and rented accommodation thus cannot be denied. Yet historically, and today, the housing finance system operates discretely and unevenly as between owner occupiers and those who rent and, with regard to the latter group, as between those renting from local authorities and private landlords and housing associations. There are even further differences between tenants of authorities and those of associations, and indeed, yet other differences between individual tenants and individual landlords depending on a variety of issues such as the legal classification of the tenancy held ('secure' or 'assured', for example), geographical location and whether or not the tenant qualifies for income support.

Nuttgens also introduces us to a further skein in the tangled pattern of housing (which links us to the public/private divide issue and the question of property rights) namely, that there is a strong element of town planning, either public or private, in its history, and that housing development is very much concerned with how land is used and allocated. These issues further reinforce the point that all housing is social, for the housing design and planning of all accommodation, no matter who its provider or what its tenure, has a profound impact visually and in terms of demand for services and utilities, traffic flow and the entire notion and ethos of communities.

This aspect of housing is, of course, its 'gallant and high hearted happiness'. The argument, traceable back to Pugin and Ruskin in the mid-nineteenth century, and in their fellow thinkers who believed that there is a connection between human goodness and good buildings, is that well designed and planned housing and town provision can create, to quote Howard, 'New hope, a new life, a new civilisation', though a civilisation which to some had to have roots deep in a traditional English past. Housing is part of a total environment —for good or ill—and a creator or inhibitor of civilised community existence. As such housing's 'social aspect' clearly encompasses not just provision, management and finance, but also its layout, mode of building, its contribution to the mental and physical health of its occupants and the wholeness of the community in which it is situated.

Public landlords made, as Nuttgens shows, notable contributions throughout the inter-war years to the stock of dwellings, trying to implement the above ideals. However, as he also points out, there has always been a degree of pragmatism in the provision of social housing, to which Jane Darke's chapter adds instances of a lack of sympathy with aesthetics. Though pragmatism in housing provision is not necessarily exclusive of idealism in housing design, there have been periods, notably from the 1950s to the early 1970s, when pragmatic solutions to housing problems were *thought* to dictate a need for higher-rise development, use of limited sites and industrialised systems-building techniques; that such theories were often ill-founded is demonstrated by Jane Darke. When that pragmatism was combined with enhanced subsidies for high-rise building and the allurement of the rapid provision of large numbers of 'units of accommodation' the result was the production of less than ideal housing, the vast majority of which is still with us today as a problem of today and tomorrow. This housing is a further problem in that it is almost exclusively to be encountered in the public sector.

The legacy of the post-Second World War high-rise boom is judged by most to be a disaster for the legitimacy of social housing and, above all, judged by the residents as an unpopular form of accommodation. There is no easy way out. For architectural determinists, spearheaded by Alice Coleman, to 'prove' errors in the design of mass housing and show how to modify them is no real solution (Coleman, 1985). It may well be that the grafitti and the muggings are reduced in renovated and modified blocks, but only to reappear elsewhere. At the same time *flats* for the elderly, or the young and aspiring in Docklands, at Salford Quay, by the River Ouse in York, sell like hot cakes, while many of the worst social problems in the social rented sector of housing are to be found on inter-war housing estates, areas that exude impeccable design features—low rise, plenty of surveillance, cottage-style dwellings and so on. High rise is not necessarily universally unpopular, and even the 'worst' of the slab block estates provided, behind the privacy of the front door, a haven for thousands of families under pressure from other aspects of their lives. As Patrick Nuttgens observes in his chapter, high rise did make some useful contributions: 'Ultimately it highlighted the necessity of having a sociological basis for housing, and for consulting people . . .'.

Prospect

What is the nature of social housing that emerges from a consideration of what is truly *more* than a century of development? There is no clear pattern. Social housing has not developed according to any grand design, as is clearly illustrated by Jane Darke's chapter. It is rather the product of a mixture of proactive principle and reactive pragmatism, high ideals and misleading vision coupled with public parsimony. The story of social housing is one of both triumph and tragedy. One aspect of the tragedy has been the failure to realise the social nature of all housing, and to think of social housing as that provided by governmental and voluntary agencies only. The consequence has been that while owner occupation has gradually developed as the preferred, and most accessible, form of housing tenure in this century of rising incomes, social housing has followed a separate path of development and has been identified primarily with council housing and also with welfare housing, this latter preoccupation being traced back to the 1950s, as Jane Darke argues. The stark result is the residualisation of social housing.

For the future a number of issues appear relevant. The first is to stress the wider social role of all housing. In a society in which the number of elderly people is set to increase as a proportion of the population as a whole, and in which a growing number of those elderly people will be aged over eighty; in which the pattern of family life has changed and seems set to change further, with an increased divorce rate, a considerable remarriage rate, and a larger number of people of all ages living alone or as single parents; where there is an increasing incidence of homelessness; in which care in the community for many who might in past years have been institutionalised is bound to create a demand for specialised housing provision (the legitimate demand of the disabled for accommodation enabling them to lead whole and independent lives) the wider social aspect of housing cannot be ignored. Truly social housing provision is concerned with the way in which *all* housing is financed, built, designed and managed, irrespective of tenure. Currently law, policy and practice all ignore this basic issue, as is perhaps most clearly illustrated by the continued failure to realise that mortgage interest relief for owner-occupiers is clearly a housing subsidy and not treated as an item of national expenditure. It is at least arguable, however, that it is only the realisation of all housing's social nature that will bring about a convergence of the interests of all its consumers so that, irrespective of tenure, they can demand responsiveness from those who provide, plan, design and finance accommodation.

In consumer terms the interests of, for example, a person living in a high-rise flat or in a so-called 'luxury apartment' or an owner-occupied sheltered long leasehold unit are similar: all are concerned that their homes should be properly serviced, managed and maintained, in both the long and the short term; that they are adequately consulted by those who supply them with housing services, and that there are adequate and effective means of account-ability and grievance mediation. It is true, of course, that somewhat different considerations apply to owner-occupied freehold property, but even here the supply of mortgage finance is a housing service where greater degrees of openness and accountability by the providers of mortgage finance is desirable. This is especially true where the attractions of home ownership and readily available mortgages have led consumers to commit themselves overmuch, subsequently finding themselves unable to meet mortgage commitments as a result of, for example, illness, relationship breakdown, loss of employment or rising interest rates. It is also arguable that as mortgage interest relief is truly an Exchequer subsidy for owner-occupiers, its grant should be made dependent on its recipients undertaking to contribute to long-term housing repair and renewal, to ensure in future years a supply of finance to meet major items of expenditure and so reduce the need to invest public money in renewal strategies. The very existence of such strategies, which have largely benefited owner-occupiers, is, of course, further evidence of the social role of all housing.

Turning specifically to housing provided for rent by public and voluntary landlords—social housing in its more usual sense—it is necessary to ensure that the debate on the deficiencies, or otherwise, of council housing does not obscure the pressing issue of the need for social housing provision. Warning voices about social polarisation of owner-occupiers and council tenants have been heard for some thirty years, as David Hughes alluded to in Chapter 7, and the 1970s certainly witnessed considerable debate on the desirability of local authorities acting as landlords. Throughout the 1980s the consequence of that was a sustained central government attack on council housing, motivated, at least in part, by poor central/local government relations, and the lack of any clear view of what functions it is appropriate for local government to undertake and how they should be organised and financed. In the main the attack took the form of continuous prescription of yet more doses of owner occupation, especially in the various manifestations of the 'right to buy'. However, by the late 1980s attention had shifted to the dispersal of the council stock by means of schemes such as housing action trusts and tenants' choice initiatives under the Housing Act 1988, and the mooted proposal to further advance owner occupation amongst council tenants by treating payments of rent as if they are payments under a mortgage. More significant than these, perhaps, has been the withdrawal from housing provision on a voluntary basis by some local authorities—often the small districts—using the device of the stock transfer. Such moves have been prompted sometimes by ideological commitment, sometimes by pressure from officers, sometimes by financial

constraints, including the realisation that 'right to buy' sales may have depleted
an authority's stock to such an extent that it can no longer afford to maintain
its existing housing department and staff—often the largest numbers of staff
employed by district councils. Furthermore the emphasis in central policy is
that in relation to housing provision local authorities should be 'enablers'—
which seems long on vague aspirations but short on specifics. And if the
housing role of local authorities is to be thus 'strategic' it would seem to imply
that other bodies are to have a tactical function. As yet there is little sign of that
function being implemented in anything approaching the scale of deployment
needed, as Jane Darke comments in her chapter. In addition, as Richard Best
has demonstrated, the history of past attempts by housing associations to build
unsubsidised housing gives little cause for sanguinity about how such bodies
might fare in the future on reduced levels of public support.

The conclusions of most of our writers have been sombre, and it is hard for
this volume to end on anything but a sombre note. Throughout the last
hundred years housing has been the subject of intense debate and controversy,
out of which has emerged an uneven pattern of housing provision. In the first
place it is encouraging that, overall, the housing stock nationally is in quite
good condition. The English House Condition Survey of 1986, published in
1988, indicates that only 2.5 per cent of the housing stock lacks five basic
amenities. Seventy-five per cent of dwellings were centrally heated, and only
4.8 per cent of dwellings were 'unfit' according to the definition of the term in
the Housing Act 1985—though it has to be added that the law's requirements
for a dwelling to be 'fit' were not particularly stringent, dating, in effect, from
the early years of the present century. (The requirements have now been made
more demanding under the Local Government and Housing Act 1989.) While
the 'bricks and mortar' state of the nation's housing stock may overall be in
good condition, it can still be questioned whether the management of its long-
term maintenance is effective no matter what its tenure. It may also be asked
whether the housing we have is suitable for the needs of a changing
population. Housing is still thought of very much in 'family' terms, and in
terms of youthful vigour. How much provision is to be made for those not
living in nuclear families, and how should homes be adapted to meet, for
example, the needs of the elderly and the disabled—is it not still the case that
electricity sockets are generally situated at skirting-board level?

In the second place the continued existence of housing which is in one way or
another substandard does mean social inequity, while for some there is no
housing at all. This volume has concentrated on housing, largely in physical
terms, and it has not been appropriate to include a chapter on the issue of
homelessness. However, that does not mean that enhanced social housing
provision is not required to provide for, in part, the needs of the increasing
numbers of homeless people. The 1989 Report by the Audit Commission
indicated a rise in the number of homeless applications *accepted* by local
authorities from 7,652 in 1970 to some 116,000 in 1988, and it must be
remembered that while, for example, in 1986–7 110,000 applications were
accepted, a further 109,000 for one reason or another, were not. A recent
report by John Greve and Elizabeth Currie showed that the figure for
acceptances had risen in 1989 to 140,000 (a total of about 400,000 people,

half of them children). The report further showed that about 40 per cent of homelessness acceptances were of single-parent families (Greve and Currie, 1990). The Audit Commission (1989) showed that only about one-third of those accepted as homeless are directly rehoused: many have to spend time in temporary accommodation, and the incidence of this as a feature of accommodating the homeless has increased sharply since 1982. Both the Audit Commission's and the Greve and Currie reports pointed to a lack of access to housing opportunities and a need for low-cost housing as the underlying causes of homelessness, with the decline of the private rental sector being identified as a contributor to the rise in homelessness, as well as that of the public sector. In a number of areas there is little freedom to allocate council housing to those other than the homeless, and the various 'priority need' groups existing under legislation have become something of a tenant selection system in their own right. The entry into the council sector of increasing numbers of homeless applicants who, generally by definition, lack the resources to be able to afford any solution to their housing problems tends still further to confirm the residualised welfare role of, at least, council housing.

What, then, are the possibilities for the new century of social housing? Owner occupation bids fair to continue as the dominant form of housing tenure, though nothing is certain—who would have said in 1890 that private landlordism would decline within one hundred years to its 'shadow of a shade' position in the housing market? Even so, assuming the continued dominance of owner occupation, the changing needs and structure of the population may lead to greater stress being placed on this type of housing's social aspect, especially with regard to management and service provision in relation to the needs of the elderly, the disabled, the single young, and so on. Within the rented sector some form of social provision will continue. The council sector is too large to disappear rapidly and housing associations are targeted to continue as providers of rental accommodation. Taking up points made by Jane Darke, the real issues are (as they have traditionally been) not just whether there will be social housing, but rather more, *how* much, *where*, and of *what* sort, design and specification. Crucial to all these questions will be the amount and the manner of finance; but there will be further matters which will need to continue to be core issues, namely the style of management of the housing that is provided, and the relationship between landlords and tenants, managers and occupiers, with the question 'whose home is it, anyway?' being a key concept. Continued greater responsiveness to tenants' needs and opinions, not just in the management of social housing but in its mode of provision and design, to ensure that what is built is what is truly needed and wanted, must surely be key features of social housing's future if 'social' is not to become a euphemism for 'residual welfare'.

References

Audit Commission (1989) *Housing the Homeless: The Local Authority Role* London, HMSO.

Bowley, M (1945) *Housing and the State: 1919–1944* London, Allen and Unwin.

Coleman, A (1985) *Utopia on Trial* London, Hilary Shipman.

Daunton, M J (ed) (1990) *Housing the Workers* Leicester, Leicester University Press.

Gyáni, G (1990) 'Budapest', in M J Daunton (ed) *Housing the Workers* Leicester, Leicester University Press.

Greve, J and Currie, E (1990) *Homelessness in Britain* York, Joseph Rowntree Memorial Trust.

Kemeny, J (1981) *The Myth of Home Ownership* London, Routledge and Kegan Paul.

Index